Hegel and Theology

Hegel and Theology

Martin J. De Nys

t&t clark

Published by T&T Clark International
A Continuum imprint
The Tower Building   80 Maiden Lane
11 York Road   Suite 704
London SE1 7NX   New York, NY 10038

www.continuumbooks.com

British Library Cataloguing-in-Publication Data
A catalogue record for this book is available from the British Library

ISBN-10: HB: 0-567-03280-9
          PB: 0-567-03281-7
ISBN-13: HB: 978-0-567-03280-5
          PB: 978-0-567-03281-2

Typeset by Newgen Imaging Systems Pvt Ltd, Chennai, India
Printed on acid-free paper in Great Britain by MPG Books Ltd, Bodmin, Cornwall

For Rachel and Jessica,
shining lights.

Contents

Preface

I began to study the texts of Hegel's mature philosophy in graduate school. My first encounter with Hegel led to decidedly mixed reactions. I was in many respects intrigued, but also critical and put off by what seemed to be the needless obscurity of his philosophical prose. The second encounter was more positive. It involved reading texts in the philosophy of religion in conjunction with Emil Fackenheim's *The Religious Dimension in Hegel's Thought*. Fackenheim enabled me to find an entrée into Hegel's philosophy, and to begin a process of inquiry that has taken on a variety of forms in the intervening decades. At times that inquiry has required that I take a distance from Hegel's powerful and overwhelming philosophical achievement, in order to learn to draw on the resources of other philosophers, especially Aquinas, Kierkegaard, Husserl, and Ricoeur, for my own philosophical work, and in order to learn critically to assess Hegel's own claims. But Hegel's magisterial presence regularly required a return to his texts. I am very grateful for the opportunity to do this book, in that it has afforded the opportunity to think in a sustained and disciplined way about critical limitations that belong to, and about the essentially productive contributions that belong to, Hegel's philosophical understanding of religion and Christianity.

My efforts at coming to grips with Hegel's philosophy have been, as is the case for a number of other philosophers in the United States, greatly assisted by the meetings of and the collegiality of the Hegel Society of America, and more lately by the publications made available in the journal of the HSA, *The Owl of Minerva*. The Hegel Society has always encouraged philosophers newly arrived in the domain of Hegel studies, as well as those established in that domain, to participate fully in the deliberations that the society promotes. At the same time, its meetings are uniformly of the highest scholarly and philosophical caliber. I am grateful to the Society for the support that it has offered to myself and many other philosophers attempting to come critically to terms with Hegel's philosophy for over three decades. I am especially grateful for the decades of conversations about Hegel, philosophical issues more generally, religion, and theology that I have been able to enjoy with Ardis Collins, presently editor of *The Owl*. Ardis has been an important philosophical interlocutor, and a long-standing and deep personal friend. Much of what I have come to think about Hegel, and about many other matters, has taken form in conversations with her.

In many ways, Hegel's philosophical views cut against the grain of much that is commonly maintained in contemporary philosophy, and more specifically in much of the received wisdom that defines the American reception of what is called continental philosophy. Hegel presents a rich and capacious notion of reason that insists that reason is autonomous, evidential, and demonstrative. He maintains that the most fundamental possibility that belongs to rational inquiry is the ability critically to probe the most basic categories that determine both the activity of thinking and the intelligible actuality that one grasps and apprehends in thought. Because of this, his efforts at realizing the possibilities that belong to the essential principles that determine modern philosophy is at one and the same time arguably a recovery of some most basic aspects of the classical philosophical tradition. His insistence on thinking categories such as identity, unity, otherness and difference in terms of their dialectical oppositions to and connections with each other challenges the postmodern critique of the conception of reason that Hegel promotes. These characteristics, along with Hegel's claim about the ability of reason to grasp and comprehend the infinite reality that both presents itself in and distinguishes itself from the world of finite things and affairs, make his philosophical views ones which should command the attention of those who pursue inquiry in religious studies, philosophy of religion, or theology.

Preface

I would be remiss if I did not conclude these brief remarks by offering endless gratitude to my spouse, Mary, for the support she has lent me as I have worked on this project, and for the boundless support that she gives to and joy that she brings to my life. I hope I am somehow able to respond in kind. I dedicate this book to our children.

Introduction

In a well-regarded study of Protestant theology in the nineteenth century, Karl Barth once asked, 'Why did Hegel not become for the Protestant world something like what Thomas Aquinas was for Roman Catholicism?'[1] The father of neo-orthodox theology is strongly critical of some central views that Hegel presents in his philosophy of religion and of Christianity. Barth does not hesitate to say that 'Hegel, in making the dialectical method of logic the essential nature of God, made impossible the knowledge of the actual dialectic of grace, which has its foundation in the freedom of God.'[2] But in speaking of Hegel's philosophy, Barth also says that 'everything that seems to give theology its particular splendor and special dignity appears to be looked after and honored by this philosophy in a way incomparably better than that achieved by the theologians themselves (with the possible exception of Thomas Aquinas).'[3] He believes that Hegel 'completely and finally disposed of the God who had somehow stood in opposition to reason, who was in some way an offence and a foolishness to reason, and who could perhaps be denied by reason.'[4] He says that Hegel 'saw God's aliveness well, and saw it better than many theologians,'[5] even though this insight is linked to an understanding of revelation that a theologian must, Barth maintains, ultimately challenge. In fact, Barth observes, 'It was only in the course of centuries that Thomas Aquinas acquired the position at present accorded to him in the Roman Catholic world. It may be that the dawn of the true age of Hegel is still something that will take place in the future.'[6] Given the complexity that must belong to a theological reception of Hegel, this possibility presents 'a great problem,' but also 'a great promise.'[7]

These comments suggest that while one can and perhaps must, from a theological standpoint, challenge some central positions belonging to Hegel's philosophical achievement, Hegel's

1

philosophy is at the same time both a resource for theological work and a challenge to contemporary theological endeavors. The aim of these pages is to discuss Hegel's philosophy in a way that focuses on his considerations of religion and Christianity and that examines the connections between that philosophy and theology in terms of the complex relations that Barth's comments suggest.

An examination of Hegel's philosophy that centers on his considerations of religion and Christianity is quite appropriate in the light of Hegel's understanding of his own work. Philosophy, for Hegel, is nothing other than 'the quest for truth, but with the consciousness of the nature and worth of the thought relationships that bind together and determine every content.'[8] This truth is not simply unavailable before philosophy comes on the scene. 'Religion is the mode, the type of consciousness, in which the truth is present for all men, or for all levels of education; but scientific cognition is a particular type of consciousness of the truth, and not for everyone, indeed only a few men undertake the labour of it. *The basic import is the same*,'[9] even though religion, as I will discuss below, expresses the truth in the forms of what Hegel calls feeling and representation, whereas philosophy operates with what he calls the concrete concept. Indeed 'there may be religion without philosophy, but there cannot be philosophy without religion,'[10] since religion presents on the level of individual and social life the truth the philosophy critically reenacts and comprehends in thought. There have been and are widely different interpretations of Hegel's views as to the relation between the truth as presented from a properly religious standpoint and the outcome of a philosophical reconceptualization of the meanings that religion on its own terms makes available. But that Hegel claims that the truth that philosophy attains is a conceptual reenactment of the truth that religion presents is not disputed. This is why it is legitimate to offer a consideration of Hegel's philosophy of religion and Christianity as an entrée into his philosophy as such.

In considering Hegel's achievement as a resource upon which contemporary theology might critically draw, and as a source of challenges to contemporary theology, it is useful to remark on the era in which Hegel found himself and to which he responded, and the comparability of his times to our own times. The German lands in the late eighteenth and early nineteenth centuries were the scene of profound economic, social, cultural, political, and intellectual transformations. Hegel was deeply alert to these processes, and to the insecurity and uncertainty they brought about. In practical terms, many found that the effective presence of the traditional religious and social communities that situated the lives of individuals had diminished, while the possibility of developments that would transform and renew the social domain so as to overcome the resulting fragmentation and isolation of individuals was open to question. In intellectual terms, traditional religious understandings had been sharply called into question by enlightenment critique. Moreover the critical philosophy, as Kant presented it and as many philosophers and theologians received it, challenged the very idea that one might, through reason, address the basic matters to which religious understandings refer so as to provide defenses of those understandings.

These concerns need, and will receive, more substantial discussion. The point now is simply that, in his philosophical work and certainly in his reflections on religion and Christianity, Hegel was attempting to respond to these matters in a focused and incisive way. If so, then he was responding to issues of importance to his own times and, of course in a historically specific way, to our own times. In our current situation individuals and groups find themselves with distressing frequency to be, for economic, cultural, and religious reasons, fragmented from the social contexts that affect them. For us the global scale that alienation and conflict can and do assume exacerbate this issue, as do well founded doubts as to the likelihood of the development of a truly global community. At the same time the capacity of reason to address fundamental problems in a comprehensive way, including problems about the intelligibility and legitimacy of religious understandings that arise in the context of a heightened consciousness of cultural pluralism, is today essentially contested. The current critique of reason proposes that the attempt to interrelate differences through rational understandings must, in the last analysis, annul rather than preserve them in their difference from each other. This critique also proposes that an attempt to address fundamental problems about reality and value in a rationally comprehensive way is undone by the limits that finitude imposes on the rational enterprise, as is suggested by the so-called end of metaphysics. These are matters of concern to social scientists and philosophers and to theologians as well. If Hegel, in his philosophy and specifically in his philosophical reflections on religion and Christianity, was engaged with issues of this sort as they appeared in his time, his work may well be a resource on which we can draw in reflecting on the problems that belong to our time.

Some brief comments about Hegel's life can extend the preceding remarks. The observations about Hegel's writings that will be included in those comments are important in relation to the work that will be done in these pages.

Georg Wilhelm Friedrich Hegel was born on August 27, 1770 in Stuttgart and died on November 14, 1831 in Berlin. He studiously avoided references to the details of his life and personal experiences in his philosophical writings. Nonetheless his life has been the subject of detailed investigation in the nineteenth century and since. For the contemporary student, the finest resource available for an understanding of Hegel's life is Terry Pinkard's excellent and accessible *Hegel: A Biography*.[11] In *Hegel In His Time*, Jacques D'Hondt presents an important account of the nature and development of Hegel's political views, with emphasis on Hegel's years in Berlin.[12] Peter Hodgson makes valuable comments about Hegel's life and career, his writings about religion, and the condition of the theology of his time in *Hegel and Christian Theology*.[13] These are useful resources for one who wants to pursue an understanding of Hegel's life and career that goes beyond the limits of my brief remarks.

The family into which Wilhelm, as he was called, was born, resided in the duchy of Württemberg. While his father, who had studied law at Tübingen, was a secretary at the ducal court, many of Hegel's forbears had been Lutheran pastors, and his mother desired that her oldest son continue in that tradition. After his years of elementary education, during which time his mother died, his father sent him, in 1794, to the Stuttgart Gymnasium, which introduced its students to traditional Protestant humanism as well as to the more current thought of the Enlightenment.

In 1788 Hegel entered the Protestant theological seminary at the University of Tübingen. During his four years at the *Tübingen Stift,* Hegel formed close friendships with Friedrich Hölderlin and F. W. J. Schelling, developed a commitment to the ideals of the French revolution, and made an initial acquaintance with the philosophy of Kant. Through his experience at Tübingen he also came to believe that the life of a clergyman was not suited to his desire to become a public intellectual who would make accessible the understandings needed for the emergence of Germany into modernity. As a way of supporting himself after graduating from the seminary and of being able to continue his intellectual work, Hegel became a private tutor in Berne, from 1793 through 1796, and in Frankfurt from 1797 through 1800.

In 1801 Hegel moved to the University of Jena, where Fichte had lectured, Schelling was lecturing, and the German Romantic movement was soon to emerge. Hegel's six years at Jena were of essential importance for his philosophical development. They culminated with the writing that is generally identified as the first of his mature philosophical publications. They ended as Hegel's situation at the University became financially untenable due to the decline of the University in the wake of the Napoleonic victory at the Battle of Jena in October, 1806. In 1807 Hegel became editor of a newspaper in Bamberg. In 1808 he became Rector of a *Gymnasium* in Nuremberg, a position he held for seven years. In 1816 Hegel finally secured an appointment as a Professor of Philosophy at the University of Heidelberg. In 1818 he became Professor of Philosophy at the University of Berlin, a position he held until his death in that city.

Hegel's mature philosophical career began with the publication of his 1807 *Phenomenology of Spirit.* My focus in these pages will be on publications and other documents produced between 1807 and 1831 that present Hegel's mature philosophical thought. But some attention to writings by Hegel prior to 1807 is also in order, especially insofar as they exhibit the significance of Hegel's early reflections on religion and Christianity, and the roles that those reflections play in the development of his philosophical thought.[14]

As early as 1793 Hegel produced an essay, the 'Tübingen Fragment,' in which he extolled the idea of a folk religion that engages the hearts and imagination of a people, emerges from that people's customs and practices, and places at its center the few very moral principles that are truly universal and fundamental. He pursued these thoughts further in fragmentary writings that he produced while at Berne. By 1795 Hegel had more fully developed a position that understood religion in terms of morality, and that understood morality through principles belonging to the practical philosophy of Kant. In 'The Positivity of the Christian Religion,' written in that year, he maintained that 'the aim and essence of all true religion, our religion included, is human morality, and that all the more detailed doctrines of Christianity . . . have their worth and sanctity appraised according to their close or distant connection with that aim.'[15] And in the reconstruction of the Sermon on the Mount that belongs to the 1795 essay 'The Life of Jesus,' Hegel's Jesus proclaims that ' "To act on a maxim that you can will as a universal law among all men, binding for you as well"—this is the fundamental law of all morality, the substance of all moral legislation and the sacred books of all people.'[16] Earlier in the same reconstruction Hegel's Jesus announces, 'You have been told to love your friends and your country, although you may hate your enemies and foreigners. But I say, if you cannot love your enemies, at least respect the humanity in them.'[17] Respect for humanity follows from respect for the moral law. Respect for the moral law requires acknowledging that moral obligation both prevails over and thus stands opposed to impulses and inclinations, and follows from rational self-legislation rather than from statutory commands.

While Hegel's understanding of morality in 1795 did include these Kantian oppositions between duty and inclinations on the one hand, and wholly external or positive commands on the other hand, it also went beyond these oppositions. This is seen as well in his writings on religion and Christianity. For example the figure whom Hegel constructs in 'The Life of Jesus' says, 'Reason does not condemn natural impulses, but governs and refines them,'[18] thus implying that natural impulses are capable of a refinement which renders them compatible with, and therefore not just opposed to, reason. He also says that 'if the light of the soul, the light of reason grows dim, how are our drives and inclinations to receive their proper bearing?'[19] This implies that drives and inclinations, which are to be distinguished from reason, can nonetheless assume a direction or bearing in the light of reason, a rational bearing, in which case opposition is not the final word about the connection of drives and impulses with reason.

Opposition is also not the final word about duty in relation to moral precepts that are given as statutes in public and cultural institutions. Moral autonomy certainly excludes conformity to precepts whose status follows wholly from external authority and that are 'positive' in that sense. But a belief or precept can present itself 'as something given throughout or as something given qua free and freely received.'[20] Moral autonomy does not exclude the affirmation of beliefs or conformity to precepts that are both given and freely appropriated by a subject. Moreover religious institutions play an important role in this regard. Authentic religious institutions present the beliefs and precepts they promulgate through imagery linked to the history and culture of a people. That imagery arouses trust and therefore renders the beliefs and precepts in question more readily appropriable by a people.[21]

The conception of morality, then, that determines Hegel's early considerations of religion and Christianity, is Kantian in opposing autonomous practical reason to given inner inclinations and given external precepts, but also includes the position that autonomous practical reason can take up into itself both inclinations given in inner nature and external precepts. Hegel tried to resolve the ambiguities inherent in this position in 'The Spirit of Christianity and its Fate,' an essay that he began in 1798, especially through the notion of 'love' that belongs to that essay. The love that Jesus embodied and that most essentially defined the mind and heart of original Christianity, according to Hegel in this essay, responds to a situation in which the various relations that obtain between God, external nature, inner human nature, and human beings themselves, are supposed to be relations of opposition. Hegel expressly says in this essay that 'Opposition is the possibility of reunification';[22] the dynamism that can bring about the reconciliation or reunification of these oppositions is love in its religious and Christian manifestation. Since the world in which this possibility became manifest had as its basis the 'most prodigious disbelief in nature (*ungeheuerste Unglaube an der Natur*),'[23] Christianity was fated in its historical development to assume a form that favors the preservation rather than the reconciliation of oppositions. Nonetheless we can still understand that healing and reconciling love defines the original spirit of this religion.

H. S. Harris notes that, in 1798, Hegel did not precisely assert the primacy of love over rational thought. Rather, 'he believed like Plato and Kant, in the natural authority of reason, and he believed, like Plato, that love is itself the most important manifestation of reason as a living force.'[24] In bringing about the reconciliations that it effects, love exhibits the rational truth of the terms that it reunifies and of their reunifications. This implies that these integrations can be the achievement of reason as such. But in 'The Spirit of Christianity' Hegel was critically unable to probe this implication. While he maintained that love as such and in its religious form was a rational power, he also identified reason with the reflective thinking that mirrors given realities and fixes distinctions and oppositions. A more substantive and comprehensive conception of reason is needed if the reconciliation of oppositions is to occur as a rational achievement. That conception of reason is the outcome of an examination that discloses in a methodic and evident way the possibilities that belong most radically to rational knowing. To attain that outcome, in turn, is to arrive at the standpoint that is in the last analysis required in order to do philosophy.

During his years at Jena Hegel worked at developing the examination of rational knowing to which I just referred, as well as the philosophy that is the result of the outcome of that examination, in the context of critical dialogues with philosophical work contemporary to him. In 1801 he published his first philosophical book, *The Difference Between Fichte's and Schelling's Systems of Philosophy*. In 1803 he published 'Faith and Knowledge' in *The Critical Journal of Philosophy*, which he was editing together with Schelling. In this work he examined basic issues pertaining to the relation of religion and philosophy, and developed a critique of the identification of rational knowing with reflection, through a consideration of the philosophies of Kant, Fichte, and Jacobi. He also produced three drafts of his philosophical system, along with other writings. And he completed his first mature philosophical work, the masterful *Phenomenology of Spirit*, for publication in 1807.

For Hegel, the *Phenomenology* was both the introduction to and the first part of his philosophical system. The system unfolds in subsequent publications. Hegel published the *Science of Logic*, a systematic examination of the categories that most basically determine thinking and the intelligible actuality of things, in three volumes between 1812 and 1816. The *Encyclopedia of the Philosophical Sciences* is a three-volume work that appeared in three editions in 1817, 1827, and 1830. He published the *Philosophy of Right*, a text in political philosophy, in 1820. In the year of his death, Hegel revised the first volume of the *Science of Logic* and was working on a revision of the *Phenomenology of Spirit*.

Since these works represent Hegel's mature philosophical achievement and are the volumes that he himself saw through to publication, they must be the resources on which all interpretation of and critical commentary on Hegel's philosophy chiefly rely. However with regard to Hegel's philosophical considerations of religion and Christianity one must also pay particular attention to the *Lectures on the Philosophy of Religion*. These, like all of the other works on diverse areas of philosophy that are entitled *Lectures* and that are attributed to Hegel, are in fact compilations of his lecture notes as well as notes taken by students in his courses, edited and published after Hegel's death. Hegel lectured on the philosophy of religion on four occasions in Berlin, in 1821, 1824, 1827, and 1831. In addition, he gave a series of lectures in 1829 on the proofs concerning the existence of God. The first editions of the *Lectures on the Philosophy of Religion* constructed a text using sources from each of the four years in which Hegel lectured on that topic. However, the most recent edition of these *Lectures* is also a truly critical edition, in that it presents each of the lecture series as an independent text based on the best available resources.[25] This is of particular importance because, as Peter Hodgson points out, in Hegel's various iterations of these lectures 'The fundamental point of view and theological-philosophical conclusions do not change, but the structure and details of the arguments do, and ideas are often formulated in slightly different ways that disclose now angles of meaning.'[26] The *Lectures* give us privileged access to the ongoing development of Hegel's thinking on religion and Christianity. They extend and enrich the positions on those matters for which he argues in his published texts.

I maintain, therefore, that while the interpretation of any aspect of Hegel's philosophical achievement must in the last analysis be controlled by attention to the mature, published texts, the *Lectures on the Philosophy of Religion*, along with the 1829 *Lectures on the Proofs of God's Existence*, are an invaluable resource that one must consult in developing a full and substantial appraisal of his views regarding religion and Christianity. That is the policy that I will follow in these pages.

The pursuit of that policy will take the following form. Chapter 1 will deal with Hegel's idea of philosophy and its relation to religion and Christianity. I will show how Hegel's idea of philosophy is the outcome of an exposition of the critical and methodical process of self-examination through which cognitive self-consciousness arrives at a warranted understanding of the fundamental truth about itself. Hegel presents this exposition in the *Phenomenology of Spirit*. He calls the understanding that it reaches 'absolute knowing'. This is a position whose justification makes evident the self-determining nature of rational cognition as well as the legitimacy of the claim that it is through rational cognition that we attain knowledge of that which truly is. Hegel also discusses his idea of philosophy by commenting, in the *Encyclopedia*, on the aims and dimensions that belong to knowing. I will examine these comments in this chapter. The process through which one reaches the position on 'absolute knowing' both does and must include considerations of religion in general and of Christianity in particular. To see why this is the case is to begin to grasp the relation that obtains between religion and Christianity on the one hand and philosophy on the other hand, as Hegel understands that relation.

Chapter 2 will present a more focused and detailed consideration of the understandings of religion and Christianity that Hegel presents in the *Phenomenology of Spirit*. I will comment briefly on the way a general understanding of religion appears at various points in the *Phenomenology*, and in more detail on the understanding of religion the emerges from a consideration of the dialectic that concludes the phenomenological examination of morality. This understanding links religion with self-transcendence, self-consciousness, and Spirit, given Hegel's understanding of the same. It provides the context for the interpretation of Christianity that Hegel develops in the *Phenomenology*. That interpretation presents ideas and claims that are of fundamental and permanent importance for all of Hegel's subsequent work regarding religion and Christianity. It also leads to the claim that Hegel expresses in 1807 regarding the connection of religion and Christianity with absolute knowing. That claim is also one that Hegel takes up and develops in fundamentally important ways in subsequent work.

In the light of material discussed in the first two chapters, Chapter 3 will consider Hegel's later reflections on religion and Christianity with reference to the issue of the relation of philosophy to theology. Hegel insists that philosophical considerations of religion and Christianity cannot confine themselves to an exclusive occupation with religious experience or human religious involvement, but must proceed to disciplined reflection concerning God. But it is also the case that one moves to reflection concerning God through a proper consideration of the components of religious involvement. Those components are faith understood with reference to certitude and feeling, and what Hegel calls representational thinking, which in this context coincides with what we might call religious discourse on the contemporary scene. Representational thinking includes symbolic images, narrative discourses that take up and elaborate those symbolic images, and conceptual elements that are linked to but also different from symbolic images and their narrative elaborations. In connection with representational thinking, Hegel's most essential claim is that such thinking both calls for and requires reconceptualization or reenactment through a process of thought that is philosophical and strictly conceptual and that, while supposedly retaining the content of representational thinking, is different in form from representational thinking as such. Both the meaning and the legitimacy of this claim are disputed. I will offer an interpretation of this claim, a defense of the claim in the light of that interpretation, some comments on the relation of Hegel and Schleiermacher in connection with the question of representational thinking, and discussion of Hegel's view about the relation of theology and philosophy in the light of his claim regarding representational and philosophical thinking.

The issues discussed in Chapter 3 are entirely germane to the problem that Chapter 4 will consider, namely, the problem of God and the world in Christian and Hegelian thought. In addressing this problem it will be necessary for me to return to the issue of representational thinking and to discuss what I will call the speculative resources inherent in representational thinking. This will lead to critical discussion of the understanding of God and of the relation between the world and God that Hegel reaches through a process that he claims to be one that reenacts the content of the religious representation in speculative, that is to say properly philosophical, concepts. In historical terms, this discussion will include comment on Hegel's relations with theologians who, in the later years of the 1820s, were critical of this work. In philosophical and theological terms, this discussion will introduce a consideration of the adequacy of Hegel's conception of divine transcendence in relation to what is required by a Christian understanding of the same.

Chapter 5 will consider Hegel's discussions of the Christian mysteries. I will begin with comment on Hegel's discussion of the divine Trinity. This comment will include critical discussion of what seems to be the position on the relation between the immanent and the economic Trinity in Hegel's thought. Then I will consider his discussions of the doctrines of creation and the Fall; the Incarnation, reconciliation and redemption; the Resurrection and the indwelling of the Spirit in the gathered community. Especially the last of these issues will lead to consideration of Hegel's remarks about cult and worship and about what he calls ethical life, remarks that are of significant importance in interpreting and assessing his understanding of religion and Christianity.

My final two chapters will consider Hegel's positions on religion and Christianity in relation to contemporary philosophical and theological inquiry. Chapters 6 will deal with some critical problems that one might find in Hegel's essential proposals regarding religion and Christianity. I will discuss his treatment of specific Christian mysteries and of the concept of mystery as such. The latter discussion will include an assessment of Hegel's position on the relation of the symbol and the concept in speculative or philosophical theology. I will consider an existential objection to Hegel that focuses on the nature of religious practice in its specificity. And I will consider an ethical objection to Hegel's position concerning the relation of religion and society which claims that the speculative comprehension of social reality that Hegel requires excludes the possibility of fundamental social critique and thus of contemporary appropriation of the prophetic sources of Christianity.

Chapter 7 will consider Hegel's thought in relation to contemporary philosophy of religion and theology by addressing ways in which his understandings of religion and Christianity might present resources for and challenges to current inquiry. I will begin by discussing religious discourse, differing hermeneutical approaches to religious discourse, and the specific hermeneutics of religious discourse made possible by what Hegel calls speculative thinking. This discussion leads to a challenging position about goals that are not only possible aims but arguably required aims for theological inquiry. It is a position that is closely connected with Hegel's insistence that reflection on religion must not be confined to considering religious experience or religious involvement but must proceed to a genuinely conceptual consideration of God. I will then revisit the question of divine transcendence in connection with Hegel's understanding of God and of the relation between God and both the natural and the historical world. Finally, I will briefly discuss the implications of Hegel's position regarding the historical nature of rational thought for a contemporary understanding of religious truth and of Christianity in relation to the other religions of the world.

I would like to conclude these introductory remarks with one additional comment. As I have already noted, Hegel insisted that the proper concern of philosophy, and of course he would say of theology as well, is with truth. That is to say, philosophical work is not simply the work of framing or considering proposals regarding how some or other matters might be understood. It is more earnestly the task of trying to understand such proposals as fully and thoroughly as possible so that one can then ask what the conditions are that would allow, require, or forbid one to affirm them, and whether or not those conditions are fulfilled. By extension, in studying a philosopher such as Hegel, it is of course of indispensable importance to come to an understanding of what he meant that is as full and accurate as possible. But if one's study of this or any philosopher is philosophical, the point at which one can say 'I've got him right' is not the point at which one is finished. Further questions remain. 'Is what he says, or some of it, true? Is what he says, or some of it, not true? Can I determine these matters? If not, what further work do I need to do? And what is the relation between those elements of Hegel's thought that I affirm, deny, continue to grapple with, or choose to set aside, and my own hold on the truth, my own ongoing inquiry into the truth?'

I am, of course, deeply concerned in these pages with getting Hegel right. But in relation to current philosophy and theology, the most important purpose for the study of Hegel or of any comparable figure is associated with the role that one's critical considerations, affirmations, doubts about and denials of understandings offered by that figure play in one's assessments of what is true. I believe that such a concern animates the attention that Barth gives to Hegel in the essay I cite at the beginning of these remarks. I invite the reader to join me in that concern.

Chapter 1

Hegel's idea of knowledge and philosophy

Since philosophy is a rational and self-reflective enterprise, Hegel believes that doing philosophy requires a warranted understanding of the essential nature of rational cognition. Only such an understanding can secure the standpoint required for philosophical inquiry. In turn, since philosophy is the radical realization of the capacities that determine rational cognition, an authentic understanding of the nature of rational cognition entails a conception of philosophy itself. Hegel made an important suggestion about the nature of rational cognition and philosophy when he wrote, in 1801, 'Dichotomy is the source of the *need for philosophy*; and as the culture of an era, it is the unfree and given aspect of the whole configuration.'[1] A dichotomy in this context is a culturally given and fixed opposition between terms. As given, it is a condition that thought must simply acknowledge, which limits the freedom of thought. As a fixed opposition, it is a condition that requires that we consider it from the standpoint of one or the other of its terms, which undercuts the possibility of integrated comprehension. These factors stand in the way of rational cognition insofar as such cognition is an autonomous process that aims at integrations of opposed terms that lead to liberating possibilities within culture and that also represent the comprehensiveness that yields genuine knowledge of what is actual.

But can we suppose without further ado that rational cognition does attain genuine knowledge of what is actual? Hegel raises this question in the 'Introduction' to the *Phenomenology of Spirit*. The *Phenomenology* presents a demonstration for a position on the nature of knowing that is supposed to supply a standpoint for philosophical inquiry. It is not possible to give a brief and also substantive discussion of the argument that belongs to this complex, labyrinthine work. But to ignore that argument and simply to present elements of the conception of knowledge that Hegel maintains would be deeply false to his philosophical approach. Hegel maintains that one can never truly consider a philosophical position apart from an understanding of the reasoning from which it emerges and which is supposed to supply its demonstration. I will try, therefore, to discuss in a general but hopefully accurate way the principle phases of that reasoning as it appears in the *Phenomenology*. I will also comment on Hegel's conception of philosophy by referring to the first volume of the *Encyclopedia of the Philosophical Sciences*. Especially in discussing the argument that belongs to the *Phenomenology* in this chapter I will address the ways in which considerations of religion and Christianity emerge in that argument and contribute to its conclusion. This will, among other things, provide a context for the more detailed focus on religion and Christianity in the *Phenomenology* in Chapter 2.

It is natural for philosophers of his day, Hegel notes, to assume that before one can develop philosophical knowledge of reality 'one must first of all come to an understanding of cognition, which is regarded either as an instrument to get hold of' what truly is, 'or as the medium through which one discovers it.'[2] After all, there are different sorts of cognition. One needs to use the right sort for philosophical purposes. But this attitude quickly leads to skepticism regarding the very possibility of cognition of what truly is. If cognition is like an instrument or a medium, then it does not leave the item to which it is applied, or the thing it filters, unaffected. If so, then anything that we know is known in virtue of its being modified by this instrument or medium. If one could correct for the modification, the object would then revert to its unmodified state and would be unknown. To regard cognition as an instrument or a medium that one can examine before putting it to work suggests the impossibility of coming to know what is in and of itself actual.

Of course much is taken for granted in the view of knowledge just mentioned. It is not evident that cognition is something like an instrument or a medium, or that there is the kind of difference between ourselves and this instrument or medium that would allow us to examine it for the sake of determining its possible uses. It is especially problematic to suppose that the nature of cognition both excludes the possibility of access to that which in itself is and at the same time opens the possibility of truth.[3] It may be that the fear of error that disposes one to begin philosophy with a critique of cognition is in fact a fear that blocks access to truth. Perhaps one should just abandon the view of cognition that gives rise to that fear. Then one could just suppose that rational cognition of actuality is possible and begin straightaway to pursue that possibility.

But this will not do either. '*One* bare assurance is worth just as much as another.'[4] By itself, the claim that knowing can attain genuine cognition of actuality is as much a bare assurance as the view about knowing that suggests a contrary position. Even if this claim is true, 'in coming on the scene it is not yet Science in its developed and unfolded truth.'[5] We require an account of knowing that includes a demonstration of the truth of that claim. This coincides with an exposition of 'the path of the natural consciousness which presses forward to true knowledge,' and which finally achieves, 'through a completed experience of itself, the awareness of what it really is in itself.'[6]

Natural consciousness consists of all forms of consciousness in which we assume but do not show the validity of an account of knowing. It comes in an array of shapes. A shape of natural consciousness presents some understanding of the nature of the object of consciousness, the nature of consciousness itself, and the relation between them. A shape of natural consciousness also presents the claim that the terms and relations that define its structure make possible genuine cognition of the object. On its own terms, a shape of natural consciousness holds within itself both the ability to test this claim and the criterion needed to make that test. One makes the test by endeavoring to know that which, given any particular shape of natural consciousness, is supposed to be there to be known, in the way in which it is supposed to be knowable. Suppose that, in the course of this attempt, a contradiction arises. Then it becomes evident that one's concept of the nature of the object of knowledge does not conceptualize that object in its integrity, but rather presents an understanding of the object that natural consciousness entertains and that stands in contrast with the object itself. 'Hence it comes to pass for consciousness that what it previously took to be the *in-itself* is not an *in-itself,* or that it was only an in-itself *for consciousness.*'[7] One's experience of the object is a process in which one forms a new concept of the nature of the object, as well as a new understanding of the nature of consciousness, the relation between consciousness and the object, and the manner in which what is available to be known is supposed to be knowable.

Phenomenology is, for Hegel, the 'Science of the *experience of consciousness.*'[8] In doing phenomenology one observes the '*dialectical* movement which consciousness exercises on itself and which affects both its knowledge and its object,'[9] the process through which new shapes of consciousness emerge from preceding shapes due to tests of and revisions of specific claims regarding the conditions of genuine cognition. The phenomenologist brings order and necessity into the process through the analyses that are part of these observations. Since any of its shapes present some claim regarding the conditions of genuine knowing, natural consciousness on its own terms exhibits at least the abstract concept of genuine cognition. But that is exactly what it exhibits. 'Natural consciousness will show itself to be only the concept of knowledge, or in other words, not to be real knowledge.'[10] The science of the experience of consciousness will demonstrate that the terms and relations supposed from the standpoint of natural consciousness to allow for genuine cognition fail as conditions of that possibility. In this sense, the course of experience that natural consciousness traverses can 'be regarded as the pathway of *doubt,* or more precisely as the highway of despair.'[11] But since a warranted account of genuine knowing does emerge as a consequence of the experience of natural consciousness, the presentation of that experience is 'the detailed history of the *education* of consciousness itself to the standpoint of Science.'[12]

The various shapes that belong to the experience of consciousness fall into more general structures that are ordered and linked in the light of phenomenological observation. The first phases of the experience of consciousness belong to a structure for which Hegel simply uses the word 'Consciousness' itself as the title. Consciousness in this sense sees its object as independent of and external to itself, and as that which makes the essential contribution to cognition. Knowledge comes about insofar as one allows the object to present itself to consciousness. One learns through the course of the development of this structure that one must do more and more in order to allow this to happen. Still, as long as consciousness in this sense is in place, the object is defined in terms of its otherness from consciousness, and the relation of consciousness to its object is the relation of an essentially receptive consciousness to something other. But it finally becomes manifest that it is the very activity of cognitive consciousness itself that realizes the intelligibility of the object that one grasps in understanding. The intelligibility that one grasps in understanding is made actual therein just through cognitive activity. This means that an understanding of the object is as such, if only implicitly, an understanding of one's own explanatory activities. The relation of consciousness to its object is not only a relation to something other. It is even more essentially a relation to itself.

With this a new general structure, 'Self-Consciousness,' emerges in phenomenological inquiry. Self-Consciousness is defined by the attitude that the relation of consciousness to the object is in truth a self-relation. The object is most essentially defined as the vehicle, as it were, through which consciousness achieves self-relatedness, and thus in terms of its being-for-another, for consciousness, as contrasted with its independent being. Of course 'the whole expanse of the sensuous world' continues to stand before consciousness. But that is so only insofar as this appearance 'is connected with the second moment, the unity of self-consciousness with itself';[13] self-consciousness needs its object to exhibit this connectedness in the manner in which that object presents itself. Self-consciousness is essentially determined by the 'Desire' (*Begierde*) that its object present itself in this manner.[14]

According to Hegel, with the emergence of self-consciousness we have 'entered the native realm of truth.'[15] This is in part because self-consciousness, determined by desire, can experience itself as living, and can experience the world that situates it as a dimension of its own life and as comprised of living things.[16] And it is indeed the case that the concept of the relation of consciousness to its object that belongs to self-consciousness overcomes the one-sided attitude that defines the object as simply given and external to consciousness. But there is also a kind of abstraction or one-sidedness that belongs to the concept of the relation of consciousness to its object that initially defines self-consciousness. The dialectic of the experience of self-consciousness will correct this.

The desire that belongs to self-consciousness, as already noted, demands that the object present itself in a way that shows the essential connectedness of the object with the self. This is possible only if another self defines itself in terms of its recognition of oneself. Thus the desire that belongs to self-consciousness defines the situation that determines the self as one of relations between selves. The self by its very nature subsists in a context that is essentially intersubjective. Its desire is, one might say, the desire for the desire of another.[17] Both the confirmation and the occurrence of the identity of the self follow from recognition by the other. Recognition, in turn, can occur in an adequate way only if the other offers recognition on the basis of its own initiative. This means that the self must acknowledge the other self, as well as its object in a more general sense, as possessing intrinsic being. Even though desire seems to relate the object essentially to the self, self-consciousness must 'learn through experience that the object is independent.'[18] Even if self-consciousness presents us with 'the native realm of truth,' the standpoint that defines consciousness must receive its due, and the two standpoints must come together.

The process through which the self learns this, and is transformed by what it learns, begins with the search for recognition. Hegel shows in a brief but penetrating analysis that genuine recognition requires a reciprocal relation between selves.[19] But the outcome of the search for recognition in its first occurrence is not reciprocity. In that instance the search takes the form of a struggle that ends when the victorious self dominates and enslaves another, requiring recognition from the other in virtue of that domination. The manifest relation of master and slave presents the first as independent and the second as dependent. The latent and true significance of the relationship reverses matters. The master enjoys products while doing no work, and receives recognition from one considered inessential, with the consequence that the recognition is itself inessential. The slave receives an experience of self-identity in fearing death at the hand of the master, consciousness of the self as one who is in principle independent in recognizing the person of the master, and a sense of personal agency in the performance of work. The slave can integrate these moments into a conscious experience of independence in the face of the master, external circumstances notwithstanding.

This makes possible an attitude that defines the world and one's situation in the world just in terms of one's understanding of the same. This attitude leads to the possibility of reversing one's judgments about even the seemingly most evident truths about the world, and then of reversing those reversals. In this circumstance the self finds itself determined by a relation between a self-identity that is stable and is its own essential reality, and a whirl of unstable differences that coincide with the endless reversals that the self brings about. Over against the self in its mutable facticity a reality stands which is essential reality, its own essential reality, and one that is beyond it. The self yearns for unity with this transcendent essence that is its own. It cannot attain this unity, because any effort at so doing is an assertion of itself, that is, of its mutable particularity over against essential reality. Self-consciousness is now the 'unhappy consciousness.' But, Hegel maintains, we can see in this situation of alienation the conditions that allow it to be overcome. The last moment of the effort the self makes at uniting itself with the reality that is essential to it and beyond it is the surrender of its own will. In surrendering its will, the mutable, particular self is both acting, asserting itself, and surrendering that about itself that requires that it stand outside of the reality that is essential to it. Given this, that reality can present itself from its side as independent of the self and as the same time connected with the self as its very essence. Alienation is in principle overcome. The self now stands in relation to an independent reality that is, in its independence, the condition of the relation of the self to itself. The object of consciousness is simultaneously independent and the vehicle of the self-related unity of consciousness with itself. Consciousness in turn is related to an independent object and is, in just this situation, a self-related unity.

This situation presents a kind of reconciliation of consciousness and self-consciousness. I say a kind of reconciliation because the form in which it now appears to us, which Hegel entitles 'Reason,' is only its initial form and requires development. Very briefly, the first form of the 'unity of self-consciousness and being'[20] that determines this reconciliation comes about as one finds that nature, including one's own corporeal nature, possesses an intelligibility that one accesses by thoughtful observation. But an attempt to understand the nature of self-conscious thought by observing things reduces thought to a thing. One must, as a response to this, revive an understanding of the active, self-realizing character of rational self-consciousness. This entails a definition of the self as one engaged in a process of self-actualization, and of the world as a world of selves engaged in such a process, a social world. The experience that follows from these definitions shows that the individual is not one who pursues the task of self-actualization by realizing within a social context the possibilities provided to one by something like a given particular nature. Rather, the individual is one whose actions function along with the actions of all to bring about the social context that in turn presents a field of possibilities for individual self-actualization. Individuals who pursue self-actualization in a way that is situated and enabled by this context find themselves integrated with others in the community that is the outcome of their actions and that grounds the possibility of individuals defining their identity in terms of their relations to each other and to the community itself. With this, Spirit makes an appearance in the science of the experience of consciousness.

This is not the first reference to Spirit in the *Phenomenology*. Once the self appears as one whose identity is confirmed and realized by recognition of another, 'we already have before us the concept of *Spirit.* . . . this absolute substance which is the unity of different independent self-consciousnesses which, in their opposition, enjoy perfect freedom: the "I" that is a "We" and the "We" that is an "I".'[21] The community that interrelates different selves and that, as the context of possibilities for action and self-actualization, is the substance of their lives, becomes something that the self

> opposes to itself as an objective, actual *world,* but a world which has completely lost the meaning for the self of

something alien to it, just as the self has completely lost
the meaning of a being-for-self separated from the world,
whether dependent on it or not. Spirit, being the *substance*
and the universal, self-identical, abiding essence, is the
unmoved solid *ground* and *starting-point* for the action of
all, and it is their purpose and goal, the in-itself of every
self-consciousness expressed in thought. This substance is
equally the universal *work* produced by the action of all
and each as their unity and identity, for it is the *being-for-self*,
the self, action.[22]

According to Hegel, 'Reason is Spirit when its certainty of
being all reality has been raised to truth, and when it is conscious of itself as its own world, and of the world as itself.'[23] The
social world situates the practical and cognitive acts through
which the self relates to nature, as well as the specific activities
and the normative understandings that pertain to our efforts at
self-actualization and our particular interactions. That is to say,
it is the context and situates and enables everything that has
heretofore appeared and received examination in the science of
the experience of consciousness. Moreover, this world presents
itself as both standing over against the self, and as the outcome
of the actions and interactions of each one and of everyone who
belongs to this world. Thus the independent being of this world
is at the same time a being-for-the-self. The self finds, in its
connection with this independent social substance, its own self-
related unity. This means that a further reconciliation of consciousness and self-consciousness has occurred, one that pertains
not only to the self in its connection with nature, or with the
other whom one encounters in particular interactions, or with
its own self, but to the self in its connection with the world that
makes possible all the actions and understandings that are related
to all of these matters. The reconciliation of consciousness and
self-consciousness that makes an initial appearance in Reason
has, with the appearance of Spirit, been 'raised to truth.'
Even this version of the reconciliation of consciousness and
self-consciousness, however, needs development. It has already
become evident in the science of the experience of consciousness
that 'Unity, difference, and relation are categories each of which

is nothing in and for itself, but only in relation to its opposite, and they cannot therefore be separated from one another.'[24] The situation that finally obtains in virtue of the reciprocity of these categories must present itself from the standpoint of each of them. This means that the individual self and the social world need to present themselves as connected with each other in a self-related unity, as different from each other, and as interrelated in a way that preserves both unity and difference. The complete reconciliation of consciousness and self-consciousness requires that each of these presentations occur independently of the other in the domain that Hegel entitles 'Spirit.' All these issues are in play as the dialectic of the experience of consciousness goes forward from this point in the *Phenomenology*. It is especially in this phase of the science of the experience of consciousness that considerations of religion begin to play a determining role.

The social world that Hegel discusses under the heading 'Spirit' first presents itself as a tranquil unity that integrates the different spheres that belong to it. Insofar as this world occurs in explicit connection with those who act and interact within it, it is the sphere of human law. Insofar as this world presents an inner reality of its own that stands over against the individual self, it is a sphere of divine law. The individual who acts in the public domain associates with others as a citizen. One carries out the natural actions and associations that are conditions of and therefore antecedent to civic association as a member of the family. Human law specifically pertains to one who is acting as a citizen. Divine law, which represents the inner reality of the world as contrasted with the domain of the city, shelters the individual insofar as the individual stands apart from civic associations, and commands that the dead be memorialized and honored. The obligations of both human and divine law are binding on all. But there is a more specific connection between human law and the actions of men, who are guardians of the city. And there is a more specific connection between divine law and the actions of women, who are guardians of the family.

Only one thing is needed to bring the terms that this tranquil unity integrates into explicit opposition, namely, the action of the individual. And the individual must act. As the tragedy of Creon and Antigone suggests, that action brings the family and the city, man and woman, human and divine law into express conflict. The world that integrates these spheres and identities falls apart. The action of the individual that has this consequence for the world also has a consequence for the individual. Insofar as the world is a tranquil integration of different spheres and identities, '*This* particular individual counts only as a shadowy unreality.'[25] In acting in the world in a way that tears the world apart, the individual asserts the sheer particularity of the self over against the world. This dimension of selfhood must receive its due. Once this occurs, however, the self becomes one particular individual along with other particular individuals. The law of the world now simply stands over against individuals and accords them the status that they have as persons. The individual who has asserted sheer particularity is deprived of concrete self-identity.

One who is thus deprived of concrete self-identity cannot recover the same through one's own resources alone. Therefore the individual must surpass the particularity of the self by reconnecting the self with the world. That world stands over against the self as a domain whose might threatens to overwhelm the individual and as a domain whose goods sustain the individual. The world presents itself in terms of power and wealth. The spheres that belong to the world are good insofar as identification with them leads the individual to surpass mere particularity, and bad insofar as identification with them simply serves that particularity. But unfortunately, the individual inevitably comes to identify efforts to serve power and to benefit from wealth as both good and bad. In this situation the individual defines the self in terms of its difference from the world and the reality of the world in terms of the presence that that reality has in one's thinking. That presence can take two forms. One can suppose that the reality of the world finally resides in another world beyond the immediately present one, a world that presents itself to our thought in symbols and in which we have faith. Or one can suppose that the reality of the immediately present world is discovered in the mediating understanding of that world itself at which we arrive through enlightened insight.

Faith and enlightened insight themselves come into conflict. Faith succumbs to enlightenment critique because it cannot, by itself, move beyond symbols to the concepts that would allow it to understand its own truth. Since, for enlightened insight, the reality of the world is defined in terms of the presence the world has to our thought, that is to say in terms of its connection with the self, the world that stands over against the self is now understood with regard to its utility for the self. If one defines the world in terms of its connection with and utility for the self in a thoroughgoing way, then one is disposed to negate any reality, certainly any social reality, that would present itself with an intrinsic identity that one would have to acknowledge, and to which one would to that extent at least have to conform. This leads to an absolute and destructive reign of terror that attacks all social institutions, including the ones the reign of terror creates, an orgy of destruction that finally destroys itself.

The self who has defined the world in terms of its utility for the self, which has terror as its outcome, learns through its experience that it has defined the world that differs from the self in relation to its own will. Since the world that stands apart from the self represents what is the case, the definitions that the will presents represent what ought to be. The reality of the world in which we act and live is now defined by a moral will, and moral imperatives, in turn, are the outcomes of the autonomous activity of that will. The will determines on its own terms what as such ought to be done, that is, what counts as a moral imperative for all rational agents. Those imperatives define what is essential regarding the world. Precisely for this reason the oppositions that at first seem to obtain between one's moral will and outer nature, the given aspects of one's own inner nature, and the holy lawgiver who sanctifies duty, disappear. Now one defines the external social world and others whom one encounters, ones own inner experience, and the voice of God, in terms of one's own conscience. In this situation, conflict inevitably arises between those who act and those who judge actions. The opposition between the acting and the judging self both indicates and is grounded in the finite nature of each. This allows each one, in a consciousness of the finitude of the other, to be conscious of the finitude of the self. Since each in its consciousness of the other recognizes itself, a word of reconciliation is spoken. This reconciliation expressly interrelates and thus transcends the opposition between selves who define their identity with reference to particular conscience, and also preserves that opposition by preserving the immediate individual identity of each self.

In the next chapter I will more fully consider the dialectic of the conscientious self, and the conflict of the acting and the judging selves to which that dialectic leads, in order to discuss the important understanding of religion that is the outcome of that dialectic. But what is to be said of that outcome now, within the limits that define the task of this chapter? As a consequence of the resolution of the conflict between the acting and the judging self, each self now discovers that it and all others are members of 'a collectivity of individualized actions, a collectivity which therefore forms the arena, the ground for their actions,'[26] and that also comes about through the actions of each of its members individually and all of its members together. The self finds this social world, this reality which situates every other reality that the self encounters, is, or becomes, to be a ground that stands over against the self and to have an identity that includes within itself activity that the self knows as its own. An explicit reconciliation of consciousness and self-consciousness that is more thoroughgoing than its predecessor because it pertains precisely to this social world results from the resolution of the conflict between the acting and the judging self.

The self-consciousness that emerges in this reconciliation occurs in connection with an awareness of something that is supposed to surpass the finitude of the finite self and of all finite realities. The object of this awareness is therefore understood simultaneously as a reality that 'contains within itself all essence and all actuality,'[27] and as the ground of the self's consciousness of itself. This marks a reintroduction of the idea of divinity into the science of the experience of consciousness and leads to an extended consideration of religion as such. At each stage of the dialectic of Spirit the idea of the divine has appeared: as the substantial power manifest in divine law, as the object of the faith that conflicts with enlightened insight, and as the holy legislator who sanctifies duty. Throughout, the social world mediates to the self not only the presence of nature, other selves, and itself, but of divinity. Now the divine presents itself as that absolute reality in connection with which one acquires consciousness of one's own identity and of the identity of the social world that presents the possibilities that enable one to form an identity.

The examination of religion that follows meets two needs. There is the need to integrate religious consciousness with a consciousness of one's being-in-the-world. And there is the need to examine in an ordered fashion those representations that express consciousness of the divine and specify conceptions of divinity. Thus Hegel's phenomenology of religious consciousness begins with a consideration of the most simple and immediate ways in which the divine can be represented through natural phenomena or things, proceeds to examine representations that human beings make, and then to consider the situation in which human beings become conscious of the possibility that all the access to the divine that we have is due to things or art works that we make. The anguish and the irony to which this consciousness can lead are reversed in a representation of God as self-revealing.

God reveals Godself through creation, and most fully through uniting Godself with human nature. God's uniting Godself with human nature enables one to experience human individual and social history as a kind of participation in the divine life. This is the ground of the possibility of integrating religious self-consciousness with a consciousness of one's being-in-the-world. The conception of God as one who reveals Godself by relating to God's own self in creation and in God's unity with human nature allows one to think of the relation between God and the created and human world, and the nature of God revealed in that relation, not as something beyond rational comprehension but as that which reason comprehends when it attains its most far-reaching possibility. That attainment, in turn, is required for the rational self-appropriation of religious consciousness. This must occur if that consciousness is to be a form of self-consciousness in the fullest sense. It is also the final form of the reconciliation of consciousness with self-consciousness. This completes the process of the reconciliation of consciousness with self-consciousness that begins with Reason and that occurs in a more thoroughgoing way through the dialectic of Spirit. The completion of this process coincides with the full self-appropriation by rational self-consciousness of itself. Hegel calls this 'absolute knowing.'

In discussing Hegel's position on the relation of religious consciousness to absolute knowing, Quentin Lauer says that one can understand this position to mean, as Feuerbach might say, that 'the only "absolute" of which the human spirit is ultimately conscious is itself. But one can also interpret it as meaning that consciousness of self short of consciousness of the "absolute" is not consciousness of the whole self.'[28] This is an issue to which I shall return on several occasions. And in the next chapter I will consider with greater care not only the appearance that religious consciousness makes at the conclusion of the dialectic of morality and conscience but also the treatment that Christianity receives in the phenomenology of religious consciousness. But for now, consider the idea of philosophy that Hegel presents in the light of the warranted understanding of rational cognition he claims to have attained in the *Phenomenology*, along with Hegel's suggestions as to the place that religion and Christianity occupy in philosophical inquiry. Each of these matters is of great importance for my subsequent discussion.

Hegel understands the nature of rational cognition in terms of the full and fully demonstrated reconciliation of consciousness and self-consciousness.[29] This means that rational knowing is an activity that (i) relates itself to an object insofar as the object is other than consciousness itself, (ii) and thus to the being that belongs to the object in its integrity, to the being-in-itself of the object, (iii) and simultaneously brings or allows the object to come into relation with itself, to stand as something whose being is a being-for-another, for consciousness, (iv) which is to say an intelligibility that can be realized, comprehended in thought, through rational processes. Since rational knowing relates itself to the being-in-itself of that which is known, its outcome is actual knowledge of that which truly is. Since rational knowing brings that which is known into relation with itself, constituting that object as an intelligibility that can be realized or comprehended through the processes of thought, it is, in relation to the object, a self-related unity. This last statement implies that rational knowing is a self-determining or autonomous activity. It is the activity of rational knowing itself that constitutes and realizes intelligibility. This is why Stephen Houlgate is correct in saying that Hegel's account of thought is an account of the conditions that allow 'thought to determine itself *freely*,' and that at the conclusion of that account 'thought has become explicitly what it always has been implicitly, namely the determination of thought by *itself*.'[30] At the same time, I maintain, it is important to emphasize that, according to Hegel, rational knowing attains actual knowledge of the intelligible structure that belongs as such to that which is known. If rational activity is fully autonomous because it both constitutes and comprehends intelligibility through its own self-directing processes, it is also the case that being itself is most essentially determined by a rational structure that it discloses in and to rational thought. This is the meaning of the often-cited statement that Hegel makes in the *Philosophy of Right*, 'What is rational is actual, and what is actual is rational.'[31] Reason has to do with nothing other than and nothing less than actuality in its essential character. Reciprocally, actuality in its essential character is determined by an intelligible structure accessible precisely to rational thought.

The process through which one arrives, according to Hegel, at a fundamental and warranted understanding of rational cognition, as well as the self-determining nature of thought made evident by that understanding, carry important implications regarding the nature of history, the relation of philosophy to history, and again more specifically to religion and Christianity. The science of the experience of consciousness examines specific shapes of consciousness that exhibit, separately and together, the determinations that account for the genuine self-relatedness of rational self-consciousness. Absolute knowing, understood with reference to the reconciliation of consciousness and self-consciousness that defines this self-relatedness, occurs through a release of those determinations from the determinate shapes of consciousness in which they appear, and an integration of them in a pure conception of knowing. But the development of the science of the experience of consciousness requires that the shapes of consciousness that are immanently ordered and identified within that science appear in life so that they can come forward again in phenomenological thought. Those appearances happen in the historical activities that bring about the social world that is the work of each and all, and that at the same time stands on its own as the substance of the lives of those whose work it is. It is in this world that people sense, perceive, and understand, attain self-awareness, struggle for recognition, observe nature, act for the sake of self-actualization, bring about communities, act on conflicting convictions, build reconciled communities that preserve conflicting differences, and gather in devotion. Indeed it is just through these sorts of activities that the social world comes into being. The action that has the social world as its work at one and the same time has as its work the production of thought in the multitude of its forms. Or, the historical and social self-production of human beings and of humanity is definable as the process of the self-production of thought.

Hegel would say that the process of the self-production of thought is the process that Spirit performs in its journey toward self-knowledge. And he expressly says with regard to this that 'The movement of carrying forward the form of its self-knowledge is the labour which it accomplishes as actual history.'[32] Actual history stands over against phenomenology, in the Hegelian sense, as its other. It is the domain in which the diverse possibilities that belong to knowing develop in a contingent and non-systematic way. These possibilities include developments in philosophy itself. The philosophy of an era, when it is at its best, represents the cognitive standpoint of that era. Thus Hegel says, again in the *Philosophy of Right*, that a philosophy is 'its own time apprehended in thought.'[33]

It would not be correct to say that phenomenology 'presupposes' actual history. The identity and order of the shapes of consciousness as they appear in phenomenology is, Hegel claims at least, determined with necessity by the immanent process of phenomenology itself. At no point does the science of the experience of consciousness appeal to actual history for the intelligibility or justification of claims that are presented. Nor does the science of the experience of consciousness even refer to actual history, as contrasted with the shapes of consciousness whose definitions and order are immanent to that science. But the shapes of consciousness whose ordered dialectic has as its outcome absolute knowing must have appeared in actual history in order for that same history to have attained the standpoint that makes possible the cognitive self-understanding that absolute knowing is, and the science of the experience of consciousness that is the demonstration of the sense and truth of that self-understanding. In this way, phenomenology is on its own terms a systematically necessary reenactment of what has already occurred in a contingent and nonsystematic way in history.

But history, the context for what I have called the social self-production of human beings and humanity and the self-production of reason, must be understood with reference to the social world as a concrete whole. In Hegel's words, 'Only the totality of Spirit is in Time, and the "shapes" which are "shapes" of the totality of *Spirit*, display themselves in a temporal succession; for only the whole has true actuality and therefore the form of pure freedom in the face of an "other," a form which expresses itself as time.'[34] Hegel makes it very clear in this context that the structures in the *Phenomenology* that he has called Consciousness, Self-Consciousness, Reason, and even Spirit are '*moments* of the whole'[35] but not the whole itself. One adequately conceives of the social world as a concrete whole when one integrates what Hegel considers with reference to the rubric of Spirit in the *Phenomenology*, which subsumes into itself the shapes of consciousness that fall under the headings of Consciousness, Self-Consciousness, and Reason, with the conception of religion that develops as the outcome of the dialectic of Spirit. It is the social world understood with reference to its political, cultural, and moral institutions and interrelations and with reference to its religious dimension that is a concrete whole and the concrete domain of actual history.

Moreover, the religious dimension of the social world is not just one dimension among others. It occupies a special place. I have already remarked that, as an outcome of the struggle between the acting and the judging self that concludes the dialectic of morality, the divine presents itself as an absolute reality in relation to which the self acquires consciousness of its own identity and of the identity of the social world that is the ground and context of the formation of the identity of the self. Hegel says this by saying that an understanding of religion as 'the self-consciousness of Spirit'[36] is the outcome of the dialectic of morality. This is an understanding of the social world and the self in connection with an absolute reality, and therefore of what is most fundamental about the world and the self, as well as an understanding of absolute reality on its own terms. This is a mode of self-consciousness, Hegel says, 'which is conscious of being all truth and contains all reality within that truth.'[37] Philosophy completes itself, one might say, in an autonomous conceptualization of the intelligibility that religious consciousness presents. More specifically, phenomenology attains the full and final form of the reconciliation of consciousness and self-consciousness that defines that nature of rational knowing through a conceptualization of the outcome of the dialectic of religious self-consciousness. That dialectic, in turn culminates in the appearance and consideration of the religion of revelation, Christianity in Hegel's understanding. It is not surprising, therefore, that throughout the mature authorship Hegel expends the greatest care and energy in the task of trying to understand the truth about religion and Christianity. The task is central and essential to the philosophical project, as Hegel understands it. Perhaps this is what John Findlay has in mind in saying that 'If Hegel was nothing better, he was at least a great Christian theologian.'[38] The sustained analyses that belong to his efforts at understanding the truth about religion and Christianity certainly recommend him to readers who approach philosophical work with theological interests.

Given the standpoint of absolute knowing, one moves in philosophical inquiry first to the determination of the pure categories that most radically determine the activity of thinking as well as the actuality of things as known in thought. Hegel refers to the philosophical science in which one makes these determinations as logic. He thus maintains that logic, as he understands it, 'coincides with *metaphysics*, with the science of *things* grasped in *thoughts* that used to be taken to express the *essentialities* of the *things*.'[39] In view of what logic attains, one then proceeds to an ordered consideration of more determinate subject matters in the remaining parts of the philosophical system, namely the philosophy of nature and the philosophy of spirit. The penultimate section of the philosophy of spirit presents the systematic consideration of religion and Christianity. There, as in all of his discussions of religion and Christianity, Hegel addresses the issue of what he calls the religious representation and the relation of the representation to philosophical thought. This is an issue that

I will discuss in detail on several occasions. At this point, however, in order to conclude these remarks on Hegel's understanding of the nature of rational cognition and of philosophy, one must observe that Hegel does not discuss the representation or representational thinking only with reference to religious consciousness or discourse.

In fact, Hegel says of philosophy generally that it 'does nothing but transform representations into thoughts—although, of course it does go on to transform the mere thought into the Concept.'[40] Representational thinking (*vorstellendes Denken*) is a process through which we place matters before ourselves for consideration. Representations can be images drawn from sense experience, as when the experience of a heavy object, a burden, becomes associated with guilt in the consideration of guilt as burdensome. Or representations can be more strictly conceptual, as in the consideration that not all but some guilt feelings are neurotic. Through representations 'several isolated and simple determinations are strung together; but they remain external to each other, in spite of the link that is allotted to them in their subject.'[41] Thinking in the strictest and fullest sense, namely philosophical thinking, is the business not simply of placing things before ourselves for consideration but of undertaking that consideration by thinking through the intelligibility of what we have placed before ourselves.

Fully rational thinking, Hegel maintains in the first volume of the *Encyclopedia of the Philosophical Sciences*, embraces the activities of understanding, dialectic, and speculative reason. Through understanding one deals with a 'fixed determinacy and its distinctness vis-à-vis other determinacies; such a restricted abstraction counts for the understanding as one that subsists on its own account, and [simply] is.'[42] Understanding fixes distinctions, such as the distinction of universal and particular, or of cause and effect, and considers the terms that belong to those distinctions to be essentially other than each other, and therefore terms that require separate consideration. Insofar as thinking functions as understanding, its principle 'is identity, simple self-relation.'[43] To conceive of identity as 'simple self-relation,' however, is to deal with that concept in a one-sided and abstract manner. Thus understanding, while always a necessary and indispensable function of rational thought, also needs to be surpassed.

Dialectical thinking surpasses the limitations of the understanding insofar as, in dialectical thinking, 'the one-sidedness and restrictedness of the determinations of the understanding displays itself as what it is, i.e., as their negation.'[44] Through dialectical thinking one discovers the terms that understanding separates from each other in fixed distinctions to be indeed other from each other and in that sense isolated, but also indissolubly interrelated, with the consequence that each is opposed to the other and to itself in a relation of negation. Hegel gives the example of life as bearing 'the germ of death within itself,' such that we may not regard 'dying as having its ground only in external circumstances' but as the outcome whose possibility is always ingredient in the very nature of what it is to be living.[45] The example is a concrete instance of what Hegel has in mind when he says that dialectic 'must in no way be regarded as present only for philosophical consciousness; on the contrary, what is in question here is found already in all other forms of consciousness, too, and in everyone's experience. Everything around us can be regarded as an example of dialectic.'[46] Negation, opposition and contradiction are not constructions of thought. They are ingredient in things. Dialectical thinking displays them.

But the opposed determinations with which dialectical thinking deals are at one and the same time interrelated in their very opposition. This is the situation that speculative reason comprehends. 'The *speculative* or *positively rational* apprehends the unity of the determinations in their opposition, the *affirmative* that is contained in their dissolution and in their transition.'[47] Reason overcomes opposition and contradiction by at one and the same time interrelating and preserving differences. On this account, the integrations that belong to rational comprehension present 'not *simple, formal unity*, but a *unity of distinct determinations*. For this reason philosophy does not deal with mere abstractions or formal thoughts at all, but only with concrete thoughts.'[48] Through the operation of reason one aims in philosophical thinking at comprehending not abstract but concrete identities, genuinely differentiated unities that are genuine unities for just that reason. For Hegel, to say this is to say that speculative and philosophical comprehension has to do with the genuine actuality of that which one considers in philosophical inquiry. Thus he maintains that 'When thinking is taken as active with regard to ob-jects, as the *thinking over* of something, then the universal—as the product of this activity—contains the value of the *matter*, what is *essential, inner, true*.'[49] Thus what is essential and true regarding things is not to be found in our immediate consciousness of them, but in our consciousness of things insofar as this is mediated by rational thinking. He adds a bit later that 'Thinking it over *changes* something in the way in which the content is at first [given] in sensation, intuition, or representation; thus, it is only *through the mediation* of an alteration that the true nature of the *ob-ject* comes into consciousness.'[50] Philosophical thinking transforms the content that is given in sensation and then more adequately in representation by reenacting that content in a fully rational process that engages the operations of understanding, dialectic and reason. In this way, Hegel claims, philosophical inquiry attains actual knowledge of that which truly is.

I have already pointed out that it is crucial, for Hegel's philosophical purposes, to determine the truth about religion and Christianity. He also maintains that it is just through the processes of fully rational and philosophical thinking, of which he comes to a justified conception in the *Phenomenology* and on which he comments in the first volume of the *Encyclopedia*, that one can determine the truth about religion and Christianity. After all, 'Religion leads us to a universal, which embraces everything else within itself, to an Absolute by which everything else is brought forth, and this Absolute is not [there] for the senses but only for the spirit and for thought.'[51] If philosophy requires that one determine the truth about religion and Christianity, philosophical thinking also allows one to determine that truth. My subsequent considerations will develop comment and reflection on what Hegel presents as he claims to make that determination. It is important, in developing those considerations, to examine in a more thorough and focused manner some of the defining analyses of religion and Christianity that Hegel offers in the 1807 *Phenomenology*. That will be the task of the next chapter.

Chapter 2

Religion and Christianity in the *Phenomenology of Spirit*

Hegel's procedure in reflecting philosophically on religion and Christianity pursues a two-sided aim. On the one hand, he aims at understanding religion through concepts that are rational and speculative in a way that is unique to philosophy. The resulting understanding will, therefore, be one that is also specific to philosophy and to some extent unavailable to those who are religiously involved but not engaged in philosophical reflection. On the other hand, he aims at establishing a philosophical understanding of religion and Christianity that grasps and expresses the consciousness that develops in a properly religious standpoint. To the extent that this end is attained, a philosophical understanding of religion will not only distinguish itself from and surpass, but also incorporate within itself and articulate, religious self-understanding. The first of these characteristics may well be more evident than the second in many of Hegel's texts or at least to many of his readers. The second, I maintain, is always discernable and always something he requires of himself.

Each of the sides of the aim that I have attributed to Hegel is discernable in the considerations of religion and Christianity in the *Phenomenology* that I will discuss in this chapter. The first discussion will involve a return to the examination of conscience and the acting and the judging self that concludes the dialectic of morality. It is in the outcome of the conflict between the acting and the judging self that religious consciousness appears in a way that leads to the dedicated consideration of religion in the penultimate chapter of the *Phenomenology*. The second consideration I will discuss will be the treatment of Christianity that Hegel presents, under the heading of 'The Religion of Revelation,' at the conclusion of the penultimate chapter of his 1807 work.

These phenomenological considerations are of great importance both on their own terms, and because of the enduring contributions they make to Hegel's later thinking about religion and Christianity.

As Hegel points out, and as I have in part noted, religion, understood as a 'consciousness of *absolute Being* as such,'[1] appears on several occasions in the *Phenomenology*. Even in the final section of the dialectic of Consciousness, understanding, which is at one moment oriented toward an intelligible world that transcends appearances, represents a kind of consciousness of absolute being and something of a manifestation of religion. Unhappy consciousness, at the end of the dialectic of Self-Consciousness, represents a definite religious possibility. And at different moments in the examination of Spirit there appear a consciousness of divine as contrasted with human law, a consciousness of a transcendent domain that is the object of faith, and a holy legislator whose voice speaks within the consciousness of the moral subject.

But a new and distinctive appearance of religion comes forward at the conclusion of the dialectic of conscience and of the acting and judging selves that one finds in the final section of the chapter on Spirit in the *Phenomenology*. I have already briefly commented on Hegel's characterization of this appearance of religion as the self-consciousness of Spirit. Now is the time for a fuller and somewhat more detailed discussion of the dialectic that has that appearance of religion as its outcome.

The definition of the self in terms of conscience comes about in virtue of the collapse of the oppositions between duty and outer nature, duty and inner nature, and the consciousness of the moral subject and the voice of the holy lawgiver, that the postulates of practical reason, as Hegel formulates these, entail. As a consequence, the moral subject defines itself wholly in terms of particular conscience. One knows one's duty in virtue of an inward conviction: the opposition of duty and inner nature is overcome. One does one's duty through the action that one performs in the external world, and to this extent overcomes the opposition of duty and external nature. In addition, through the language used in speaking with others, the self declares that its action is the expression of its conviction, and 'this declaration is the true actuality of the act, and the validating of the action.'[2] Finally, the conscientious self 'knows the immediacy of the presence within it of the absolute Being as the unity of that Being and its own self'[3] by knowing that the voice of the holy lawgiver coincides with the voice of conscience.

The conscientious self defines its own inner nature, outer nature, other selves, and God in terms of its own self-knowledge. That is to say, its self-knowledge is the source of its definition of everything. For this reason, with the conscientious self 'we see self-consciousness withdrawn into its innermost being, for which all externality as such has vanished'; whether this self directs its attention to external reality or to its own identity, 'its consciousness is only this knowledge of itself.'[4] This condition entails two possibilities. The self may endeavor to preserve its self-relatedness at all costs. Then the self 'flees from contact with the actual world' and becomes the 'beautiful soul'[5] who shuns action. Or one may remember that self-knowledge is knowledge of the self as one whose conviction determines duty, and that duty requires action. Then one will act. To do this, of course, is to present one's deed and one's declaration about that deed, to the self who shuns action but is still capable of judging the actions of others.

The judge knows that any action supposed to express duty may be assessed as following from personal inclination rather than duty. This is the chief reason why the judge shuns action in the first place. To act is to offer someone else the opportunity to assess one's action, and thus to present a definition of one's identity that conflicts with the definition that one has formed in virtue of conscientious self-knowledge. But the judge seems to confront no such danger in assessing the action of another. So the judge assesses the self who acts to be base, by claiming that the act follows from inclination rather than duty, and to be hypocritical, because the actor declares that the deed expresses duty as determined by the actor's conviction. By making this assessment, the judge brings himself into relation with the self who acts. In doing this the judge has put himself on the same level, one might say, with the acting self, and the actor can examine the judge. The actor sees that the judge has become base by insisting that the act be assessed with reference to personal

inclination rather than conscientious conviction, and hypocritical by substituting judging for acting, thus making duty a matter
of words. But the actor also sees that he must attribute to himself
the same characteristics that he attributes to the judge. The actor
does choose his deed by referring to personal inclination, since
this is the ultimate ground of his conviction, and does make
duty a matter of words, because he expects others to recognize
the quality of his action on account of what he says regarding it.
The actor, in other words, in seeing the judge, sees himself in
the judge. The actor 'does not merely find himself apprehended
by the other as something alien and disparate from it, but rather
finds that other, according to its own nature and disposition,
identical with himself.'[6] Seeing this, the actor confesses it to the
judge. The confession 'is not a one-sided affair, which would
establish his disparity with the other; on the contrary, he gives
himself utterance solely on account of his having seen his identity with the other,'[7] and expects the other to do the same.

But this response is not what the judge wanted at all. The
judge defines his own self-relatedness as an opposition to the
other and 'rejects any continuity with the other.'[8] However,
the judge also believes that his conviction gives him access to a
genuine understanding of duty, that is, of an obligation that is
universal, that holds for all particular individuals, and in this way
interrelates those particular individuals. In rejecting the actor's
confession, the judge rejects the actor's contribution to the process of realizing a condition of interrelatedness, rather than
opposition, between the actor and the judge. For just this reason
the judge must see, precisely in the context of his rejection of
the confession of the actor, that the judge's claim to represent an
understanding that interrelates particular individuals is made in
a valid way not by what the judge is doing, but by what the actor
is doing. In other words, the judge sees the truth about himself in the self who acts and makes confession. The judge then
responds to the confession with forgiveness and extends a 'word
of reconciliation'[9] that interrelates those otherwise contrasting
and opposed selves and institutes community among them.

The dialectic of the acting and the judging self exhibits a paradox of which one may have become mindful at the very beginning of that dialectic, namely that 'if conscience is absolute, and

individuals who act out of conscience differ in their conscientious judgment over the same matter, then conscience as absolute is relative.'[10] One must understand precisely the outcome of the dialectic that presents that paradox. It is of course a reconciliation of selves who have been opposed. But it is also a reconciliation that preserves each of those selves in its difference from each other, and in this way both surpasses and preserves the opposition between them. Each self continues to define itself in relation to the particular conviction of conscience that is its own. Since this is a conviction that is particular and stands in contrast with other particular convictions, it is limited or finite and is constitutive of the finite identity of the self who maintains it.

Joseph Flay points out that as an outcome of the dialectic now under discussion, 'The community of finite individuals, grounded in conscience but nevertheless finite and only attempting to participate in that universal ground, comes into being by mutual recognition of each other's attempts. The community gains existence and concreteness through language, the word of reconciliation, the recognition of finitude.'[11] The community is a 'universal' ground in which finite individuals attempt to participate because it interrelates particular individuals, which is what a universal in any sense of the word does. This point deserves emphasis. Each of the individual selves is a differentiated individual, set in opposition to others in particular ways, and an individual that nonetheless has and understands its being only in virtue of its connections with those others. It is in virtue of being related to others that the self is related to itself in just the way that preserves its differentiated particularity and the oppositions that follow from that particularity.

Joseph Flay also says that 'the religious community is born in the community of conscientious actors and conscientious judges, reflectively oriented towards the absolute standpoint by their quest for that standpoint.'[12] I have already pointed out that, in the case of each of these conscientious selves, there is a reciprocity between its differentiated particular being and the being that belongs to the self in its relation to others. The community that these individual selves bring about among themselves is the result of their enacting that reciprocity. But it cannot be the case that these selves are interrelated wholly by the community that they bring about through their mutual acts of recognition. The self that sees itself in the other realizes that it has not known the truth about itself until that moment, and therefore knows that its being or identity is determined by its connection or relation with the other even before it sees that this is the case. Thus, on the one hand, finite selves bring about community among themselves through acts and words of recognition. On the other hand, these selves find that the interrelatedness that obtains among them, and is an intrinsic determination of their being or identity, is something already accomplished before the finite efforts that they make at bringing about community among themselves. Finite selves, in the context of those efforts, come to recognize this interrelatedness as something to be acknowledged as already accomplished.

I believe that these statements validly interpret the final sentence of the section on Morality in Hegel's *Phenomenology*. 'The reconciling *Yea*, in which the two "I's" let go their antithetical *existence*, is the *existence* of the "I" which has expanded into a duality, and therein remains identical with itself, and, in its complete externalization and opposite, possesses the certainty of itself: it is God manifested in the midst of those who know themselves in the form of pure knowing.'[13] Those who institute community among themselves by speaking a word of reconciliation experience and are aware, in their speaking, of an interrelatedness that already obtains among them. The manifestation of that interrelatedness in the efforts they make at instituting community is the appearance of a situation that obtains prior to their finite efforts, and therefore the word of reconciliation that they speak in making those efforts permits them to acknowledge a word that has already been spoken. That situation and that word, therefore, supervene upon the finite actions of finite selves and at the same time stand in contrast with them, allowing for the appearance in the actions and lives of those selves of something that presents itself as infinite. In commenting on the words of Hegel I have just cited, Emil Fackenheim says that the community that finite individuals institute through the word of reconciliation 'could not be accomplished by the unaided moral self-activity which lives in and between the two extremes' of the acting and the judging selves. 'The tension is transcended only because what the moral self—in both its poles—produces, and forever is yet to produce, already *is* as Substance, and because in recognizing and accepting what already is, the *moral* self turns religious.'[14] I would add that this recognition and acceptance involve one's understanding the being of the self in terms of a finite particular identity and simultaneously in terms of a relation to something that is other than the self, that transcends the self, and that is supposed to present itself, within the actions and lives of finite selves, as transcending the finitude that determines them. The moral self who 'turns religious,' to use Fackenheim's words, does so in finding its identity to be determined by finite self-relatedness and by a specific sort of self-transcendence.

I believe the last claim to be quite important on its own terms. But at the moment I am discussing it only in relation to the understanding of religion that Hegel presents in the section of the *Phenomenology* now under consideration. Joseph Flay, in a remark on this section, says that 'we who have traversed the *Phenomenology* now realize the foundation of all religiosity, our recognition of our finitude.'[15] Certainly our recognition of our finitude is crucial to the appearance that religious consciousness makes at the end of the section that Hegel devotes to Morality. But I think there is a bit more to the understanding of religion that appears there. Religious consciousness is determined by recognizing what I have called one's finite self-relatedness and by at the same time finding one's identity to be determined by one's being in a self-transcending relation to something that presents itself, in the domain of finite life, in terms of its contrast with finite life. I understand this as self-transcendence in its specifically religious form. Acknowledging finitude in and of itself does not entail this. Without this, the specificity of religious consciousness and religious existence is lacking.

This link in human self-understanding between an awareness of finite self-relatedness and a specifically religious form of self-transcendence gives us, in Hegel's words, religion as the self-consciousness of Spirit. That is, among other reasons, because given this link the self is, in its awareness of the transcendent other, conscious of its own identity. Moreover, the self in this instance is not an isolated individual. Rather, the self is an individual who is essentially situated in a domain of social relations that are constitutive of self-identity, and therefore conscious, in its awareness of itself, of the connection of its identity with that social domain. This yields a reconciliation of consciousness and self-consciousness with regard to an awareness of social identity that the understanding of religion as the self-consciousness of Spirit would seem to require. It may be useful to note in this connection the implication that, given this understanding, religion can never wholly or even principally be an occupation that belongs to private inwardness, as contrasted with social or public involvement. Perhaps Hegel's version of this position makes him potentially vulnerable to Kierkegaard's critique. But Hegel would require that critique to face the claim that, if God manifests Godself in the domain of finite action and life, that occurs in an essential way in the actions and lives of individuals making efforts to build community among themselves while they also assert the particular identities that differentiate them from each other, with all the complications that process entails.

I should also note that when Hegel refers to God in the passage cited above he does not think that he is making an inference in view of what is given in the experience of consciousness being observed. Nor does he think that an inference is being made within the structure of that experience itself. His claim is that those who speak and respond to the word of reconciliation find, in their finite actions and lives, the appearance of a reality that stands in contrast with finite reality and which they can recognize as divine. This should not be surprising. Recall once more that each of the shapes of the social world that present themselves in the course of the dialectic of Spirit mediates some manifestation of divinity. And indeed, Hegel could not claim in the *Phenomenology of Spirit* to present a thoroughgoing demonstration of the reconciliation of consciousness and self-consciousness if that demonstration did not take religious and specifically theistic consciousness into account. Of course, the forms of religious consciousness that that demonstration takes into account must appear with immanent necessity in the dialectic of the experience of consciousness that unfolds in the *Phenomenology*. I have tried to show how that is the case regarding the specific form of religious consciousness that appears at the conclusion of the phenomenological consideration of Morality.

That form of religious consciousness takes divine reality to be a reality that in some way manifests itself within finite life, and takes it to be that case that it is in being conscious of divine reality that people become conscious of their identity, and that a people becomes conscious of its identity. Given this situation, two tasks face religious consciousness. The reconciliation of consciousness and self-consciousness that belongs to religious consciousness is, in its first appearance, a simple, immediate unity, rather than a unity that results from an explicit differentiation of its distinct terms and then their reintegration. As a consequence religious consciousness 'is for-itself self-knowledge instead of simply being the consciousness of its world, as was the case in previous cases' belonging to the dialectic of Spirit.[16] Since this reconciliation of consciousness and self-consciousness absorbs, as it were, the former into the latter, 'Spirit's *existence* is distinct from its *self-consciousness* and its reality proper falls outside of religion. There is indeed one Spirit of both, but its consciousness does not embrace both together, and religion appears as a part of existence, of conduct and activity, whose other part is the life lived in its real world.'[17] This condition is problematic for religious consciousness and for mundane consciousness. 'Our life in the world and our religious consciousness are distinct; hence our religious consciousness is still imperfect and our life in the world is still without true reconciliation.'[18] The first task that faces religious consciousness is that of remedying this situation by achieving a reconciliation of consciousness and self-consciousness that is concrete and differentiated rather than abstract and immediate.

Religious consciousness is also a form of consciousness that is occupied with representations of the divine. As I indicated in the previous chapter, for Hegel representational thinking is a form of thinking that is, from a philosophical point of view, essentially incomplete. The standpoint of religious consciousness on its own terms indicates the truth of this position. Insofar as religious consciousness places before itself conceptions of the divine but does not go on to think-through the content of those conceptions for the sake of comprehending the intelligibility they present through its own activities, the reconciliation of consciousness and self-consciousness that is supposed to belong to religious consciousness is not fully achieved. Religious consciousness needs, as its second task, to deal with the representational nature of its conceptions. This involves allowing the representation of the divine to develop in the ordered manner that is possible given phenomenological observation and analysis.

The development of the religious representation is the focus of the dialectic of the experience of religious consciousness in the *Phenomenology*. That dialectic proceeds through three phases: Natural Religion, The Religion of Art, and The Religion of Revelation.[19] I will make only the briefest comments that are necessary regarding Natural Religion and the Religion of Art in order to introduce a discussion of The Religion of Revelation in the *Phenomenology*, which will be my primary concern for the rest of this chapter.

Religious consciousness in its most immediate dimensions represents the divine in terms of natural realities. The artificer who at first makes religious objects that depict natural realities becomes able to produce things whose structure is abstract in relation to those realities or things that are phantasmagoric combinations of aspects of different natural realities. In either case, the artificer is initially one whose attention is directed at the objects being produced, rather than at the thought and skill operating in their production. But the focus of attention inevitably expands so that the one producing religious objects comes to see those things as objectifications of his or her planning and action. Then the artificer has become more genuinely an artist and religion has become the religion of art.

The religion of art presents a new possibility for the reconciliation of consciousness and self-consciousness in religious consciousness. The work of art enables the artist and the community in which the artist is active to see in the object that the artist makes, and that is the focus of the community's worship, a representation of the divine that is the outcome of self-conscious action and thus on its own terms a representation of self-conscious being. This is the case for the statue, whose motionless shape makes reference to inner life. It is more fully the case for cultic worship that is carefully structured and informed by language, because here devotees speak to and hear the addresses of the divine. Epic poetry, developing the narratives to which cultic worship appeals, continues to represent divinity in self-conscious form, as does the drama performed on the occasion of religious festivals that displays the tragic hero in connection with divinity. But finally, since the work of art that is supposed to mediate the presence of the divine to human beings is entirely a human product, the self becomes able to find in the experience of the religious art-work nothing but itself. Tragic seriousness is replaced by comic irony and levity, as human beings become explicitly conscious of the humanly produced nature of representations of divinity. At one and the same time, the loss of a connection of the self with the integral and substantial reality of the divine robs the self of substance and throws the self back on the constantly changing character of its own finite particularity. The comically happy consciousness of independent selfhood has as its counterpart the unhappy consciousness that longs for union with the substantial reality that represents its deepest truth and from which the self seems hopelessly separated.

It is this self-inversion of the comically happy consciousness that marks the emergence of, and defines the nature of, revealed religion. This unhappy consciousness 'constitutes the counterpart and the completion of the comic consciousness that is perfectly happy with itself. Into the latter, all divine being returns, or it is the complete *alienation* of *substance*. The Unhappy Consciousness, on the other hand, is, conversely, the tragic fate of the certainty of self that aims to be absolute.'[20] The finite self that defines itself as absolute finds through experience that because of its finitude its reality is insubstantial and its definition of itself is falsified. Its condition is 'the loss of substance as well as of the Self, it is the grief which expresses itself in the hard saying that "God is dead."'[21] This is the direct consequence of the inability of self-consciousness, as it develops in the religion of art, to experience in its representations of the divine anything other than itself.

At the same time, this is a form of self-consciousness. The argument of the *Phenomenology* is supposed to have already shown that (1) self-consciousness must be able to know itself in its other, and that (2) this is genuinely possible only if the other is another self. Moreover, the argument that belongs to the conclusion of moral self-consciousness is supposed to have linked the awareness that such self-consciousness has of its own finitude with an awareness of its being in a self-transcending relationship with something that escapes the finitude that belongs to the finite self and that is the ground of the reality of the finite self. This suggests a proposition that is also evident in the light of an earlier dialectic, namely, that 'the grief which expresses itself in the hard saying that "God is dead"' cannot exhaust the nature of unhappy consciousness. Unhappy consciousness is not simply the awareness of the absence of a substantial reality that escapes finitude stands over against the self, and is the ground and truth of the self. It is the awareness of the loss of such a thing. Without loss there would be nothing to grieve. In its earlier appearance, unhappy consciousness experiences this loss as a desire for union with a reality from which it is separated and with which it cannot unite itself by any effort it makes. In its later appearance unhappy consciousness experiences this loss in the context of its inability to experience in its representations of the divine anything other than itself. The sense of loss is still there, just because of the link in the consciousness of the finite self between its awareness of its own finitude and its awareness of its own self-transcending nature.

In virtue of its awareness of its self-transcending nature, the finite self has a conception of a reality that is other than the finite self because it escapes the finitude that determines that self. The diverse representations of the divine with which the finite self is familiar have come to be ones that construe that reality as possessed of selfhood. Since the finite self has come to find itself in those representations, it can construe infinite or divine reality in terms of that unity of that reality with the human self. These ideas need to be integrated, and are integrated in the belief that God 'is *immediately present* as a self-conscious Being, i.e. as an *actual man*, that the believer is immediately certain of spirit, *sees*, *feels*, and *hears* this divinity.'[22] This belief entails the idea that this incarnation is one in which God manifests or reveals Godself in and through God's own action. If so, then the finite self does not, in its relation to this incarnation, find only itself. It finds God. At the same time, the Incarnation enables the finite self to know God precisely as a divine being whose identity consists in being a self, consists of self-consciousness. Thus God is both other than the finite self and one in whom the finite self can genuinely know itself. These remarks indicate that the religious consciousness that comes about in virtue of the belief in the Incarnation of God is a form of self-consciousness that meets the requirements laid down on the occasion of the very first appearance of self-consciousness in the *Phenomenology*, namely, (1) that self-consciousness must, in its relation to its object, know itself, and thus attain self-relatedness, and (2) that self-consciousness must recognize the object in terms of the being-for-another of the object and in terms of the independence of the object.

I leave aside the question about whether Hegel could successfully claim that the shape of religious consciousness now under discussion emerges, as must every shape of consciousness in the *Phenomenology*, with necessity in the dialectic of the experience of consciousness. One should note at this moment, however, that Hegel may seem, given the account of the religious consciousness that emerges in connection with the belief in the Incarnation, to be developing a position that coincides with views that Schleiermacher will come to present. In this connection one should also note, however, that in 1807 Hegel anticipates some of the criticisms he will make of Schleiermacher more substantially in the 1820s. In speaking of religious consciousness as that is now understood, Hegel insists that this 'Consciousness, then, does not start from *its* inner life, from thought, and unite *within itself* the thought of God with existence; on the contrary, it starts from an existence that is immediately present and recognizes God therein.'[23] A consequence of this attitude is the awareness that 'in this religion the divine Being is *revealed*. Its being revealed obviously consists in this, that what it is, is known.'[24] In the religion of the Incarnation 'the divine Being is known as Spirit', in that 'Spirit is the knowledge of oneself in the externalization of oneself; the being that is the movement of retaining its self-identity in its otherness.'[25] God unites Godself with human nature in its otherness from the divine, maintains self-relatedness in so doing, reveals in this unity of the divine and human natures God's own being as God knows Godself to be, and thus knows Godself in this externalization of Godself. Hegel adds that to know that God is self-revealing is to know that God

is essentially a *self-conscious Being*. For there is something hidden from *consciousness* in its object if the object for consciousness is an '*other*' or something *alien*, and if it does not know it as *its own self*. This concealment ceases when the absolute Being *qua* Spirit is the object of consciousness; for then the object has the form of a *Self* in its relation to consciousness, i.e. consciousness knows itself immediately in the object, or is manifest to itself in the object.[26]

I will return in Chapter 6 to several statements made in this text. For now, notice two of those statements. First, in that God is self-revealing and reveals Godself as Spirit, God reveals Godself as 'essentially a self-conscious being.' It is not only the case that, as in the religion of art, humanly produced representations of the divine make reference to self-consciousness. Divine self-revelation discloses self-consciousness. Thus in its consciousness of this revelation, the finite self comes to know not only itself, but also Godself. But second, in its consciousness of this revelation the finite self does indeed come to know itself. In recognizing its divine object as another self, the finite self finds in its connection with that object a kind of self-recognition and thus a kind of union. For this reason, Hegel remarks, 'The hopes and expectations of the world up till now have pressed forward solely to this revelation, to behold what absolute Being is, and in it to find itself.'[27]

Hegel anticipates later treatments of Christianity by holding, in the *Phenomenology*, that the understanding that the religion of revelation presents must be considered in terms of the pure concept that conceptualizes the essential moment of that understanding, the elaboration of this concept through representations, and the process through which we reenact in thought the significance of those representations and attain a new form of self-consciousness. I have already discussed the pure concept of the essential understanding that the religion of revelation presents. It is the concept of God as one who unites Godself with human nature, reveals Godself therein, and enables us to know in this revelation both Godself and ourselves. Hegel adds that our knowledge of God in the religion of revelation makes reference not only to the historical, time-bound existence of the individual in whom God is incarnate, but also to this individual as one who lived, died, and was raised to dwell in the life of the gathered community. To know God in these terms is to know that, 'just as formerly He rose up for consciousness as a *sensuous existence*, now He has arisen *in the Spirit*.'[28] Consciousness of the individual in whom God is incarnate is integrated with 'the *universal self-consciousness* of the [religious] community,' with the consequence that 'not the individual by himself, but together with the consciousness of the community and what he is for this community, is the complete whole of the individual as Spirit.'[29]

The pure concept just mentioned is in need of elaboration. Even given belief in the Incarnation, it would be possible, in the light of this concept alone, to think of God essentially as 'pure substance.'[30] But this is insufficient, given the necessity to think of God as concrete, and also infinite, self-conscious life. The different aspects of this necessity require a conception of God as an inwardly self-differentiating unity. Thus 'it is said that the eternal Being *begets* for itself an "other." But in this otherness it has at the same time immediately returned into itself; for the difference is the difference *in itself*, i.e. it is immediately distinguished only from itself and is thus the unity that has returned into itself.'[31] This trinitarian process encompasses the moments of being, being-for-self through self-related unity in relation to the other, and knowledge of self in knowledge of the other.[32] Representational thinking does not deal with its content in terms of these speculative determinations. Rather, 'it has the content but without its necessity, and instead of the form of the Concept it brings into the realm of pure consciousness the natural relationships of father and son.'[33] Overcoming this limitation in the conception of God now under consideration will require a reconsideration of the content of representational thinking by speculative thinking.

There is another limitation that belongs to the conception of God now under consideration. This limitation must be met by a further development of representational thinking as such. In the immanent, trinitarian life of the godhead, otherness emerges only to be immediately superseded by God's knowledge of Godself in the other and thus by self-related unity. 'In this *simple* beholding of itself in the "other," the otherness is therefore not posited as such; it is the difference which, in pure thought, is immediately *no difference*; a *loving* recognition in which the two sides, as regards their essence, do not stand in antithetical relation to each other.'[34] This statement may seem to anticipate what one commentator sees as Hegel's reliance on Jacob Boehme, in whose theosophy 'the "Immanent Trinity" as holy gets explicated in such a way as to suggest deficiency, deficiency, moreover, which is only relieved when the so-called pure divine opens itself to the finite and enters into its impurity, finally, of course, subjecting it to transmutation.'[35] One may well find a problem, even a deep problem, with this aspect of Hegel's understanding of the immanent Trinity. I in no way want to deny the possibility of such a problem. I do not, however, want to explore that possibility now. It is better explored in the light of both the *Phenomenology* and of later Hegelian texts that I will consider below.

For now, the point is that the understanding of God as infinite, self-conscious Spirit requires that one conceive of God by referring to a relationship that preserves divine infinity and is at the same time a relation between God and something whose otherness from God is not immediately superseded. 'Thus the merely eternal or abstract Spirit becomes an "other" to itself, or enters into existence, and directly into *immediate* existence. Accordingly, it *creates* a world.'[36] The world that is created includes nature and created selves or finite spirit. In its most immediate moment, the finite self is one whose consciousness is focused on the world that surrounds it and on its creator. As such 'it can be called "innocent" but hardly "good." '[37] In fact, in order genuinely to be a self the finite self must 'become an "other" to its own self, just as the eternal Being exhibits itself as the movement of being self-identical in its otherness.'[38] Since the finite self initially directs its consciousness to what is outside of itself, it becomes an 'other' to itself by withdrawing into itself and focusing most essentially on itself. Furthermore,

> Since this withdrawal into itself or self-centeredness of
> the existent consciousness immediately makes it self-
> discordant, Evil appears as the primary existence of the
> inwardly-turned consciousness; and because the thoughts
> of Good and Evil are utterly opposed and this antithesis is

not yet resolved, this consciousness is essentially only evil. But at the same time, on account of just this antithesis, there is also present the *good* consciousness opposing it, and their relation to each other.[39]

Now the consideration of the relation of God and creation has become more specifically a consideration of the relation between divine goodness and creatures who set themselves in opposition to God and bring about evil. Hegel mentions the possibility, as H. S. Harris points out, of an account of the coming into being of evil that antedates the creation of the human world. One finds that account in 'Boehme's myth that Lucifer was the First Born Son, that he fell because he was self-obsessed, and he was replaced by Jesus Christ.'[40] But such an account would not help resolve the central problem that now presents itself.

That problem has to do with the conditions under which it is possible to overcome the opposition between God and creatures that has arisen on account of the coming into being of evil. Overcoming this opposition would not be possible if on account of it God and creatures were simply set over against each other, without a link between them that joined them together. But of course God and creatures cannot simply be set over against each other. Even the *'wrath of God'* that evil elicits represents a link that joins God and creatures, because it is God's response to creatures who incur divine wrath by estranging themselves from God.[41] Moreover, since the centerpiece of the religion of revelation is the belief that God unites Godself with human nature, it is here 'already *asserted* that *in themselves* the two are not separate; likewise in the declaration that the divine Being *from the beginning* externalizes itself, that its existence withdraws into itself and becomes self-centered and evil, implies, though it does not expressly assert, that this evil existence is not *in itself* something alien to the divine Being.'[42]

Hegel takes pains to insist that this statement does not mean that good and evil are in some sense finally the same, rather than different from and opposed to one another. 'If Evil is the same as Goodness then Evil is just not Evil, nor Goodness Good: on the contrary, both are suspended moments—Evil in general is self-centered being-for-self, and Goodness is what is simple and without a self.'[43] These definitions state what evil is as it appears in human creatures, and therefore what goodness initially is, with reference to those same creatures, insofar as being opposed to evil is what determines goodness. These definitions also indicate a problem. To be without a self, for a being whose nature is essentially a potency for selfhood, is a kind of evil. The withdrawal into inwardness, insofar as this is constitutive selfhood, is a kind of good. This implies that the condition of the human creatures is not finally one in which good and evil stand over against and in opposition to each other, but a condition whose deepest possibility is realized by transcending this opposition.

In turn, the truth about the relation between God, who is good, and human creatures, who bring about evil, finally appears not in the opposition that estranges humans from God but in the reconciliation that overcomes that opposition. It is the Incarnation that initiates this process of reconciliation. In uniting Godself with human nature, God shows that the truth about human nature has to do with union with God, rather than with the estrangement from God that is the consequence of the withdrawal into self-centeredness. In that God enters fully into human nature, in such a way that the God-man undergoes suffering and death, one can find in the Incarnation 'the propitiation of the absolute Being' for the evil that humankind has brought about.[44] In virtue of its recognition of the process into which God has entered toward the end of reconciling humankind with Godself, the finite self looks into itself once again. Before the withdrawal into self resulted in self-centeredness and evil. Now 'its withdrawal into itself consists, therefore, in *convincing itself* that natural existence is evil.'[45] This allows for a transcendence of self-centered estrangement from God and a transformation that brings the self into union with God.

With this step a new form of self-consciousness has emerged in the phenomenology of religious and Christian consciousness. There are at least three notable aspects that belong to this achievement. First, religious consciousness can now understand the unity in difference that interrelates its diverse representations of the divine. Creation, incarnation, death and resurrection, reconciliation and divine indwelling, are not separate events, but distinct and also integrated components of a single, unified divine process. Second, this process, and therefore the moments that are components of it, is not only or even primarily confined to a remote historical past, but more essentially is ongoing in the life of the community whose self-consciousness is determined by its consciousness of this process. Thus, Hegel says, 'The dead divine Man or human God is *in himself* the universal self-consciousness' of the community; 'this he has to become *explicitly for this self-consciousness*.'[46] This occurs, given the nature of the consciousness that belongs to the community, insofar as 'death becomes transfigured from its immediate individual meaning, viz. the non-being of this *particular* individual, into the *universality* of the Spirit who dwells in His community, dies in it every day, and is daily resurrected.'[47] The consequence of this daily or 'spiritual resurrection' is 'the coming into existence of God's individual self-consciousness as a universal self-consciousness, or as the religious community.'[48]

There is a third notable aspect to the specific achievement of self-consciousness that has occurred within the development of Christian religious consciousness. The religious community does and can integrate its diverse representations of the divine into an understanding of a single comprehensive process, and can find that process most essentially to be one that is ongoing in the life of the community. That is to say, it is through the activities that the community does, in living the life that the community does live, that the community allows the divine process that is indwelling in it to become manifest to it. Moreover, human, communal participation in the divine process represented in the conceptions of creation, incarnation, death and resurrection, reconciliation and divine indwelling, is a dimension of that process itself. God acts in ways that make possible human responses and takes those responses up in to the process that divine action initiates and directs. Thus human action, the action that comprises the life of the human religious community, is both a dimension of the process that is grounded in divine action and is what makes it possible for that process to be manifest to the community.

But the limits of representational thinking are such that this understanding is not fully available to religious self-consciousness. That self-consciousness is the product of a reenactment of the significance of the representations that focus religious consciousness. But that reenactment, and the self-consciousness that is its product, still belong to the level of representational, as contrasted with fully conceptual, thinking. Thus Hegel says that religious consciousness, in the culminating moment of its development, returns 'into self-consciousness, but not according to the proper form, for the religious aspect is the aspect of the *in itself* which stands over against the movement of self-consciousness.'[49] In this instance, the 'religious aspect' of the consciousness in question coincides with that consciousness having the form of representational thinking. Consciousness that has the form of representational thinking can on its own terms attain a kind of self-relatedness or self-consciousness in connection with its object. But that self-consciousness is necessarily imperfect and incomplete, just because it is attained by a kind of thinking that falls short of fully conceptual thinking.

Hegel says this, in the discussion of the religion of revelation, by observing that, on account of the nature of the conception of divine being and action that belongs to religious consciousness, 'the Self does not grasp and truly comprehend it, or does not find in it its *own* action as such.'[50] The position to which this statement refers maintains, according to Quentin Lauer, that to know God as God is known in the religion of revelation 'is to know man; not that the propositions "God is man" or "man is God" are true, but the process of God's becoming "Spirit" or of man's becoming "spirit" is the same process.'[51] The form of self-consciousness attained by properly religious consciousness in the light of the religion of revelation is capable of arriving at this recognition, but not of articulating this recognition for itself, not of grasping it adequately and comprehending it truly. That is because properly religious consciousness, defined by the representational nature of the thinking that belongs to it, cannot explicitly know that 'determinateness is just as much its opposite, unity in otherness, i.e. the spiritual relationship, is an accomplished fact, just as the opposite meanings were united previously for us, or in themselves, and even the abstract forms of "the same" and "not the same," of "identity" "and non-identity" were reduced to moments.'[52] This knowledge is fully available only to that form of cognitive consciousness that has articulated and justified for its self its own most radical self-understanding, that is to say, absolute knowing.

But what, in the last analysis, is the outcome of a speculative rethinking of the content of the religious representation in relation to the religious self-understanding that Hegel also tries to grasp on its own terms? At one point, Hegel contrasts religious consciousness and speculative knowledge by saying that 'God is attainable in pure speculative knowledge alone and *is* only in that knowledge, and is only that knowledge itself, for He is Spirit, and this speculative knowledge is the knowledge of the *revealed* religion.'[53] This plausibly suggests that religious consciousness, on account of its representational character, cannot grasp the knowledge that the religion of revelation has the capacity to deliver, and that such a grasp is available only to speculative comprehension. But if that is Hegel's view, what are its implications? Consider just two statements he makes in the examination of the religion of revelation. In discussing the idea of creation, he says,

> 'creating' is representational thinking's word for the
> Concept itself in its absolute movement, or to express the
> fact that the simple which has been asserted as absolute,
> or pure thought, just because it is abstract, is rather the
> negative, and hence self-opposed or 'other' of itself; or
> because, to put the same thing in another form, that
> which is posited as *essence* is simple *immediacy* or *being*, but
> *qua* immediacy or being lacks Self, and therefore, lacking
> inwardness is *passive*, or a *being-for-another*.[54]

Again, in speaking of the understanding of redemption and reconciliation available to religious consciousness, Hegel says that that understanding is,

> for that self-consciousness not a grasp of this Concept
> which knows superseded natural existence to be universal
> and therefore reconciled with itself; but rather a grasping
> of an imaginative idea, that by bringing to pass its own
> externalization, in its historical incarnation and death,

the divine Being has been reconciled with its natural existence.[55]

This understanding stands in contrast with a speculative grasp of what the religious representation in this instance conveys, with the 'knowledge of Nature as the untrue existence of Spirit,' and the recognition that 'this immanently developed universality of the Self is *in itself* the reconciliation of Spirit with itself.'[56] In addition to provoking impatience in the reader, language like this may suggest that, for Hegel, a speculative grasp of the conceptions that occupy religious consciousness departs in perhaps important respects from the understanding of those conceptions that belongs to religious consciousness and from religious self-understanding as such.

There is indeed an important body of commentary on Hegel's philosophy in general and on the *Phenomenology* in particular that supports this view. Thus H. S. Harris holds that, for Hegel, philosophical comprehension of the content of the religion of revelation shows that 'its God is just the "intelligible force" of Reason, whose very essence is to "manifest" itself,' and that the historical development that the *Phenomenology* recapitulates 'reached its climax in a human self-consciousness that was clearly aware of its identity with God.'[57] And Merold Westphal, developing as it were these views that Harris presents, says that Hegel, for all that he does hold that religious representational thinking in a way grasps truth, also claims to disclose 'the fundamentally deceptive character of religious knowledge as a self-knowledge which does not know itself to be that.'[58] On the other hand, Quentin Lauer is hardly alone in reading the final chapters of the *Phenomenology*, and Hegel's philosophy as a whole, in a very different way. I myself have tried to defend a reading of the treatment of revealed religion in the *Phenomenology* that finds continuity rather than opposition in views put forward there about the relation between religious self-understanding and philosophical comprehension.[59]

I make these comments with three points in mind. First, the reader should know that there is controversy about the relation between religious and Christian self-understanding and the philosophical comprehension of that self-understanding that Hegel proposes. The *Phenomenology of Spirit* is an important source on which persons who take positions on that issue draw. Therefore it is appropriate to be explicit about the controversy that obtains among those positions in connection with a discussion of the *Phenomenology.*

Second I am going to address the issue of the relations between religious and Christian self-understanding and Hegel's philosophical comprehension of religion and Christianity not at this point, but in discussions that consider his later writings. I believe that one considers this issue in a more productive way if one takes those texts into account, rather than staying with the *Phenomenology* alone. But one can also not leave the *Phenomenology* behind, and several of my later discussions will return to ideas and texts presented in this chapter.

This will be necessary because, third, the understandings that Hegel establishes in the *Phenomenology* play a determining role in his later considerations of religion and Christianity. Hegel always identifies religion in its consummate form with Christianity, and always emphasizes the essential importance of revelation for this religion. Hegel always devotes attention to the central Christian mysteries: God, the Trinity, Creation, Incarnation, redemption and reconciliation, the indwelling of the Spirit in the gathered community. His identifications and later understandings of these mysteries, and of mystery itself, follow in important ways from views established in the *Phenomenology.* Hegel always understands religion as a corporate and social phenomenon, rather than as being essentially private or individual, and links religious consciousness with a self-consciousness that integrates understandings of human finitude and self-transcendence. One can hardly do better than begin a study of Hegel's philosophical consideration of religion and Christianity with a discussion of the *Phenomenology.* The 1807 text in important ways sets the agenda for his later work.

But of course it is the later work that pursues that agenda. An important part of that pursuit involves developments in Hegel's understanding of the nature and tasks of philosophical reflection on religion and of the relation of philosophy to theology. Those are the issues I will consider in the next chapter.

Chapter 3

Philosophy, religion, and theology

I have already said that, for Hegel, one who reflects philosophically on religion and Christianity pursues a two-sided aim. Now I must add that in pursuing this two-sided aim, one focuses reflection on two dimensions of the phenomenon of religion. These dimensions are intimately interrelated but nonetheless different. On the one hand, one must focus on the object of human religious involvement. Adopting a theistic idiom even when inquiring into religions of many different varieties, Hegel names this object with the word 'God.' On the other hand, one must also focus on the way in which humans are involved with this object, the components that must belong to that involvement if humans are to be adequately connected with its object. Each of these foci must belong to philosophical reflection on religion and Christianity, Hegel maintains, and they must be properly interrelated.

In this chapter I will begin a discussion of each of the dimensions of religion and Christianity upon which, according to Hegel, philosophical reflection must focus. This issue is important for its own sake. It will also lead to comment on Hegel's position concerning the relation of philosophy to theology, and to a more developed remark on Hegel's criticisms of one of the most important theologians of his era, Friedrich Schleiermacher.

Hegel often emphasizes the relatedness of the different but interrelated aspects of religion that command philosophical attention. Thus in the 'Introduction' to the *Lectures on the Philosophy of Religion* of 1824 one reads that the subject matter of those lectures 'is not just God as such; the content of our science is religion.'[1] This is because God must be understood as spirit, and 'this concept includes the subjective side within it, the side that is introduced into this concept when it is defined as religion.'[2] Hegel adds,

> Out concern here is not with God as such or as object, but with God *as he is [present] in his community.* It will be obvious that God can only be genuinely understood in the mode of his being as *spirit*, by means of which he makes himself into the counterpart of a community and brings about the activity of a community in relation to him. Thus it will be evident that the doctrine of God is to be grasped and taught only as the doctrine of *religion.*[3]

The point here is that, as spirit, God actively and dynamically relates Godself to that which is other than Godself, and in so doing retains self-related unity. An adequate comprehension of divine reality must grasp this. We can grasp this by grasping God's dynamic presence to Godself and to us in the religious community. And falling short of this comprehension is not philosophically acceptable. A key challenge that philosophy of religion presents is that of establishing, precisely in relation to an understanding of the nature of our religious involvement with God, a comprehension of God as God is in Godself.

Hegel insists that such a comprehension is both possible and necessary, even though such a claim was greeted with skepticism on his contemporary scene, just as it is on our own. He notes in 1827 the prevalent view that our knowledge cannot be of God as such but only of our relation to God. Since religion is supposed to comprise our relation to God, this means that we can have knowledge not of the nature of God, but of the nature of religion.

> That is why it is that nowadays we merely hear religion talked about but find no investigations into God's nature or what God might be within himself, how God's nature must be defined. God as such is not made the object [of inquiry] himself; God is not before us as an object of cognition, and knowledge does not spread out within this sphere. Only our relation to God, or religion as such, is an object [of inquiry] for us. Our discussion concerns

religion as such and does not, or at least does not very much, concern God.[4]

There are at least two problems with this view. Previous comments have already referred to the first problem. If God is to be conceived as spirit, then in relating Godself to the community that is religiously involved on account of this dynamic, divine activity, God manifests Godself, God's own nature and identity, to that community. In other words, to have genuine knowledge of our relation to God is to have knowledge of the God to whom we stand in relation.

The second problem does not have to do with the specifically Hegelian notion of spirit, but with an essentially Aristotelian understanding of teleology that Hegel adopts as his own. Religious involvement is essentially a process that aims at a goal or end. Let us call that end a reconciled relationship with God. If a process is one that aims, not accidentally but essentially, at an end, then one must understand the end in order to adequately understand the process. But one can understand a reconciled relation with God only if one understands who and what God is. Thus, to paraphrase Hegel, if our discussion of religion does not very much concern God, then it does not very much concern religion. An understanding of religious involvement requires an understanding of that with which people are religiously involved.

A suitable formulation of that understanding requires that one give a proper account of the nature of knowledge of God and distinguish that account from competing claims about the nature of knowledge of God that in various ways and to various degrees fall short. Hegel discusses such claims in many texts, including the *Lectures on the Philosophy of Religion* and the *Encyclopedia*. One such claim begins with the position that 'our consciousness has immediate knowledge of God, that we have an absolutely certain knowledge of God's being.'[5] If no more were said that, this Hegel would be, rightly or wrongly, content. According to him, 'Not only does philosophy not repudiate this position, but it forms a basic determination within philosophy itself.'[6] But with regard to the claim in question matters are not so simple. 'What it maintains is not simply that consciousness of God is conjoined with self-consciousness, but rather that the relationship with God is only and exclusively an immediate one.'[7] Hegel associates this view with Jacobi, for whom conceptual thinking is a 'progression through *sequences*, from one *conditioned* item to another *conditioned* one, where each condition is itself just something conditioned once more.'[8] Since God is supposed to be unconditioned and infinite, it follows that God cannot be known through thinking that is conceptually mediated. Therefore knowledge of God must be a kind of immediate knowing, a kind of faith. And if reason, as contrasted with understanding, is defined as the capacity to grasp the unconditioned, then reason must be understood in terms of immediacy and subsumed into faith.[9]

As already indicated, Hegel believes that there is a certain truth that belongs to the claim under consideration. He expresses an admiration for Jacobi that is qualified but genuine. 'What this immediate knowing knows is that the Infinite, the Eternal, or God, that is [present] in our representation also is—that within our consciousness the certainty of its being is immediately and inseparably combined with our representation of it.'[10] The problem with the claim about immediate knowledge of God is not this view, but the related view 'that *immediate* knowing can only have the truth as its content when it is taken *in isolation*, to the *exclusion* of mediation.'[11] Hegel maintains, as I will discuss below, that the religious representation on its own terms calls for a conceptual determination of its content through the mediating activity of autonomous, rational thought. Thus knowledge of God must take on a rationally and conceptually mediated form and integrate this with the immediacy whose legitimacy Hegel also acknowledges.

A more specific form of the claim that knowledge of God is essentially immediate interprets immediacy through the idea of feeling. Hegel understands this position to maintain 'that religion has feeling as its source, and that the relationship of the human spirit to God is to be confined only to the sphere of feeling and is not to be transposed into thought or into comprehension.'[12] The question is how, on the basis of this position, one could attribute any objectivity to the concept of God? After all, 'feeling as such, the mode of feeling, is one thing, while the content

63

of feeling is another.'[13] Very obviously a feeling, even a passionately strong feeling, that something is the case, in and of itself does not at all guarantee that the state of affairs in question obtains. In fact it is the materialists who are consistent in understanding the implications of the position that consciousness and knowledge of God belongs exclusively to the sphere of feeling. They have recognized that 'Feeling as such is the general form of what is sensible,'[14] and have on this basis 'reduced spirit and thought to feeling and sensation, and accordingly have taken God and all representations [of God] as products of feeling, and denied objectivity to God. The result is then atheism. God is thus a product of my feeling, of my weakness—a product of pain, hope, fear, joy, cupidity, and so forth.'[15] This is not to say that feeling plays no role in religious consciousness. It plays an essential role, as I will note below. Hegel's critical comments at this moment have to do with a specific claim about feeling in relation to knowledge of God, and do not address the more comprehensive question of the role of feeling in religious consciousness. This criticism will appear again in Hegel's comments on Schleiermacher's views. One might note at this point, with reference to those who would assimilate Hegel's understanding of religious consciousness with that of Feuerbach, that Hegel is at least in one text quite explicit in identifying and rejecting an account of religious consciousness that appeals to the ideas of projection and illusion.

If one cannot legitimately claim that knowledge of God has an exclusively immediate form or occurs exclusively in the form of feeling, one also cannot legitimately claim that knowledge of God comes about through the abstractly rationalistic procedures that Hegel associates with the Enlightenment. Enlightenment rationalism, Hegel maintains, 'left the doctrinal system in place and also left the Bible as foundation, but arrived at its own divergent views and sought to interpret the word of God in a different way.'[16] More specifically, this form of reflective thinking left the specificity of doctrinal teaching and the positivity of Biblical faith behind, and endeavored to form and legitimize understandings of God that were, as a consequence, one-sidedly abstract. 'The consequence is that no meaning for the expression "God" remains any more in theology than in philosophy, save only the representation, definition, or abstraction of the supreme being—a vacuum of abstraction, a vacuum of "the beyond." '[17] This consequence entails the view that one can legitimately know that God is, but not what God is. Hegel does not consider this view in relation to the variety of ways in which it has been put forward in the history of Christian theology, but only in relation to the interpretation he gives to this view in association with his comments on the Enlightenment. His comment is that 'Inasmuch as we know [only] *that* God is, God is an *abstractum*. To cognize God means to have a definite, concrete concept of God.'[18] Given the tenets of abstract rationalism, such a concept is not forthcoming.

As Walter Jaeschke points out, Hegel's attitude toward the Enlightenment is in fact complex. He 'criticizes the Enlightenment inasmuch as in its final form as reflective philosophy it proceeds to surrender the idea of God or take from it its significance for philosophy, and thereby its significance in general. On the other hand he is a follower of the Enlightenment inasmuch as in it the rationalization process only finds its at that time latest, highest form.'[19] Nonetheless, the form that reason finally assumes in the Enlightenment calls for rational critique. Hegel undertakes that critique by elaborating a philosophy 'that rectifies the false premises that led the Enlightenment to renounce' the possibility of a concrete concept of God 'not by stepping back behind the Enlightenment, except by directly refuting *in part* the critique which the Enlightenment directed against the former metaphysics.'[20] I will show in a subsequent discussion that this refutation is directly connected with Hegel's understanding of the nature of a speculative rethinking of the content of the religious representation, and with his understanding of the relation that must obtain between reflection on human religious involvement and reflection on the being and nature of God.

Thus for Hegel an acceptable understanding of rational knowledge of God does not identify that achievement with immediate cognition, with a form of consciousness that is exclusively determined by feeling, or with an empty rationalism that aims at an understanding of God that abstracts from all dogmatic and positive content and that must conclude that, at best, it is possible for us to know that God is but not what God is. Recognizing the inadequacy of these views clears the way for the development of a philosophical inquiry into the being and nature of God whose goal is defined in a more productive and adequate manner. But of course, that inquiry is illegitimate from the outset if our knowledge is limited to finite matters and cannot extend to a reality that is infinite. Hegel must contend with the position that asserts this. For many philosophers on his contemporary scene, and on our own, it is that case that 'There seems to be a lack of proportion between us men, limited as we are, and the truth as it is in and for itself; and the question arises of the bridge between the finite and the infinite. God is the Truth; how then are we to be cognizant of him?'[21] The 'ugly, broad ditch' which Lessing imagined as a seemingly unbridgeable chasm between historical and eternal truths had, by Hegel's time, extended to the separation that many at least supposed to obtain between finite matters and infinite reality, at least insofar as those are conceived of as objects of rational, conceptual cognition. Hegel believes that he can show that a consideration of finite matters on its own terms shows that those matters point beyond themselves to an infinite reality with which they stand in a necessary and essential relation, and that this demonstration exhibits the legitimacy and the necessity of moving in thought from an occupation with finite matters to an examination of a reality that is infinite. A discussion of this belief will be an important part of my consideration of Hegel's claims about the speculative rethinking of the religious representation and of his positive claims about rational knowledge of God.

But as I have already noted, one attains that knowledge, for Hegel, in connection with an understanding of the nature of what I am calling human religious involvement. That understanding requires a careful analysis of the components that must belong to religious involvement and the relations that must obtain between them. In Part One of the 1827 Lectures, which will be the resource on which I will draw in the following comments, the discussion of most of the components of religions involvement that I will examine occurs under the editorial heading 'Knowledge of God.' That is because the opening division of this part of these lectures, that deals with the understanding of God that, according to Hegel, philosophy needs to grasp and justify, has as its heading 'the Concept of God.' 'Knowledge of God,' in this context, is the knowledge that we gain, through participating in religious consciousness and religious life, and finally through a speculative consideration of what we come to know, through that participation, of the content that the concept of God presents. Thus, in this instance at least, 'Knowledge of God' is an appropriate rubric for Hegel's discussion of religious consciousness and religious life on their own terms.

Hegel's discussion of religious consciousness and life, of what I term religious involvement, includes, as the immediately preceding remark indicates, a consideration of the speculative reenactment of knowledge attained through religious involvement. I am going to separate these topics in my treatment of them. It is important, I believe, to see the extent to which Hegel considers religion on its own terms, before going on to develop his position regarding the nature and outcome of a philosophical rethinking of the significance that religious understanding presents. Given the examples he uses in this consideration of religion, it is clear that Christianity stands as the model to which he appeals in developing his views. Thus this consideration of religion on its own terms is also Hegel's effort at presenting a specific consideration of Christianity on its own terms, before going on to attempt a philosophical rethinking of the content of Christian self-understanding.

Hegel identifies essentially three components of religious involvement: faith, representation, and the cultus. One needs to consider each of these components in its complexity, and in connection with the relations that bind each of these components with the others.

The discussion of faith considers once again and in this context to some extent rehabilitates two ideas considered in a critical way in the treatment of problematic claims about the nature of knowledge of God: immediacy and feeling. Faith is the first of the specific aspects that belong to religious consciousness, considered on its subjective side, rather than with regard to the object toward which it is directed. Faith is 'certainty inasmuch as it is *feeling* and exists in feeling.'[22] Even though the English translation emphasizes only one word in this statement, Hegel is referring to two matters that are conceptually distinct, albeit apparently inseparable in faith, as he understands it. The first is certainty, which he understands in this context as a kind of immediacy. 'Certainty is the immediate relation of the content to myself. If I wish to express this relation forcefully, then I say, "I know that as certainly as [I know that] I myself am." '[23] Clearly in this instance one's conviction has to do with something that is supposed to be an external reality, rather than with one's own existence or with some fact about oneself. And it is also obvious that the occurrence, even the persistent occurrence of a representation of something for one's consciousness does not as such guarantee the reality of that thing. Nonetheless for the instance of immediate knowledge now under consideration, certainty has to do with God 'not merely [as] my own or [as] a subject within me, but [as] independent of me and of my acts of representing and knowing. God is in and for himself: that is implied in the content itself.'[24] But at the same time the God whom I know as being in and for Godself is the God whom I know in terms of God's being for me, as one who is in myself. This is the source of the certainty that belongs to faith, as Hegel construes it.

Hegel goes on to note that one needs some additional comments about faith itself for a more adequate understanding of the certainty that belongs to faith. Faith is often considered in opposition to knowledge. This Hegel takes as problematic, although faith is certainly different from knowledge, just as certainty is different from and not a guarantee of truth. Still, insofar as 'faith' refers to the 'certainty that there is a God,' the word is used 'inasmuch as we do not have insight into the necessity of this content. And to that extent we say that "faith" is something subjective, as opposed to which the knowledge of necessity is something objective.'[25] Additionally, while faith is said to have grounds only in an extended sense, the idea is important. Certainly faith as such does not have the sort of proper, objective grounds that belong to knowledge in the strictest sense. 'But again the grounds themselves can be of a subjective nature, whereupon I let my knowledge pass for a proven knowledge and say "I believe." '[26] Most often, these grounds are the authority of others in whom we have confidence, the testimony of others, perhaps to some marvelous occurrence.

> But the absolutely proper ground of belief, the absolute
> testimony to the content of a religion, is the witness
> of the spirit and not miracle or external, historical
> verification. The genuine content of a religion has for
> its verification the witness of one's spirit, [the witness]
> that this content conforms to the nature of my spirit and
> satisfies the needs of my spirit.[27]

In the last analysis, one might say, one finds in faith the being and actuality of God by finding that God speaks to and satisfies the deepest needs of the self.

This remark leads to a consideration of the connection between faith and feeling. Hegel's discussion in this context repeats some criticisms noted earlier in comments on feeling in relation to knowledge of God, but also underscores the important, indeed the essential and necessary role that feeling plays in relation to faith and religious consciousness. 'We will find,' he says, 'that possession in feeling is nothing else but the fact that a content is *my own* and indeed is my own as this particular individual—the fact that it belongs to me and is for me, that I have and know it in its determinateness and at the same time know myself in this determinateness.'[28] Hegel understands the manner in which feeling makes something 'my own' very concretely. 'The particularity of our own person is its corporeality so that feelings pertain to the corporeal side. With [aroused] feelings the blood becomes agitated and we become warm around the heart. That is the character of feeling.'[29] Whether warmth around the heart is a universal characteristic of feeling is not quite the point. Hegel very definitely recognizes the particular and quite bodily character of feelings, and wants to integrate this recognition into his account of faith and religious consciousness.

That integration leads to the statement that 'It is required not only that we know God, right, and the like, that we have a consciousness of them and are convinced about them, but also that these things should be in our feeling, in our heart. This is a just requirement; it signifies that these interests ought to be essentially our own—that we as subjects are supposed to have identified ourselves with such content.'[30] Of course in and of itself a feeling is neither good nor bad. That depends, among other things, on the determinate character of the feeling and the situation in which it is operating. And certainly it is not the case that one can appeal to feeling for verification of that which is felt, even though this claim is made in relation to religious maters. 'In our consciousness we know very well that, in order to know that a content is of the right kind we must look about for grounds of decision other than those of feeling. For it is true that every content is capable of being in feeling: religion, right, ethics, crime, passions.'[31] On can, however, say that feeling is the source or seed of knowledge of God, although, Hegel adds, 'that is not saying very much.' 'The enveloped being of the tree's nature, the simple seed, is the product or result of the entire developed life of the tree. And in feeling, too, the entire genuine content is within our subjective actuality in this enveloped fashion.'[32] In this comment, and throughout the discussion of feeling, Hegel may be on to a great deal. In addition to acknowledging the bodily character of feelings and the intentional directedness of at least some feelings, Hegel seems to understand that feeling allows us to experience meaning in a holistic way that conceptual thinking recovers only through elaborate and often laborious, albeit necessary, processes of analysis and synthesis. This understanding would certainly contribute to an assessment of the important role that feeling plays in religious consciousness.

Hegel's discussion of faith in terms of immediate knowledge, certainty, and feeling is supposed to give an analysis of religious consciousness as its subject experiences it. It is more than possible to take exception to aspects of this discussion. Paul Tillich might object to Hegel's seemingly unqualified identification of faith with certitude, and insist that faith genuinely occurs with doubt as a dimension of itself. Kierkegaard would object to Hegel's identification of faith with a kind of feeling, and to the omission of any mention of the religious task that Kierkegaard calls appropriation. The reason Hegel does not concern himself with such matters is that his interest is not so much in the phenomenon of faith for its own sake, or in the struggles that belong to faith so understood, but in faith as a phenomenon whose consideration belongs of necessity to an inquiry that aims at philosophical knowledge of God. For good or ill this interest sets the limits that circumscribe Hegel's consideration of faith. It also allows for the possibilities realized in that consideration.

To turn from thinking about the manner in which the subject experiences religious consciousness to questions about the significance grasped in religious consciousness is to turn to an analysis of the religious representation. Because of the issues Hegel addresses in his treatment of the religious representation, the examples he uses in considering those issues, and the way in which current philosophy addresses those issues, I think it is best to consider Hegel's analysis of the religious representation as a proposal regarding the nature of specifically religious discourse. The first component of this proposal is the observation that 'sensible forms or configurations belong to the representation. We can distinguish them by the fact that we call them *images* [*Bilder*].'[33] The prime characteristic of such an image is that it 'is something symbolic or allegorical and that we have before us something twofold, first the immediate and then what is meant by it, its inner meaning.'[34] As an example, Hegel points to something to which he also refers in the *Phenomenology*, namely the use of the imagery of God as one who 'begets' and the begotten as a 'Son,' used to express an understanding of the divine Trinity. We of course know that this 'is not meant in its immediacy, but is supposed to signify a different relationship, which is something like this one. The sensible relationship has right within it something corresponding for the most part to what is properly meant with regard to God.'[35] Other examples are images of the wrath of God, of the tree of knowledge of good and evil in the story about the Fall, and of someone giving instruction, as in stories about Prometheus. These examples show that the images in question can derive from outer experience or, as in the case of wrath, from inner experience.

The examples also show that these images do not occur in isolation. They belong to more extended discourses, and these discourses are in the first instance narratives, stories. The narratives develop and elaborate the significance of the images. The images endow the narratives with a meaning that is itself symbolic or allegorical. Some of these stories, such as those of the

Homeric deities, can be called myths in a rather simple sense of that word. Others, such as those concerning the birth, passion, and death of Jesus, are what one might call sacred histories.

> The story of Jesus is something twofold, a divine history. Not only [is there] this outward history, which should only be taken as the ordinary story of a human being, but it also has the divine as its content: a divine happening, a divine deed, an absolutely divine action. This absolute divine action is the inward, the genuine, the substantial dimension of the story, and this is just what is the object of reason.[36]

That is, an understanding of the story moves through its manifest or outward meaning to its latent or inner meaning, and in this way grasps the properly religious significance of the story. In an interesting way, Hegel anticipates more recent views concerning the symbolic nature of religious discourse and narrative theology proposed by such figures as Paul Tillich and Paul Ricoeur. He maintains that, for what he calls 'ordinary consciousness,' religious meaning essentially presents itself in symbolic and narrative form.

> The content is empirical, concrete, and manifold, its combination residing partly in spatial contiguity and partly in temporal succession. But at the same time this content has an inner aspect—there is spirit within it that acts on spirit. To the spirit that is in the content the subjective spirit bears witness—initially through a dim recognition lacking the development for consciousness of this spirit that is in the content.[37]

But that recognition calls for greater clarity. This comes about insofar as 'nonsensible configurations also belong to representation.'[38] The 'nonsensible configurations' in question are conceptions. They come about as a consequence of efforts at making sense of the meanings that symbolic images and narratives present. Those efforts result in understandings that, as they develop, can be called theological. Thus reflection and theological understanding occur, to some extent at least, at the level of representational thinking as such. Hegel maintains that the matters with which representational thinking deals call for a kind of autonomous, rational consideration that exceeds the capacities of representational thinking as such. It is also important to note that, for Hegel, reflection and understanding also develop within representational thinking.

There is a contrast between this aspect of Hegel's treatment of the religious representation and Ricoeur's analysis of religious discourse that is interesting because of the light it sheds on Hegel's position. In discussing discourse concerning God, Ricoeur says,

> the very word 'God' primordially belongs to a level of discourse I speak of as *originary* in relation to utterances of a speculative, theological, or philosophical type, such as: 'God exists,' 'God is immutable and omnipotent . . . ,' 'God is the first cause,' and so on. I put theological utterances on the same speculative side as philosophical utterances inasmuch as theology's discourse is not constituted without recourse to concepts borrowed from some speculative philosophy, be it Platonic, Aristotelian, Cartesian, Kantian, Hegelian, or whatever.[39]

In his analysis of the religious representation, Hegel recognizes what Ricoeur identifies as originary religious discourse. Hegel's analysis of the symbolic and narrative dimensions of the religious representation is very similar to Ricoeur's understanding of originary religious discourse. And Hegel believes that theology does and needs to make use of philosophical concepts. Nonetheless, he at least in some respects links theological discourse with symbolic and narrative religious discourse and distinguishes a fully speculative or philosophical consideration of God and of divine matters from all of these. That is because, for Hegel, the speculative concepts needed for the sake of a rational consideration of God and of divine matters are fully available only to self-determining, philosophical thought. An implication of this is that theology, in order to completely reach its aim as a form of rational inquiry, needs not simply to make use of philosophical concepts but to be a kind of philosophy. I will return to this idea below.

One reason for the difference in the ways in which Hegel and Ricoeur make distinctions in their understandings of religious discourse may well have to do with the different interests that they bring to their considerations of that discourse. Ricoeur certainly intends his consideration of religious discourse to be a philosophical hermeneutic. At the same time, immediately after distinguishing originary discourse from theological and philosophical discourse, he says, 'For the philosopher, to listen to Christian preaching is first of all to let go (*se depouiller*) of every form of onto-theological knowledge. Even—and especially when—the word God is involved.'[40] Hegel is quite aware that at least some philosophers are hearers of the word. But his interest is not in a hermeneutic that would understand the nature of religious discourse so as to determine, among other things, the possibilities available within that discourse for proclamation. His interest is rather in religious discourse as a domain of meaning whose consideration leads finally to rational knowledge of God. Such knowledge is itself of religious significance, he maintains, and it is the object of his inquiry.

I have already mentioned why Hegel discusses faith and the religious representation under the heading 'Knowledge of God.' Faith, informed by the representation, does deliver knowledge of God, even if not in the radically conceptual form that such knowledge demands in the last analysis. Through such knowledge, one's connection with God is, Hegel says, 'theoretical.' This needs as its compliment another, 'practical' connection. That connection emerges in the cultus.

To the extent that the relationship with God is exclusively cognitive or theoretical 'I am immersed in the object and know nothing of myself.'[41] In pure cognition, Hegel suggests at this point, one is entirely occupied with the object and not focused on one's relation to the object. But the religious subject, of course, is not simply one who has pure knowledge of God. This subject stands essentially in a relation to God. Knowledge of God and knowledge of one's relation to God need integration. 'I have not only to know the object, to be filled, but to *know myself* as filled by this object, to know it as within me and likewise myself as within that object that is the truth—and so to know myself in the truth.'[42] Cultic action, one's own actual participation in the cultus, enables one to know oneself and God in this way. Through this participation one becomes concretely aware of the otherness of God and the self, and of the union of God with the self, and of the self with God that bridges this otherness. The outcome of this participation and awareness is, according to Hegel,

> supreme, absolute enjoyment. There is feeling within it. I take part in it with my particular subjective personality, knowing myself as the individual included in and with God, knowing myself within the truth (and I have my truth only in God), i.e., joining myself as myself in God together with myself.[43]

Participation in cultic life begins with devotion, faith made vivid through prayer and worship. Reconciliation with God is made concrete through the sacraments, and through the various activities grouped together under the rubric of sacrifice. One most fully participates in the cultus insofar as one 'not only practices renunciation in external things such as possessions, but offers one's heart or inmost self to God and senses remorse and repentance in this inmost self,'[44] thus overcoming one's particular subjectivity and attaining purity of heart. Hegel adds,

> To this extent philosophy [too] is a continual cultus; it has as its object the true, the true in its highest shape as absolute spirit, as God. To know this true not only in its simple form as God, but also to know the rational in God's works—as produced by God and endowed with reason—that is philosophy. It is part of knowing the true that one should dismiss one's subjectivity, the subjective fancies of personal vanity, and concern oneself with the truth purely in thought, conducting oneself solely in accordance with objective thought. The negation of one's specific subjectivity is an essential and necessary moment.[45]

It is not unusual for Hegel to refer to philosophy as a kind of devotion or worship. Here he connects this idea with reference to a kind of ascetic dimension that philosophy must have and that also belongs to the fullest form of participation in the life of the religious cult.

It seems fair to say, given his comments on the cultus, that for Hegel participation in cultic life brings together the experience of particular relatedness that the subject enjoys in the immediacy of feeling with the directedness of religious consciousness toward its divine object, which the representation defines. Hegel comments on the integration of these dimensions of religious involvement in somewhat different terms in another context. In a forward that he wrote for H. Fr. W. Hinrich's *die Religion im inneren Verhältnisse zur Wissenschaft*, published in 1822, Hegel says,

> I understand by faith neither the merely subjective state
> of belief which is restricted to the form of certainty,
> leaving untouched the nature of the content, if any, of the
> belief, nor on the other hand only the *credo*, the church's
> confession of faith which can be recited and learned by
> rote without communicating itself to man's innermost
> self, without being identified with the certainty which a
> man has of himself, with his consciousness of himself. I
> hold that faith, in the true, ancient sense of the word, is
> a unity of both these meanings, including the one no less
> than the other.[46]

Hegel is insisting here on the integration of two aspects of faith that nonetheless do need to be distinguished for conceptual purposes: *fides qua creditur* and *fides quae creditur*. This insistence, which is certainly consistent with his later remarks about the roles of immediate certainty, feeling, and representation in religious consciousness, is at the basis of his critique of Schleiermacher and his position on the relation of philosophy to theology.

In the *Lectures*, Hegel's critique of Schleiermacher is most prominent in the 1824 text. It is also forcefully evident in the 1822 'Forward.' This critique has two important aspects. The first, not surprisingly, deals with Schleiermacher's definition of religious consciousness in terms of feeling. As Hegel reads him, for Schleiermacher religious consciousness has its origin in and derives its content from a feeling of dependence. In 1824, Hegel comments that 'If we say that religion rests on this feeling of dependence, then animals would have to be religious too, for they feel this dependence.'[47] In 1822 he makes a more pointed comment. 'If religion in man is based only on a feeling, then the nature of that feeling can be none other than the *feeling of dependence*, and so a dog would be the best Christian for it possesses this feeling in the highest degree and lives mainly in this feeling. The dog has feelings of deliverance when its hunger is satisfied by a bone.'[48] Peter Hodgson notes that Hegel falls short in understanding Schleiermacher's position regarding religious consciousness. For Hegel, feeling is 'a sense based mode of knowledge that can be filled with any content, whereas Schleiermacher intends something quite different by "feeling," namely a prereflective awareness of the whence and wither of existence.'[49] Hodgson comments elsewhere that this may be in part because Hegel had access only to the first edition of Schleiermacher's *The Christian Faith*, published in 1821, and not the second edition published in 1830. According to Hodgson, 'in the first edition as well as the second, Schleiermacher intended to distinguish between *religious* feeling and the feeling of reciprocity that we experience in relation to finite object. But he did not thematize this so sharply by designating the former as the "feeling of utter (or absolute) dependence," and by indicating that it entails an actual "relation to God." '[50] This is entirely likely, and Hegel does present something of a caricature of Schleiermacher's understanding of religious consciousness. Even so, as I have already commented, Hegel has good reason, he believes, for objecting to the position that feeling is the source of religious consciousness, and certainly for objecting to the position that feeling determines the content of religious consciousness, rather than the relation of the subject to that content. To the extent that the more nuanced statement of Schleiermacher's views regarding religious consciousness would entail the second of these positions, and perhaps some version of the first as well, Hegel would still find grounds for criticizing those views.

It does seem that Hegel is right at least in finding, in Schleiermacher's understanding of religious consciousness, the position that the content of that consciousness is determined by feeling, as Hodgson helpfully points out. 'Hegel is closer to the mark in noting that for Schleiermacher the knowledge afforded by religious feeling does not strictly include knowledge of God, whose infinite being is beyond all finite categories.' He adds, 'Schleiermacher does develop a system of divine attributes, which follow from modifications in the feeling of absolute dependence, but do not describe the divine nature but rather aspects of out relationship to God.'[51] One can state the problem Hegel finds here in terms of a comment about what is possible for understanding the content of the religious representation, and this directly presents the second part of Hegel's criticism of Schleiermacher. Given the view of religious consciousness that the latter puts forward, one can understand conceptions that supposedly have to do with God in terms of the aspects or modes of the conscious feeling of absolute dependence that they represent, but not as conceptions that have to do with God's own nature. If so, then this view of religious consciousness does indeed entail the position that we can have knowledge of our relation to God but not of Godself, and some version of the position that we can know that God is but cannot have knowledge of what God is. These, of course, are two positions that Hegel finds good reasons to reject.

The critique that Hegel directs at Schleiermacher in relation to understanding the content of the religious representation has particular importance for Hegel in relation to the conception of God that the doctrine of the Trinity presents. This doctrine, as previous comments indicate, is indeed put forward historically by the Church, Hegel maintains, in representational form. At the same time 'it is just this definition of God by the church as trinity that is the concrete determination of the nature of God as spirit; and spirit is an empty word if it is not grasped in this determination.'[52] One must treat the doctrine of the Trinity not as a representation of some form that our feeling of being related to God takes on, but as a conception that in its own way has to do with God's nature, and that we can think through for the sake of attaining an understanding of that nature.

This remark about the doctrine of the Trinity is emblematic of Hegel's understanding of theology and of the relation of philosophy to theology. One will hardly be surprised, in the light of previous comments in this chapter, to read that, for Hegel, theology cannot be concerned exclusively with our relationship to God. Theology must attempt to establish a fully rational understanding of the being and nature of God as such, and an understanding of the nature of our relation to God that is grasped in connection with a legitimate conception of the being and nature of God. Such an understanding cannot be the outcome of a process that leaves conceptual mediation behind in asserting immediate certitudes, that occupies itself with articulating the sense that is supposed to belong to our feeling of being in relation to God, or that pursues rational inquiry concerning God in a way that abstracts from the rich conceptions available in the historically established doctrines of the Church, and that is itself abstract in a problematic way for this reason.

Theology, then, must essentially be in the business of giving rational consideration to the historically established doctrines of the Church. And those considerations can neither exclusively or even principally have to do with the historical processes through which those doctrines were formed and became established. Hegel often complains about bodies of inquiry that are called theological and that either abstract from the riches of church doctrine altogether or consider that doctrine only with regard to its historical development. Either approach falls short of, and in fact expresses disdain for, 'the elaboration of doctrine that is the foundation of the faith of the Christian church.'[53] That elaboration requires a conceptual articulation of the rational intelligibility that doctrine presents. Hegel is quite clear that theology has this articulation as its task, and that the task is essentially a philosophical one.

Religion initially contains representations of God; these representations are communicated to us from our youth up as the doctrines of our religion, compiled in the Creed; and insofar as the individual has faith in these teachings, they are the truth for him, he has what he needs to be a Christian. Theology, however, is the science of faith. If theology provides a merely external enumeration and compilation of religious teachings, then it is not yet science. Even the merely historical treatment of its subject matter that is in favor nowadays (for instance, the reporting of what this or that Church Father said) does not give theology a scientific character. Science comes only when we advance to the business of philosophy, i.e., the mode of thinking that involves comprehension. Thus, genuine theology is, at the same time, Philosophy of Religion, and this is what it was in the Middle Ages too.[54]

This, one might note, is not the only place in which Hegel expresses admiration for medieval theology, or by extension for the Catholic Church in view of its medieval heritage. Elsewhere, while complaining about the separation of philosophy and theology from church doctrine, he notes that 'in the Catholic church, particularly in former times, there was no such separation between philosophy and church doctrine, for Scholastic philosophy was the philosophy of the church. Speculative philosophy has, in fact, been more in evidence in the Catholic Church than in the Protestant. This cleavage first occurred in the Protestant Church.'[55] Hegel's concern, however, is of course not with comparative denominational history, but with the concept of theology as such. He maintains that, among the essential components of the religious representation, the 'nonsensible configurations' or doctrinal conceptions hold pride of place. These conceptions convey the intelligible sense of a religious tradition to the believer. The theologian needs chiefly to be occupied with these conceptions. The aim of that occupation is the conceptualization and demonstration of the rational intelligibility and truth that doctrinal conceptions present. Conceptualization and demonstration are fully rational when they are philosophical, because philosophy is not only a rational enterprise, but an enterprise that presents a warranted articulation of the possibilities and ends that most radically determine reason itself. Therefore the theological task is simultaneously a philosophical task.

Hegel even goes so far as to say that 'philosophy *is* theology, and [one's] occupation with philosophy—or rather *in* philosophy—is of itself the service of God.'[56] One can and should consider very carefully the understanding of philosophy that this statement suggests. But one can also ask if anything is left of theology itself as an independent domain of inquiry? Peter Hodgson does ask this question, and finds the 'Hegelian embrace of theology a bit suffocating'[57] for quite understandable reasons. Consider for example only one limited problem. Hegel defines theology in connection with church doctrine. But what counts as church doctrine? Obviously dispute reigns regarding this question. A great deal of research, deliberation, and dialogue is required for any consideration of this matter. Those efforts are certainly theological and hardly philosophical in nature. And this is only one of many problems one might cite that seem to call for an integrally theological rather than philosophical consideration.

To say this, however, is not to deny that there is or at least can be substantial importance to Hegel's connection of theology with philosophy. I will discuss this matter below. Another question is of more immediate concern. Hegel's association of theology with philosophy has to do with the claim that the significance of the religious representation needs to be rethought in fully conceptual, philosophical terms if the intelligibility and truth of that significance is to be properly expressed. But, once again, what is the outcome of this process? Is the outcome at least in principle recognizable from the standpoint of religious consciousness and representational thinking? Or is the outcome one that is arguably the result of a legitimate consideration of that standpoint but nonetheless one that no longer proposes a truth recognizable in the light of religious self-understanding? Might the outcome of an Hegelian reenactment of the significance of the religious representation even be one that proposes a nonreligious or an antireligious truth?

In fact, one finds different versions of each of these positions in discussions of Hegel's philosophy of religion and Christianity. That is especially the case in relation to the utterly fundamental question about the conception of God at which Hegel claims to arrive through a speculative rethinking of the content of the religious representation. I will examine this question in the following chapter.

Chapter 4

The problem of God and the world in Christian and Hegelian thought

In this chapter I will consider some basic aspects of the philosophical conception of God that Hegel presents and the adequacy of that conception in relation to the issue of divine transcendence. The present consideration will focus chiefly on what I am going to call the speculative resources of the religious representation, and on the doctrine of creation. The consideration of the idea of God will develop further in the examination of the Christian mysteries in Chapter 5, and in the assessment of Hegel's views on religion and Christianity in the final chapter. The discussion in this chapter will establish positions to which those later examinations will appeal.

It is certainly the case, as I have already indicated, that interpretations and assessments of Hegel's conception of God differ widely. John Burbidge has a fascinating way of discussing what he takes to be the tendency of commentators on this aspect of Hegel's philosophy to find in it very different views which each takes to be either deeply right and essentially deserving of affirmation, or deeply wrong and calling for trenchant criticism.[1] Two recent and very important books exhibit this tendency. I have already referred to Peter Hodgson's *Hegel and Christian Theology*. Hodgson maintains that Hegel's philosophical theology represents one of two paradigms that develop in a dominant way throughout the history of Christian thought. 'Both,' he says, 'offer true insight into the reality of God and religion, and both have limitations.'[2] Hodgson critically identifies limitations that he finds in Hegel's philosophical theology, and at the same time holds that it represents a valid philosophical and theological option as well as a most valuable and productive resource for contemporary theological work. William Desmond takes a very different view, as he indicates in the title of his book, *Hegel's God, A Counterfeit Double?* The punctuation in the title represents a question. Desmond leaves no doubt about his response to the question. 'On the surface Hegel's thinking saturates us with God, but what it saturates us with, I have come to think, is a "God" who is not God. . . . An idol is no less an idol from being wrought from thought and concepts as from stone or gold or mud.'[3] For this reason, Hegel's thinking is certainly not a source of fruitful possibilities for current theology.

The difference between the views that Hodgson and Desmond present is emblematic of diverse readings of Hegel that were presented even in the 1830s and that have persisted in the literature on Hegel ever since, certainly in the last three decades. In a book such as this it is necessary to be quite explicit about this. That said, I am sure it will not be a surprise to the reader, especially given my earlier reference to Barth, that I am going to argue for a position in this and subsequent chapters that is far closer to the one that Hodgson takes than to Desmond's position. This is not to say that there is no merit to the kind of analysis and argument that Desmond and others present. There is a great deal of merit in those analyses and arguments, and much to be learned there. Nonetheless, I think that a far more plausible case can be made for a very different point of view. I would identify critical limitations belonging to Hegel's philosophical theology somewhat differently than Hodgson does. But I quite agree that, those limitations not withstanding, Hegel presents valuable, even indispensable resources for contemporary philosophical and theological inquiry. And on the central question of divine transcendence, I will argue that one finds in argumentation that belongs in a prominent way to Hegel's mature texts the development of a conception of God that entails a substantive and complex idea of transcendence and that is more than worthy of theological consideration.

In order to discuss Hegel's conception of God and the understanding of transcendence that is, I maintain, associated with that conception, one must return to an analysis of the religious representation. To begin with, recall the specific role that the representation plays in connection with the other necessary components of religious involvement. The representation mediates the otherwise immediate certitude of the faith that the religious subject has regarding God. It informs religious feeling, giving that feeling the definite content it requires. The representation also informs cultic practice, giving definition to the process through which the subject surpasses what might otherwise be an exclusively 'theoretical' consciousness of God through activity that brings about a consciousness of the essential relation to God in which one stands.

The religious representation itself, in turn, presents an internal complexity. Each of its elements is necessary and essential. Nonetheless, a certain primacy belongs to one set of those elements, namely to conceptual expressions or doctrines. Doctrines conceptualize and express the fundamental significance of the symbolic narratives that comprise sacred histories, just as those narratives themselves interpret the primary symbols ingredient in them. Hegel does not maintain that the narratives and, one might add, the other literary forms that make up the 'originary discourse' of a religious tradition, are of primary importance and that doctrines have the more secondary role of expressing in conceptual but also in more historically or culturally local terms the significance those narratives present. He holds that doctrines belong, along with symbols and symbolic narratives, to that 'originary discourse,' and play the role of expressing the most basic and essential significance of the other components of that discourse, although not with the concrete vivacity that belongs to those components themselves. It is telling that Hegel gives pride of place to doctrines in his comments about religious and Christian instruction.

It is not surprising, therefore, that philosophical reflection, on Hegel's view, pays special attention to the doctrinal components of the religious representation. As already noted, these components, for all that they are conceptual, still belong to the domain of representational thinking. Just as one can describe the business of philosophy in general as that of transforming representations into thoughts, philosophy of religion aims at rethinking the content of the religious representation in the form of the concept. The process is and must be a subtle one, because representational thinking as well as philosophical thinking is a genuine manifestation of '*thinking reason [denkende Vernunft]* . . . the only difference being that in philosophy the activity that constitutes religion appears simultaneously in the form of *thought [Denken]*, whereas religion, being thinking reason in naïve form, so to speak, abides rather in the mode of *representation [Vorstellung]*.'[4] Representational thinking falls short of fully rational or philosophical thinking for a number of reasons. It does or at least can make uncritical use of phenomena immediately given in external or internal experience, and of the analogies those phenomena make possible, in the process of concept formation. Even when dealing with strictly conceptual terms, representational thinking presents those terms to itself but does not think them through in a full and autonomous fashion. For this reason, 'Though they do indeed proceed from thought and have their seed and soil in thought, they are still representations on account of their form. For they are determinations that are related simply to themselves, that are in the form of independence.'[5] The terms in question are genuinely conceptual. 'But to the extent that they are not analyzed internally and their distinctions are not posited in the way in which they relate to one another, they belong to [the realm of] representation.'[6]

The last statement just cited is of overriding importance. Hegel is talking therein about the strictly conceptual terms that belong to the religious representation. He makes three comments as to why those terms are conceptual in nature and still belong to thinking that is representational in form. First, those terms are not 'analyzed internally'; for all that representational thinking is a genuine manifestation of 'thinking reason,' there is a kind of analysis of its own content that is needed and that representational thinking itself does not and cannot perform. Second, 'their distinctions are not posited'; the particular terms or elements that belong to representational thinking have not yet been clearly and expressly understood with regard to the ways in which they are different from, and must be distinguished from, each other. Third, 'their distinctions are not posited in the way in which they relate to one another'; the same elements or terms that are not clearly and expressly understood with regard to the ways in which they are different from each other are also not understood in terms of the connections that at one and the same time interrelate them and preserve the differences between them.

Of chief importance with regard to the comments just made is the observation that the dimensions of meaning that Hegel identifies all belong to the religious representation as such, that is, to the content of the representation. The religious representation has inherent in its content particular terms that are both specifically different from each other, and concretely interrelated with each other. The form that belongs to representational thinking, as well as the limitations that belong to that form, follow from the fact that these differences and relations inherent in the significance or content of the religious representation are not given explicit and autonomous rational consideration. The specifically different and concretely interrelated terms are not analyzed expressly with regard to the specific differences that distinguish them from each other and the concrete interrelations that join them together. For this reason they can appear to stand over against each other as if they were simply separate and independent.

An example that Hegel uses to illustrate the issue at hand is the statement 'God is all wise, wholly good, and righteous.' This statement suggests that the divine perfections in question both differ from each other and belong to God on account of divine nature itself, with the consequence that they need to be understood both with respect of the kind of difference that there is between them and the unity that obtains among them on account of God's unity with Godself. But the very understanding of the differences among the divine perfections along with their interrelated unity in the divine nature that this doctrinal component of representational thinking calls for is an understanding that representational thinking cannot attain. In the last analysis, that is because representational thinking sets concepts before itself but does not think through the most basic categories that operate in determining the meaning of those concepts—categories such as identity, difference, unity, sameness, and otherness. Thinking that turns to and succeeds at this task has become fully rational and speculative, and has surpassed the limitation that defines representational thinking as such. Thus, 'In saying "God is all wise, wholly good, righteous," we have fixed determinations of content, each of which is simple and independent alongside the others. The means for combining the representations are [the words] "and" and "also." '7 The statement or representation in question calls for a comprehension of the significance that it presents that is more radical than the understanding that mere conjunction attains. But representational thinking cannot attain that comprehension.

Another example quite relevant to the concern of this chapter is the doctrine of creation. To say that 'God creates the world,' or that 'the world is created by God,' is to suggest the God differs from the world and that the world differs from God in a specific way, that the differences that obtain between God and the world are what they are just on account of the relationship that in a definite way connects the world with God, and that one understands the nature of God's being and the nature of the being of the world just through understanding these differences and this relation. But insofar as the doctrine of creation is a component of representational thinking, it both calls for this understanding of its significance and is not the focus of a form of thought for which that understanding is possible.

These examples, and the principle they illustrate, concern what I call the speculative resources of the religious representation. It is indeed that case, for Hegel, that speculative thinking rethinks the content of the religious representation and attains a comprehension of that content that representational thinking as such cannot attain. It is also the case that the religious representation calls for a speculative rethinking of its own content, and does this by presenting a content that suggests both determinate differences and overarching interrelations, and thus forms of otherness along with forms of unity, that representational thinking on its own terms cannot grasp and that speculative thinking is precisely equipped to grasp.

Two implications follow. First, speculative thinking does not approach the religious representation and endeavor to rethink the meaning it presents with an aim that is alien to that meaning insofar as that meaning is considered from the standpoint of the representation as such. To put the point rather simply, if philosophy is the business of transforming representations into thoughts, the representation asks that philosophy be in that business.

Second, it cannot be the case that a speculative rethinking of the content of the religious representation by definition replaces an understanding defined in terms of opposition and difference with an understanding defined in terms of reconciliation and self-related unity. This view supposes that difference and opposition define the form of the representation as such, whereas the concept transcends the representation by replacing opposition and difference with reconciliation and self-related unity. Thus the religious representation concerning creation, as a representation, represents God and the world as realities each of which is not the other, as realities that differ from each other and stand over against each other. A speculative rethinking of the significance of the doctrine of creation would eliminate difference and opposition in an understanding of the unity of God with the human world. If the representational form expresses negation, the speculative concept surpasses that form through a negation of the negation that comprehends the unity among terms that only seem defined by the differences and oppositions between them. Stephen Crites seems to hold a version of this position. He notes that, for Hegel, 'all religious apprehension is in the formal mode of representation (*Vorstellung*); in a broad sense its mode is image, an objectification of its content as something placed over against religious consciousness.'[8] Philosophical comprehension transcends the form of the representation by overcoming this objectification and the concomitant understanding of religious consciousness as having to do with a content placed over against itself, rather than with its own self-relatedness. But to do this, of course, is to transcend religious self-understanding as such. Consequently, 'to transcend the formal limitation of the representation is to transcend religion itself.'[9] But this argument, I think, will not do. On its own terms the religious representation conveys a meaning that has to do both with difference and opposition and with concrete interrelations that reconcile and overcome opposition while preserving difference. And the self-related unity that speculative thinking grasps preserves difference as an essential and constituting moment of itself. In the light of what must be said about the speculative resources of the religious representation, and for that matter about the necessary outcome of speculative thought, it is a mistake to maintain that a speculative rethinking of the content of properly religious understandings of God and the world must, just because of the differences that there are between speculative and representational thinking, overcome the understanding of the otherness of and the transcendence of God from the world that religious consciousness, from its own standpoint, requires.

What, then, is the outcome of a philosophical conceptualization of the religious, and more specifically the Christian, understanding of the relation between the world and God that the doctrine of creation presents? One begins with a conceptualization of the understanding of God that this doctrine puts forward.

> God in his universality, this universal in which there is
> no limitation, finitude, or particularity, is the absolute
> subsistence and is so alone. Whatever subsists has its root
> and subsistence only in this One. If we grasp this initial
> content in this way, we can say 'God is the absolute
> substance and the only true actuality.' All else that is
> actual is not actual on its own account, has no subsistence
> on its own account; the uniquely absolute actuality is God
> alone. Thus God is the absolute substance.[10]

Hegel immediately adds that this conceptualization is incomplete. 'That God is substance is part of the presupposition we have made that God is *spirit, absolute spirit*, eternally simple spirit, being essentially present to itself.'[11] But this does not mean that to conceive of God as absolute spirit is to cease to conceive of God as absolute substance. It is rather to take up the latter concept into the former, thus altering and preserving it. Initially, the thought of God refers to 'the One, the eternal, this actual being in-and-for-itself. In this genuine, absolute determination, although it is not yet developed or consummated, God remains absolute substance and does so through all of the development.'[12] The process that will develop and consummate the conception of God by conceiving of God as spirit will continue to conceive of God as one, eternal, eternally self-related and uniquely self-subsistent.

That said, it is still the case that the concept of spirit surpasses the concept of substance in this understanding of God. Regarding this, Hegel observes, 'Spirit, if it is thought immediately, simply and at rest, is no spirit; for spirit's essential [character] is to be *altogether active*. More exactly, it is the activity of *self-manifesting*.'[13] Creation is the activity of divine self-manifestation, as Hegel will endeavor to show.

To say that 'God creates the world' is to say that 'God posits the world as something other, distinct from him (hence something naturally posited); [yet] the world is [also] what continues to belong to God and to be posited by him, so that it has the movement of betaking itself back to him.'[14] That is to say, a consequence of God's bringing the world into being is not that the world then stands in being wholly on its own, as it were, over against God, related to God in the way in which one independent thing is related to another independent thing. For that to be the case the world would have to be self-subsistent, but then it would not be created. Rather, the world possesses the being that is indeed its own wholly in a relation of total and unqualified dependence upon God. This is the world's 'movement of betaking itself back to him.' On this reading of Hegel's position, the being or self-relatedness that the world possesses as its own is at one and the same time a self-relatedness that is wholly and necessarily encompassed by the relation of the world to God.

God, on the other hand, who as absolute spirit is entirely active and self-manifesting, is as absolute substance unqualifiedly self-related.

> All through the development God does not step outside his unity with himself. In God's creating the world, as tradition has it, no new principle is established, nor is something evil established, something that would be autonomous and independent. God remains only this One; the one true actuality, the one principle, abides throughout all particularity.[15]

In creating the world, that is, in establishing and relating Godself to something that is other than Godself, God does not sacrifice God's own self-relatedness or self-subsistence. God does not cease to be something other than what God is in Godself by establishing and relating Godself to the world. On this reading of Hegel's position, God's relation to the world is wholly and necessarily encompassed by divine self-relatedness.

The starting point of these comments was a conceptualization of the understanding of God that the doctrine of creation represents. One could also begin with a conceptualization of the understanding of the world that the doctrine represents. The results are the same. The being of things in the natural and cultural world, by way of contrast with the being of God, is intrinsically finite. Such things do of course have being. 'The being of all these things is not of an independent sort, however, but is quite simply something upheld and maintained, not genuine independence. If we ascribe a being to particular things, it is only a borrowed being, only the semblance of a being, not the absolutely independent being that God is.'[16] The being of mundane things is, to use another word, received, rather than something that belongs to those things just through themselves. Some medieval theologians would have invoked the notion of participation in order to give an account of this understanding. Because the being of mundane and finite things is 'borrowed' or received, a consideration of the being of finite things leads of necessity to a consideration of its source. 'Because there is something finite, there must also (on that account) be something infinite and not bounded by another, an absolutely necessary essence. The finite is what is not inwardly its own ground, it is what is contingent; there must therefore be something that is not in turn grounded in another.'[17] As contrasted with finite things, God is precisely 'something that is not in turn grounded an another.' In the *Encyclopedia* Hegel says that the philosophical reader must be able to recognize 'not just that God is actual—that he is what is most actual, that he alone is genuinely actual—but also (with regard to the formal aspect) that quite generally, what is there is partly *appearance* and only partly actuality.'[18] In the *Lectures on the Philosophy of Religion* he is more expansive. He points out that 'through our treatment the world is relinquished

91

as genuine being; it is not regarded as something permanent on this side. The sole import of this procedure is that *the infinite alone is*; the finite has no genuine being, whereas God has only genuine being.'[19] A bit later he adds,

> This being is the distinction that takes itself back
> into simplicity. Involved within this essence is the
> determination of what is distinguished; but it is a
> determining of what is distinguished as it relates itself to
> itself, a self-determining. . . . Distinction does not come
> into it from the outside, for this unrest lies within it as
> being itself the negation of the negation. More precisely,
> it determines itself as *activity*. This self-determination
> of the essence within itself, namely the positing of the
> distinction and its sublation in such a way that it is an
> action, and that this self-determining remains in simple
> connection with itself, is inward *necessity*.[20]

I grant that this seems to be Hegel at his obscure best. But consider this text. In bringing creatures into being, God establishes a distinction between creatures and Godself. But simultaneously, in establishing this distinction God relates Godself to Godself. Thus while the outcome of creation is something different from Godself, God remains, in connection with that outcome, wholly self-determining. More precisely, in creating, God determines Godself as acting, and through the activity in question God brings Godself into connection with something other than Godself through a process that is nonetheless, and with necessity, wholly one of self-determination. Thus creatures, on account of the finite and received being that belong to them, have being or self-relation only in virtue of and wholly in the context of the relation to God in which they stand. In the case of creatures, to be self-related is to be related to another and to be determined by that other. Whereas in the case of God, to be related to another is at the same time to be self-related and wholly self-determining.

There are several comments that need to be made about the positions I have just presented, and the reasoning associated with them. First, the reasoning I have just presented is historically associated with various forms of the cosmological argument concerning the existence of God. Hegel notes that the form in which such an argument is typically presented can fail fully to disclose its content. On the one hand, given an argument that begins with comments on contingent beings and proceeds to the conception of a necessary being, one could suppose that 'Here there are *two entities* in connection—*one being* with *another being*—a connection that we have seen in the form of *external* necessity.'[21] But this of course is not the case. The argument is in fact based on the understanding that finite things have no being at all outside of the relationship to God, and thus certainly are not entities in their own right that stand in a connection with some other entity in a way that is necessary but at the same time external to them. On the other hand, 'there is the objection against these proofs that they are said to make the finite into the foundation for the being of God. The finite is an abiding point of departure, and in this procedure the being of God is mediated through the being of the finite.'[22] But of course, syllogistic form notwithstanding, just the opposite is the case. In the 1829 Lectures Hegel expressly makes this point in relation to the distinction between the order of knowledge and the order of being. 'It is only our knowledge of the absolutely necessary being that is conditioned by the starting point. The absolutely necessary does not exist by raising itself out of the world of contingency and requiring the world as its starting point in order that, by starting from it, it first attain to its being.'[23] This statement, Hegel believes, exhibits the essential process of thought that the cosmological argument manifests, however imperfectly because of its form.

On more than one occasion Hegel says that he finds in medieval theologians an anticipation of the work that he does in philosophy of religion. This suggests a second comment on the positions and reasoning just discussed concerning God and creatures, in the form of a comparison and contrast between Hegel and Aquinas on that issue. Aquinas maintains that creatures have being exclusively, wholly, and entirely in the context of the real relation that there is between creatures and God.[24] Creatures have the being that they do have on account of participating in being or receiving being in virtue of the divine first principle.

Aquinas also, of course, maintains that God is self-subsistent being, as such possessed of the whole power of being, with the consequence that, should God act in relation to things other than Godself, the first, proper and essential effect of that action is the being of those things. Moreover, God is most intimately present to creatures as the first cause of the entire being of each creature, and this in a manner that in no way qualifies God's utter self-subsistent being and self-determination. These positions closely resemble ones that I have attributed to Hegel in the foregoing discussion.

In view of the understanding of relations with which he operates, Aquinas must hold a position on the connection between God and creatures that differs from what Hegel asserts. On account of God's utterly self-subsistent and self-determined being, there cannot be real relations that obtain between God and creatures, as contrasted to the real relations that must obtain between creatures and God if there are creatures at all. Aquinas understands the analogical nature of the terms that signify real relations and that are predicated of God to accommodate this position. He maintains that this position is quite consistent with the assertion that God is intimately and substantially present to each creature as the first cause of the entire being of that creature. Aquinas asserts this, and that at the same time maintains that every perfection that can and does belong to God belongs to God independently of creatures.

So the comparability that appears between Aquinas's positions about the relation of creatures to God and ones that I have attributed to Hegel does not extend to the way in which each thinks about God in connection with creatures. Aquinas denies the possibility of real relations between God and creatures. Hegel affirms real relations between God and creatures, and in fact seems to think that it is impossible otherwise to affirm real relations between creatures and God. But in texts I have cited, Hegel does assert that the relations that obtain between God and creatures do not compromise the self-subsistent and self-determined nature of divine being. In this regard it is possible to say that the positions of Aquinas and Hegel approach each other. There are different ways of assessing this situation. One might say that Aquinas thought through the concept of self-subsistent being more thoroughly and radically than Hegel. Or one might say that Hegel developed a complex and nuanced understanding of relations that allowed him to think about the connection between the self-subsistent being of God and the received being of creatures in a way that was not available to Aquinas. At any rate, it seems possible, given the reading I have offered, to say that each of these writers is attempting to account for the intimate presence of God to creatures on the one hand, and the difference that obtains between the being of creatures and the being of God on the other.

But perhaps this comparison between Hegel and Aquinas should give one pause. After all, more than credible commentators from Hegel's day to the present have understood the central positions that belong to Hegel's philosophy of religion in general and to his conception of God in particular to be a far cry from anything that would resemble Aquinas's views even in a remote way. Ought not one to ask if Hegel's views are indeed as theologically plausible as I have suggested, and for that matter if what I have suggested does indeed represent views that Hegel maintained?

These questions lead to two further comments about the positions and reasoning dealing with the issue of God and creatures that I have discussed. These comments have to do with objections raised against Hegel's conception of God in his day and on the current scene.

We find Hegel himself responding to the first set of objections in the 1827 *Lectures on the Philosophy of Religion* and elsewhere. The source of these objections was 'the neopietism of F. A. G. Tholuck and other theologians who had begun to attack Hegel's alleged "pantheism" and "atheism" by labeling him a "Spinozist."'[25] If Hegel was occupied in 1824 with leveling criticisms at Schleiermacher, he was occupied in 1827 and subsequently with responding to criticisms leveled at him by Tholuck and his allies.

The basis for these criticisms is not hard to find. After all, as I have pointed out, Hegel does insist on conceiving of God as infinite and absolute substance. He does say that '*the infinite alone is; the finite has no genuine being, whereas God has only genuine being.*' He does say that everything other than God is 'partly

95

appearance and only partly actuality.' It is not hard to give statements like these an apparently Spinozistic reading, and to draw one of two conclusions. God is infinite and absolute substance. Nothing finite has genuine, that is substantial, being. Thus finite things are not properly speaking 'things' at all, but accidents, as it were, of the absolute substance. Insofar as they seem to be independent entities, they are only appearances. The degree of being that such items have is only accidental in nature. This means that the being of everything mundane is really divine, which is pantheism. Or since one can suppose that the reality of a substance is exhausted in the totality of its accidents, it means that the apparent difference between the world and God is only apparent, which is atheism.

In 1827 Hegel responds vigorously to the charge of pantheism. To begin with, he says that 'pantheism in the strict sense has never been propounded. "Pantheism" means "all is divine," and amounts to the notion that everything taken singularly is God—this [snuff] box or the pinch of snuff.'[26] Were this Spinoza's position, and Hegel's for that matter, it would entail not pantheism in the strict sense of the word but 'monotheism and acosmism.'[27] Any of Hegel's critics would reject the second of these positions, which says that there is no world of finite things. 'Our modern babblers, however, cannot break free from the view that finite things as well as God have actual being, that they are something absolute.'[28] Hegel maintains that his reasoning leads to a position that escapes both of these erroneous views: 'we have the finite as our starting point, and it turns out to be something negative, the truth of which is the infinite, i.e., absolute necessity, or, by a more profound definition, absolute vitality, or spirit.'[29] According to this position, to use language I have employed, the being of finite things is both real and received, and therefore must be understood in connection with the relation of that being to the principle from which it derives. Now granted the reasoning that reaches just this position does not by itself make it clear 'whether absolute spirit in its relationship to the finite has being as substance only or as subject, and whether finite spirits are effects or accidents of the infinite. This last is certainly a distinction, but it does not deserve so much fuss.'[30] Why not? That is because further reasoning makes it clear that absolute spirit must be thought of as subject, with the consequence that the relation between absolute spirit and finite spirit has the form of intersubjectivity, which requires that the difference and the independence of the interrelated terms be maintained. In fact, as previously noted, the reasons for insisting that absolute spirit be conceived as subject are at least implicit in the concept of absolute substance. Nothing more is needed, for Hegel, to dispose of the charge of pantheism.

In the final volume of the *Encyclopedia*, Hegel again responds to the accusations of pantheism by referring to the issue of acosmism, and also discusses the concepts of unity, identity, and relation. He begins by referring to 'the one need common to all philosophies and all religions of getting an idea of God, and secondly, of the relationship of God and the world.'[31] The position that an essential and internal necessity, rather than an external necessity, obtains in the relation between God and the world entails that between God and the world there is some sort of unity. But, some reason, unity means simple oneness. To say a unity obtains between God and the world is to say that God and the world are simply one. The outcome is pantheism, or perhaps atheism, depending on one's interpretation. Hegel responds that

> though philosophy certainly has to do with unity in general, it is not, however, with abstract unity, mere identity, and the empty absolute, but with concrete unity (the notion), and that in its whole course it has to do with nothing else;—that each step in its advance is a particular term or phase of this concrete unity, and that the deepest and last expression of unity is the unity of absolute mind itself.[32]

So understood, the category of unity comes progressively to be defined through the concepts of identity, difference, and relation. Mere identity can only be a caricature of the speculative conception of the unity of absolute spirit, or of the unity that obtains between God and the world and that must as such, Hegel suggests, maintain the difference and independent identity of each, in the context of a concrete understanding of the relation of each to the other. Indeed, Hegel maintains, for those who can conceive of the unity between God and the world only through the concept of abstract identity it must be the case that since 'in their judgment either of the two, the world as much as God—has the same solid substantiality as the other, they infer that the philosophic Idea God is *composed* of God and the world. Such then is the idea they form of pantheism and which they ascribe to philosophy.'[33] Hegel is maintaining, however, that the philosophic idea of God is not 'composed' of God and the world. There is a difference between God and the world, and thus between the concepts of God and of the world, as well as a concrete relation between each and the other that unites them and that, from God's side, confirms divine self-relatedness.

But these comments, that represent Hegel's response chiefly to the charge of pantheism and that are supposed to contribute to indicating the theological legitimacy of his conception of God, still seem to presuppose the discussion of that conception that I gave earlier. And the second question posed in the aftermath of the comparison of Hegel and Aquinas still stands. Is that discussion truly representative of positions that Hegel maintains?

One possible response is to invoke the texts that I have, I think amply, used as resources for that discussion. But that alone will not dispose of the issue. Learned commentators have given readings of Hegel's conception of God quite at variance to the one I have offered. William Desmond is prominent among them. Given the focus of this chapter, I will refer, chiefly, to Desmond's view of Hegel's conception of God in connection with the issue of creation, and to other comments by Desmond insofar as they are strictly related to that issue.

The traditional doctrine of creation, of course, asserts that creation is *ex nihlo*. Desmond maintains that 'Hegel has no way of thinking this "nothing" outside of his doctrine of *self-relating negativity*; the negative activity that in determination makes self-determination possible.'[34] This means that 'creation, for him, is not external determination, but immanent self-determination in self-externalization.'[35] Thus creation has to do with a kind of divine becoming, which is really a divine self-becoming. Moreover, Hegel 'folds all being into this process of determinate becoming, and even more so, into a process that turns out to be one of self-becoming or *self-determination*.'[36] Given this, 'God might well be called the whole of wholes,'[37] the one, all encompassing and self-determining process of which all other processes are components or dimensions. Now in the first place, 'an absolute that has to become itself to be itself cannot be an absolute to begin with, and hence cannot begin, or create, the new beginning we find as the finite between.'[38] Hegel conceives the process of divine self-becoming more specifically inasmuch as he thinks that 'God is just like subjectivity, nay, *is* absolute subjectivity (inter-subjectivity); the absolute must other itself; the restless drive, or ecstasis of self-transcending must come out of itself and take on the form of otherness in the world of finitude.'[39] According to this view, 'creation,' as philosophically understood by Hegel, is a process of divine self-becoming, an all-comprehensive whole in which all other processes and the events belonging to them are inherent, a process to be understood with reference to the conception of (inter)subjectivity, and a process that occurs with necessity. Moreover, since the conceptions of subjectivity, and more specifically of autonomous rational knowing, that are the bases for understanding this process are themselves formed with reference to human subjectivity and human knowing, 'the difference between the image and the original vanishes, the difference of man and God.'[40] If so, then 'in Hegel there seems, finally, no absolute God beyond world history. . . . Hegelian absolute knowing is a counterfeit absolute knowing, for we know nothing absolute.'[41]

As an aside, the last statement badly misconstrues what, for Hegel, absolute knowing means. But that is not central to present concerns. One might also note that Desmond's critique bears an uncanny resemblance to the objections regarding pantheism and atheism to which Hegel responded in 1827 and 1830. But Desmond may well think that Hegel failed to respond successfully to those objections, and if so he is fully right to present his case. As I understand it, that case, stated especially with reference to the idea of creation, asserts four critical claims: (1) Hegel understands creation with reference to the inadmissible concept of divine self-becoming; (2) he maintains that that process occurs with necessity; (3) he understands that process as a whole of wholes; (4) understanding the divine creator with reference to the humanly derived conceptions of subjectivity and intersubjectivity has disastrous consequences regarding the relation of God and the world, and more specifically regarding the relation of God and historical humanity. Each of these claims, for Desmond and as such, is important in relation to the conception of divine transcendence.

Since Hegel conceives of God through the concepts of substance and of spirit, he certainly does introduce the notions of activity and self-determination into the concept of God. Desmond maintains that this makes it impossible adequately to conceive of God as creator, and thus to attribute to God the transcendence that such an understanding would allow. Presumably this is because creation, understood as *creatio ex nihilo*, requires that God realize and exercise the whole power of being, and thus that God be fully actual, and thus incapable of becoming, which requires potency as contrasted with actuality. Indeed Aquinas argues in this way, and the reasoning is powerful. However some medieval theologians such as Bonaventure, and in a way Aquinas himself, in conceiving of God as subsistent *act* of being, introduce the notions of dynamism and action into God without thinking that this challenges unqualified divine actuality. This is even more expressly the case in the context of explicitly trinitarian theology, but that requires an independent discussion. Hegel himself, while explicitly referring the idea of dynamic self-determination to God, also insists that the conception of God as spirit preserves, as well as transforms, the conception of God as absolute substance, which includes the idea of self-subsistence and all that it entails. And more contemporary Protestant theology continues and develops this line of thought. Eberhardt Jüngel, for example, maintains that 'when God is understood as the one who chooses, his being is already thought of as a being in becoming,' and insists on the very same page that 'the becoming in which God's being is cannot mean either an augmentation or diminution of God's being.'[42] Perhaps a kind of eternal dynamism having to do with divine autonomy is quite compatible with an understanding of God's being as entailing unqualified actuality, thus allowing for a full conception of creation as well the ontological possibility that opens God to, or better, through which God opens Godself to, history.

However, one might well meet this response to Desmond's first criticism with his second criticism. Hegel's conceptualization of what religious discourse names 'creation' identifies a process that cannot not occur, that occurs with necessity. If God's very being requires the created world, then God does not possess the entire perfection of being in Godself alone, and then God, so understood, cannot be truly a creator and cannot transcend the world as a true creator transcends creatures.

I will both comment now on this criticism, and briefly return to the issue below in connection with discussion of the fourth criticism. It is at least the case that the interrelated issues of creation, divine freedom, and necessity are not easily sorted out with regard to major figures in the history of Christian theology. Take Aquinas again as a representative example. He certainly holds that God realizes every possible perfection in Godself alone, that there is no necessity that God be or be thought of in relation to anything other than Godself alone, and that therefore creation is entirely the outcome of divine freedom. At the same time, he maintains that God's being is infinite, that to be 'good' is a transcendental predicate of being, and that the good is self-diffusive. If God is infinitely good and if the good is self-diffusive then God is infinitely self-diffusive. If so, then how is it possible that God might not create? Moreover, God is thoroughly eternal. Therefore all God's choices are thoroughly eternal, including the choice to create the world. Thus God chooses from all eternity and inalterably to create the world. That is, from all eternity it is the case that creation cannot fail to occur. The suggestion here is that a genuine sense of divine freedom and something that it may seem quite reasonable to call 'necessity' might not at all be incompatible and may even require each other.

Desmond's third criticism asserts that Hegel understands God as a 'whole of wholes.' God determines Godself in and through the processes that representational thinking identifies with 'creation.' Since God determines Godself through those processes, they are immanent to God and their development and integration is the coming into being of God's very being. Thus, Hegel's way of characterizing creation as the necessary form of divine self-determination produces at best a caricature of divine, creative transcendence. Peter Hodgson argues against Desmond on this matter.

> A whole comprises parts. If the independence and integrity of the parts are violated, if the many are reduced to one, then holism becomes identity or sameness. Without genuine difference and otherness, without transcendence as well as immanence, there is no whole, no system of relations, no spiraling into novelty, but simply an eternal repetition of the same. God *is* this whole, the whole in which everything finite comes into being and passes away, a whole in which time and eternity transpire and God becomes concretely self-determined.[43]

There is much appeal to the view that Hodgson presents. But I think that it is not fully adequate. A whole has parts. The parts must have integrity and independence from the whole. For this reason, a whole is not just identical with its parts, taken in their integrity and their independence from the whole and from each other. But a whole is also not something that is independent of the integration of its parts and their functions. For example, my living body is a whole organism whose parts are organs. Each of the organs has integrity and a kind of independence from my body and from the other organs. Each of these organs periodically replaces its component cells and exercises functions that are its own. Still, my body is not something independent of the integration of these organs and of the occurrence and development of their functions as they promote life, growth, and more lately decline. When the integration breaks down, the functions will cease and my body will cease to be my living body.

Part of the problem, I think, is with the concepts of wholes and parts themselves. Desmond and even Hodgson emphasize these concepts in speaking of Hegel's understanding of God and creation. Hegel emphasizes unity, difference, otherness, relation, and self-relatedness. It may well be that the language of wholes and parts cannot capture the understandings that Hegel wants to present in offering a speculative conceptualization of the doctrine of creation that addresses, as it must, the issue of the relation of God and the world. Language that treats of difference and interrelation, subjectivity and intersubjectivity, is better suited to the task.

But this, of course, takes us to Desmond's fourth criticism. Hegel, he maintains, understands God with reference to the concept of subjectivity, which in turn implies intersubjectivity. This has two consequences. First the subject, the self, knows itself only in relation to the recognition received from another self. Thus, on the one hand, the other is not really defined in terms of its otherness from the self, but in terms of the connection it has with the self that delivers self-knowledge. If God knows Godself through creatures then creatures are not genuinely other than God. On the other hand if God must know Godself and can do so only through being self-related in connection with relations to creatures, then any thought of reconciling the necessity of creation with divine freedom, and for that matter of maintaining that creation follows from God's realization of the whole power of being rather than from a divine ontological deficiency, is undone.

The second consequence presents conclusions that differ from those entailed by the first, but that are equally disastrous. Self-knowledge, Hegel maintains, can come about only through recognition, only within the context of intersubjectivity. The idea of God is in fact the representation of this necessity as final and absolute. Even God knows Godself only through God's connection with creatures. Divine self-knowledge comes about insofar as God externalizes Godself and dwells in the gathered community. The community's knowledge of God is God's self-knowledge as well as the community's knowledge of itself. In fact the very conception of God is a representation of the overarching reality of the community, the intersubjective domain that each of its participants knows and in reference to which each of its participants gains self-knowledge, just as the self-consciousness of the identity of the community itself resides just in that self-knowledge. Feuerbach, Bruno Bauer, and Emil Durkheim are the authentic successors of Hegel's speculative construal of the religious representation of creation.

There does seem to be some basis for these conclusions. Consider the following text from the 1827 *Lectures*, part of which I cited earlier.

> Spirit, if it is thought immediately, simply, and at rest,
> is no spirit; for spirit's *essential character is to be altogether
> active. More exactly, it is the activity of self-manifesting.* Spirit
> that does not manifest itself or reveal itself is something
> dead. 'Manifesting' signifies 'becoming for an other.'
> As 'becoming for another' it enters into antithesis,
> into distinction in general, and thus is a *finitizing* of
> spirit. Something that is *for an other* is, in this abstract
> determination, precisely something finite. It has an other
> over against itself, it has its terminus in this other, its
> boundary. Thus spirit that manifests itself determines
> itself, enters into existence, gives itself finitude, is the
> second moment. But the third is its manifesting of itself
> according to its concept, sublating it, coming into its own
> self, and becoming *explicitly* the way it is implicitly. This is
> the rhythm, or the pure eternal life of spirit itself.[44]

Spirit must manifest itself, must do so by determining itself as other than itself, and recover itself only as a consequence of this self-determination. In this case the other is not genuinely other, spirit finitizes itself on account of an ontological deficiency and through necessity, and self-knowledge comes about only in the context of an overarching community of selves, which is therefore the final, only, and immanent absolute reality.

But one must not be hasty. Even the text I just cited does not lend itself to only this reading. And other important texts suggest both a different position, and a different reading of this text. In the *Encyclopedia* Hegel draws the following statements from a book that he quite favorably reviewed:

> God is God only insofar as he knows himself: his
> knowledge is, further, a self-consciousness in man and
> man's knowledge *of* God, which proceeds to man's self-
> knowledge *in* God.[45]

Consider these statements very carefully. God is God only insofar as God has self-knowledge. That divine self-knowledge
determines human self-consciousness. That is, God has self-
knowledge on account of God's intrinsic being, and it is also
the case that God reveals what God knows Godself to be to
human beings. Human beings then acquire the knowledge of
Godself that God reveals. That knowledge, which is itself divine
self-knowledge or self-consciousness, then becomes present in
human knowledge of God. Human knowledge of God includes
an understanding of the essential connection that humans have
with God, and thus human self-knowledge in God. This is very
different from the conclusions that the 1827 text seemed to suggest. And please note, there is nothing in that text that excludes
the possibility that God possesses self-knowledge on account of
God's intrinsic being and further manifests Godself to human
beings just because it is in the nature of spirit to do, analogous
to the way in which it is in the nature of the good to be self-
diffusive.

A text from the 1829 *Lectures on the Proofs of God's Existence*
reinforces the position stated by the propositions mentioned in
the *Encyclopedia*.

> The object of our concern, the community and
> communion [*Gemeinschaft*] of God and humanity with
> each other, is a community of spirit with spirit; and it
> involves the most important questions. It is a community,
> and this very circumstance involves the difficulty of at
> once maintaining the difference and of defining it in such
> a way as to preserve the communion. That humanity
> knows God implies, in accordance with the essence
> of community, a communal knowledge; that is to say,
> humanity knows God only insofar as God knows Godself
> in humanity. This knowledge is God's self-consciousness,
> but at the same time a knowledge of God on the part
> of humanity; and this knowledge of God by humanity
> is the knowledge of humanity by God. The spirit of
> humanity—to know God—is simply God's Spirit itself.
> It is here that the questions of the freedom of humanity,
> the union of humanity's individual knowledge and

consciousness with the knowledge by which humanity is in communion with God, and the knowledge of God in humanity, come to be discussed.[46]

Humanity knows itself in God in virtue of its knowledge of God. Humanity's knowledge of God is God's knowledge of Godself in humanity, a human participation, one might say, in divine self-knowledge. This must be the case since, if God reveals Godself to humanity, God must reveal Godself to humanity as God knows Godself to be. That self-knowledge, in turn, is and arguably must belong to God on account of God's intrinsic being. One could more than plausibly argue that if this were not the case the understanding of God as absolute spirit could not possibly subsume within itself the understanding of God as absolute substance. Hegel insists on that subsumption.

What is the outcome of this discussion? It seems that the conception of God based on the concepts of subjectivity and intersubjectivity need not have the consequences mentioned above. If self-knowledge is intrinsic to God's being and if there is both an identity and a difference between God's intrinsic self-knowledge and the knowledge that God has of Godself in humanity in virtue of revelation, then genuine difference remains in the community of God with humanity. Moreover, one can argue that the 'necessity' with which God as spirit manifests Godself, given the self-subsistent nature of divine being with which self-knowledge coincides, is once again analogous to the 'necessity' with which the infinite good is unqualifiedly self-diffusive, rather than the outcome of an ontological deficiency. These propositions in turn entail the transcendence of the God who at the same time is related to Godself through God's indwelling in the human community that knows God and knows itself in God. The position that these propositions represent integrates divine transcendence and divine immanence. That is hardly a surprising outcome given the Christian theological tradition, not to mention the originary discourse and the set of practices that constitute that tradition. That integration follows from an understanding of God based on the concepts of subjectivity and intersubjectivity, again hardly a surprising outcome given the theological tradition and the discourse and practices just mentioned.

But then, what is one to say about the widely conflicting readings that there are regarding Hegel's views on the nature of God, the relation of God and the world, and the issue of divine transcendence? It would hardly do just to say, 'Hegel's texts lend themselves to different interpretations.' Of course they do. That is a matter of historical fact. Nor can one deny that there are bases in the texts to which proponents of these conflicting interpretations legitimately appeal. I have tried explicitly to recognize that in this chapter. I believe that what one can say is that there is a substantive and central line of argumentation in Hegel's mature texts that supports the positions regarding the nature of God, the relation of God and the world, and the understanding of divine transcendence that I have presented in this chapter. Those positions assert that the unity that obtains between God and the world requires an essential ontological difference between God and the world, more specifically that the relation between God and the world does not compromise but rather exhibits God's self-subsistent being and self-knowledge, and consequently the world, in its essential relation to God, remains other than God the creator, just as God is creator is both transcendent and most deeply immanent in God's connection with the world. Whether Hegel always frames these positions in a fully adequate way and always supports them with arguments that are sufficient to them is another question. I think I have shown that he does in his own way at least assert and try to support them.

These claims of course do not settle all matters. One question seems to leap from the discussion I have offered so far. If Hegel thinks that self-knowledge is intrinsic to God's being, and that the concept of spirit entails the view that self-knowledge requires intersubjectivity, how does he reconcile these views. Part of his answer to that question is the statement that 'If "spirit" is not an empty word, then God must [be grasped] under this characteristic, just as in the church theology of former times God was called "triune." '[47] This claim is an important part of the topic to which I will now turn.

Chapter 5

The Christian mysteries

The philosophical task of rethinking the religious and Christian representation, according to Hegel, is in no way confined to reflection on the doctrine of creation. Nor is that task limited to the domain of what is sometimes called natural or rational theology, as contrasted with revealed theology. There is of course a difference between reason operating independently of revelation and reason operating in a way that is informed by revelation. But in each instance, Hegel believes, reason maintains its essential autonomy. And the aim of rational reflection on religion and Christianity is the systematic integration of the outcomes of various moments of that reflection, whatever the sources might be on which one draws. Certainly revelation must be one of those sources. In reflecting on God and the relation between God and the human world the philosopher's aim is knowledge of God as God is. In turn, God is as God reveals Godself to be.

Additional reasons for directing philosophical reflection on the data of revelation follow from the claim that such reflection understands God not only as absolute substance, but also and in a surpassing way as absolute spirit. The results of natural theology are suited to understanding God as absolute substance. These results assert predicates of God, such as God is all wise, all powerful, all good, and so forth. Predicates like these 'are stabilized by reflection—[each predicate is] a content that has attained through reflection the form of universality, of relation to self.'[1] Spirit, the category through which philosophical reflection must deal with God, 'develops itself, realizes itself; and it is complete only at the end, which is the same time its presupposition [*Voraussetzung*]. At first, it is in itself as the totality; then it sets itself forth [*setzt sich voraus*], and likewise it *is* only at the end.'[2] The predicates of natural theology allow for an understanding of substance but are not adequate to the dynamic and self-determining reality that is spirit. Moreover, spirit is essentially self-manifesting. Philosophical reflection, therefore, must consider absolute spirit in terms of its self-manifestation or self-revelation.

Hegel identifies the religion of revelation with Christianity, and calls Christianity the consummate religion. That is, he maintains that Christianity is the consummation or full realization of the possibilities that belong to religion as such and that develop in various ways through the history of religions. The account of this position calls on the concepts of consciousness and self-consciousness in a way that is familiar from the *Phenomenology*. 'Religion, in accord with its general concept, is the consciousness of God as such, consciousness of absolute essence.'[3] 'Consciousness' of God, in the strict sense of the term, is an awareness of God as an object, as standing over against the conscious self. The knowledge that this consciousness delivers is knowledge of God just with regard to God's being other than the self. Moreover this externality implies that God finds the limit of God's being in the independent being of the self, which entails a representation of God as finite.

Self-consciousness preserves and surpasses consciousness as such. In relation to religious consciousness, this entails *'consciousness relating itself to its essence*, knowing itself as its essence and its essence as its own—and that is spiritual religion.'[4] In this situation, the self's consciousness and knowledge of God has to do with consciousness of its relation to God and thus with consciousness of itself. In knowing 'its essence as its own' the self knows itself. Moreover, since the relation to God is the most fundamental determination of the being of the self, this self-consciousness is not only a form of self-knowledge, but the most fundamental form of self-knowledge available. And of course, as the dialectic of recognition that Hegel developed in 1807 has shown, genuine self-consciousness comes about insofar as the self is aware of itself as related to, and as the recipient of recognition from, another self. Thus, the integration of consciousness and self-consciousness in religious consciousness leads to a representation that depicts God as both substance and subject, that is to say, as spirit. According to this representation, 'This absolute essence distinguishes itself at one and the same time into absolute power and subject; it communicates itself in what is distinguished from it while at the same time remaining undivided, so that the other is also the whole—all this, along with the return to itself, is the concept of religion.'[5] If God is supposed to be subject and spirit, then God is conceivable as one who relates Godself to the finite self, then enabling to finite self to know itself in knowing its relation to God. And if, as absolute spirit, God's relation to finite realities is both a relation to what is other than God and an expression and preservation of God's self-relatedness, then we have a genuine representation of God's infinity.

Hegel says that this integration of religious consciousness and self-consciousness, including the representation of God that I have just discussed, defines 'the consummate religion, the religion in which religion has become objective to itself.'[6] The 'concept' of religion, that is, the understanding of what religion is that belongs to religious consciousness and that philosophical reflection articulates in its own terms, entails constitutive possibilities that are realized in a consummate way in the religion that presents this integration. This religion both emerges in the history of religions, and surpasses the religions that develop in that history, representing both an evolution of that history and a kind of break with it. That is because this religion acknowledges of the nature of spirit itself and is therefore a religion of revelation.

Hegel's speculative reenactment of the content of the consummate and revelatory religion focuses on the ideas of the Trinity, creation, the Fall, incarnation, redemption and reconciliation, resurrection and ascension, and the indwelling of the Holy Spirit in the gathered community. These ideas receive consideration in each of the lecture series on the philosophy of religion. Hegel also treats them under the heading of 'Revealed Religion' in the *Encyclopedia*. That treatment is brief but also important given the status of the text. In the *Encyclopedia* Hegel discusses what I am calling the Christian mysteries under the headings of universality, particularity, and individuality, understood with reference to the three terms of a syllogism. The relation between the first and the second or middle term is one of self-differentiation. These differentiated terms are at the same time integrated, and the outcome of that integration is the individual. Thus, 'All men are mortal, Socrates is a man, Socrates is mortal,' as an example of what Hegel has in mind. It is in Socrates that the differentiation and integration of the universal and the particular, of being man and being mortal, occurs. Hegel also envisions the discussions falling under these headings as comprising three different syllogisms, each of which has one of the different terms as its middle term.

In the *Encyclopedia* the discussions that fall under these headings have to do respectively with (1) the Trinity, (2) Creation and the Fall, and (3) the Incarnation, redemption, and the indwelling of the Spirit. Under the first of these headings, Hegel writes of

> absolute spirit, which is at first the presupposed principle, not, however, staying aloof and inert, but (as underlying and essential power under the reflective category of causality) creator of heaven and earth: but yet in this eternal sphere rather only begetting himself as his *son*, with whom, though different, he remains in original identity—just as, again, this differentiation of him from the eternal essence eternally supersedes itself and, through this mediating of a superseding mediation, the first substance is essentially as *concrete individuality* and subjectivity—is the *Spirit*.[7]

Absolute spirit is active and self-determining. Immanent to absolute spirit itself is a dynamic within which absolute spirit differentiates itself from itself and simultaneously recovers its unity with itself from the standpoint of that differentiation. Since spirit accomplishes this self-determining dynamic as subject, the immanent life of absolute spirit is one of intersubjectivity or community, and at the same time one of thoroughgoing unity.

Peter Hodgson notes that 'Hegel does not attend to any of the technicalities of the classical trinitarian debates—the questions, for example, of the *homoousian* (the equality or identity of being) of the Son and the Spirit with the Father, or the procession of the Spirit from the Father alone or from the Father and the Son.'[8] These issues, Hodgson believes, belong to thinking that, for Hegel, is representational rather than fully conceptual.

It is nonetheless unfortunate that Hegel did not attend to such issues. That attention may have strengthened his conception of the immanent Trinity, and thus helped to equip his thinking for responses to criticisms of his understanding of the relation between the immanent Trinity and the economic Trinity.

These criticisms come in two different forms. On the one hand, commentators like Dale Schlitt maintain that Hegel offers a 'philosophically reinterpreted presentation of "economic" Trinity inclusive of "immanent" Trinity. This latter, "immanent" Trinity, is the initial moment structuring the overall dynamic of divine self-revelation.'[9] In order to determine the importance of this understanding for the conception of the immanent Trinity, one must note that, also according to Schlitt, the way in which Hegelian speculative thinking both negates and preserves in a truer form, and thus develops the content of the trinitarian representation appears most clearly 'in Hegel's proposal to translate what appears on the level of religious representation as the divine freedom, namely, to create or not to create, into a logically necessary self-othering of the absolute idea in, and as, nature. This self-othering as logically necessitarian self-determination is called by Hegel "free self-release." '[10] If the economic Trinity includes within itself the immanent Trinity because the trinitarian God creates out of necessity, then it is arguable that God in Godself, that is in God's immanent trinitarian self, is insufficient. One sees this most fully, Schlitt says elsewhere, by noting that 'in Hegel's philosophy the transition from logic to nature and finite spirit, which is paradigmatic of the transition from "immanent" Trinity to created world, is not directly rooted in overflowing abundance but in need.'[11]

There seem grounds for this critical assessment. Hegel does insist that God, understood as spirit, must manifest Godself. Moreover, he says that the 'act of differentiation' through which we understand the immanent Trinity 'is only a movement, a play of love, which does not arrive at the seriousness of other being, of separation and rupture.'[12] Self-manifestation is a manifestation of the self to another. God's manifestation of Godself requires 'the seriousness of other being,' which in this case would have to mean creation. If God must manifest Godself, and if for that reason God must create, then on the further assumption that God is triune, the economic Trinity includes the immanent Trinity within itself because by itself the immanent Trinity is deficient, somehow affected by privation. This at least challenges the ability to consistently think of God as infinite. And it makes the idea of creation untenable if one holds that creation requires that God possess in Godself the whole power of being.

But the remarks I just made do not say all that is needed regarding the matter at hand. I have already commented on the difficulty of understanding divine freedom with respect of creation in a way that excludes any and all senses of what one might reasonably call necessity, no matter how 'necessity' is construed. Schlitt may be too hasty in believing that the speculative reconceptualization of the notion of creation associates creation with a sense of necessity that excludes divine freedom. Further, it is not always obvious that Hegel does conceive of the immanent Trinity as included in the economic Trinity. The passage that I cite above from the *Encyclopedia* does suggest that inclusion. But other texts present different suggestions. For example, in the 1829 *Lectures on the Proofs of God's Existence*, Hegel writes that,

> in Christianity least of all do we know God only as
> creative activity and not as spirit. Rather, what is
> distinctive for this religion is the *explicit* consciousness
> that God is spirit, that God, precisely as God is in and for
> Godself, relates Godself to God's other (which is called
> the Son) as to Godself, that God relates to Godself in
> Godself as love, essentially as this mediation with Godself.
> God is indeed creator of the world and is sufficiently
> defined by this. But God is more than this: God is the
> *true* God in that God is the mediation of Godself with
> Godself, and this is love.[13]

These statements affirm an integrity of the immanent Trinity considered in contrast with God's involvement in the economy of creation. That affirmation argues against supposing that the immanent Trinity is essentially a moment that determines God considered with respect to that involvement, which would be the result of including the immanent Trinity in the economic Trinity.

William Desmond offers a very different criticism of Hegel's understanding of the relation between the immanent Trinity and the economic Trinity. He notes that Hegel's development of a conception of the Trinity incorporates a model of community or intersubjectivity. But, he says,

> we stress here that community is a *self-communication* of the One: the one as trinitarian seems to be both source of communication and the ultimate addressee. You might say: absolute subjectivity is absolute intersubjectivity; communication is between, inter, the absolute subject and itself, in the form of its own otherness. Theologically, God communicates with God in the self-mediation of the whole. This trinitarian monism is absolutely inclusive, overreaching both the immanent mediating life of the godhead, but also the relation of God to the finite creation.[14]

He goes on to say, 'For a holistic God, otherness is no otherness at all. Nor can the otherness between God and creation be final, since this otherness cannot be irreducibly "between" the two, since it is included in the absolute holistic process.'[15] To say this is to say the God considered in terms of the immanent Trinity includes creation, and thus God considered with respect of God's involvement in the economy of creation, within Godself. Or, the immanent Trinity includes the economic Trinity as a moment of itself, and creation along with it.

Desmond's argument seems to be that, when Hegel's conception of the Trinity is considered with reference to his understanding of creation, one sees that that conception must be one in which the immanent Trinity includes the economic Trinity, since Hegel cannot maintain that the otherness between God and creation is final, cannot conceive of an irreducible otherness between the two. But as I have already pointed out, the 'problem' in this instance is not with Hegel but with the very idea of creation. Created things must be things that have the being that is their own wholly and unqualifiedly in the context of their relation to God the creator. If so, then one cannot hold that there is a final and irreducible otherness between created things and God. For something to be wholly and irreducibly other than God would be for that thing to be uncreated. If Hegel's own discourse at least sometimes argues against Schlitt's view that the Hegelian conception of the Trinity includes the immanent Trinity with the economic Trinity, the logic of the idea of creation itself stands in opposition to Desmond's argument for the view that Hegel's conception of the Trinity includes the economic Trinity within the immanent Trinity.

Peter Hodgson offers a nuanced understanding of Hegel's conception of the Trinity that points out the limitations that belong to each of the criticisms I have just discussed. As he observes,

> The elements or spheres of the trinity cannot be
> prioritized or ranked; they are co-essential. Classical
> theology accorded precedence to God's ideal self-relations,
> of which the world is an epiphenomenal reflection.
> Modern theology has prioritized the economic Trinity,
> God's appearance and work in the world as Son and spirit,
> on the grounds that nothing can be known of God's inner
> life, of what God is in and for Godself. Hegel will have
> nothing of this division, for it destroys the very heart
> of what God is. The elements are distinguishable but
> not separable. While in a discursive treatment they are
> unavoidably discussed in linear fashion, they are related
> not linearly but spirally or concentrically, with each spiral
> overlapping and encompassing the previous ones.[16]

I would suggest that these comments are both correct as a reading of Hegel, and eminently defensible, on the assumption that any discussion of a triune God is admitted at all. A passage from the 1827 *Lectures on the Philosophy of Religion*, which Hodgson himself cites, lends strong support to the first suggestion.

The absolute eternal idea is:

(1) First, in and for itself, God in his eternity before the creation of the world and outside the world.
(2) Second, God creates the world and posits the separation. He creates both nature and finite spirit. What

is thus created is at first an other, posited outside of God. But God is essentially the reconciling of himself to what is alien, what is particular, what is posited in separation from him. He must restore to freedom and to his truth what is alien, what has fallen away in the idea's self-diremption, in its falling away from itself. This is the path and the process of reconciliation.

(3) In the third place, through this process of reconciliation, spirit has reconciled with itself what it distinguished from itself in its act of diremption, of primal division, and this it is the Holy Spirit, the Spirit [present] in the community.

These are not external distinctions, which *we* have made merely in accord with what we are; rather, they are the activity, the developed vitality, of absolute spirit itself.[17]

Each dimension of the Trinity, as it were, implies or includes the other, and is implicated or included in the other, such that there is a constant interchange and an essential unity, rather than any kind of relation of priority and posteriority between the two.

And, to pursue the second suggestion mentioned above, could anything else be the case? Assuming again the conceptions of a triune God and of creation, some distinction between the immanent and the economic Trinity is inevitable. But how can we legitimately conceive of any relations of priority or posteriority, or of superiority and interiority, among dimensions of the Godhead that we distinguish? Surely any suggestion of precedence that one needs to make regarding dimensions of the triune God, or for that matter among persons of the Trinity in relation to the nature of divinity, is at the same time a suggestion that one needs immediately to remove. This seems to be exactly the idea that the passage I just cited conveys.

I would like to suggest the utility of thinking of Hegel's conception of the Trinity, and of creation in relation to that conception, in connection with the teaching of St. Bonaventure, as read by Ewert Cousins. According to Cousins, Bonaventure teaches that 'God as self-sufficient must be necessarily fecund and self-communicating. . . . *Because* God is self-sufficient, he is absolutely self-communicating.'[18] The fullness of this

self-sufficiency and self-communication is found in the immanent Trinity. 'The highest self-diffusion is found only in the
Trinitarian processions. Without the Trinitarian processions we
would not find in divinity the highest good, "because it would
not be supremely self-diffusive." '[19] At the same time, there is
a direct connection between the immanent and the economic
Trinity: ' "the more primary a thing is, the more fecund it is
and the principle of others." ' Having stated this as a universal
philosophical principle, he proceeds to apply it to the divine
essence as the fecund source of creatures. Bonaventure states:
' "the divine essence, because it is first, is the principle of other
essences." '[20] No more than Aquinas does Bonaventure want to
understand creation in a way that compromises divine freedom.
At the same time he understands creation to follow from God
in virtue of the fecundity that belongs to the divine nature on
account of God's self-sufficiency in being.

Cousins believes that these aspects of Bonaventure's theology
call us to think of Hegel. 'In modern times, the problem of
divine fecundity has been acutely felt in Hegel's philosophy,
where we find one of the most powerful statements of God as
dynamic in the history of thought.'[21] To think about Bonaventure
and Hegel in connection with one another is to probe the difficult
but also inescapable conception of God as fecund and dynamic.
According to Cousins, 'Bonaventure might lead critics to re-
examine Hegel's texts to see if, in fact, Hegel held a doctrine of
God equivalent to Bonaventure's; or if not, at least he might provide an alternative to Hegel's dynamic God which would allow
critics to accept other elements of Hegel's system.'[22] Building on
this, I would suggest that reflection on Hegel and Bonaventure
might lead one to find in Hegel's text a line of argumentation
that does indeed lead to a conception of God very much like that
which Bonaventure suggests, even if that line of argument is not
present without ambiguity, and even if that conception of God
is not present without ambiguity, in Hegel's writings. Assuming
that this claim is legitimate, it represents just the sort of combina-
tion of historical and conceptual aims that contributes to contemporary philosophical and theological inquiry.

The dynamic notion of God that Hegel proposes, integrating as it does the conceptions of the immanent and the

economic Trinities, is directly connected with the idea of creation. This introduces the second of the three divisions or moments that belong to the discussion of the consummate religion. In the *Encyclopedia*, Hegel calls this the moment of particularity.

> Under the 'moment' of *particularity*, or of judgment, it
> is this concrete eternal being that is presupposed: its
> movement is the creation of the phenomenal world. The
> eternal 'moment' of mediation—of the only Son—divides
> itself to become the antithesis of two separate worlds.
> On the one hand is heaven and earth, the elemental
> and concrete nature—on the other hand, standing in
> action and reaction with such nature, the spirit, which is
> therefore finite. That spirit, as the extremity of inherent
> negativity, completes its independence till it becomes
> wickedness, and is that extreme through its connection
> with a confronting nature, and through its own
> naturalness thus investing it. Yet amid that naturalness,
> it is, when it thinks, directed towards the Eternal,
> though, for that reason, only standing to it in an external
> connection.[23]

In the *Encyclopedia*, Hegel refers, in the second division of his comments on the revealed religion, to the creation of the natural and human worlds and to the Fall. He reserves discussion of the incarnation, redemption, and reconciliation to the third division of his comments, where he also discusses the indwelling of the Holy Spirit. In the different versions of the *Lectures on the Philosophy of Religion*, he discusses incarnation, redemption, and reconciliation in the second division of the treatment of revealed religion, and, in the third, emphasizes the connection between the indwelling of the Spirit and the development of the gathered community or the cultus. Hegel allowed himself the freedom to define and arrange the material considered in philosophical reflection on religion and Christianity in different ways, and to develop his thinking on the basis of different definitions and arrangements of that material. One should be mindful of this in reading and assessing Hegel's texts.

In discussing creation, Hegel commonly refers to the second person of the Trinity in the way that he does in *Encyclopedia*. Any number of questions can and should be raised as to the theological adequacy of saying that, in creation, the second person of the Trinity 'divides itself to become the antithesis of two separate worlds.' At the same time, one can at least say that there are ample precedents in patristic and medieval theology for identifying the Son or the Logos as a specific divine principle in connection with creation. The ultimate source of that identification, of course, is the prologue to John's Gospel.

Comments on creation lead Hegel directly to a discussion of the Fall. A common pattern belongs to all his discussions of the Fall, however significant the differences between individual discussions might also be. Human creatures, finite spirit Hegel would say, exist in an essential connection to God. This connection is one that enjoins humans to transcend their condition of immediate, natural particularity through pursuing a relation to a good that stands as the telos of human development and that surpasses that condition, namely to God, and also to the universal standards of right that determine the rational will. But the self transcends a condition of immediate, natural particularity by cultivating itself. And for the self to cultivate itself is for the self to assert itself. In turn, an essential possibility that belongs to self-assertion is the possibility of asserting itself in its particularity, and thus in a way in its natural immediacy as well, since the self, taken precisely as particular, is external to the transcendent good that stands over against natural immediacy. In this situation the self still stands in an essential connection with God. The self is still one whose development has as its telos the relation to God and to universal standards of right. But in this situation the self has also turned away from that telos and has turned upon its own particularity, that is upon its own self. The self is centered on itself, rather than being centered in a self-surpassing way on the telos that is nonetheless inescapably its own.

The account just given entails that, in the situation described, one can say neither that humanity is by nature simply good, nor that humanity is by nature simply evil. Insofar as one defines humanity in terms of the capacity to transcend natural particularity through a process whose telos is the development of a relation with a good that surpasses the particular self, humanity is by nature good. In an unqualifiedly natural condition, humanity is in a condition of innocence that is neither good nor evil. Insofar as being human involves a mode of assertion that centers the particular self on itself and on wishes or interests that are just its own, and thus natural and immediate rather than cultivated in virtue of a process of mediation that relates the self to a telos that surpasses its mere particularity and thus is universal, humanity is evil. 'This means that natural humanity is selfish.'[24] According to Hegel, 'Strictly speaking, the naturalness of the will is the selfishness of the will; in its naturalness, the will is private, distinguished from the universality of willing and opposed to the rationality of the will that has been cultivated into universality.'[25] He adds, however, that 'the fact that, insofar as its will is natural, humanity is evil, does not annul the other side, the fact that it is implicitly good, which always remains part of its concept.'[26] At the same time, 'the actuality that it has is the natural actuality that it is selfishness. The condition of evil directly presupposes the relation of actuality to the concept; this simply posits the contradiction between implicit being or the concept and singularity, the contradiction between good and evil.'[27]

The natural will exists in opposition to its own telos and thus in opposition to itself, in a condition of contradiction. This condition, of course, belongs not only to the factual condition of the self but to consciousness and self-consciousness. The self is 'conscious of the good, of the infinite demand of the good,'[28] and of its own existence as standing in opposition to that demand. This awareness determines self-understanding. 'It is not that one has transgressed this or that commandment, but rather that one is intrinsically evil, purely and simply evil in one's innermost being. This evil character is the essential definition of one's concept: this is what one must bring to consciousness. It is with this depth that we are concerned.'[29] The outcome of the experience of the depth of this self-understanding is anguish, and this anguish is 'my humiliation, my remorse; I experience anguish because I as a natural being do not correspond to what at the same time I *know* to be my own essence, to what I should be in my own knowing and willing.'[30]

The story of the Fall in *Genesis* presents the account that I have just outlined in symbolic and narrative terms. In that narrative, 'this conceptual determination appears representationally as a story and is represented for consciousness in an intuitable or sensible mode, so that it is regarded as something that *happened.*'[31] God creates Adam and Eve and places them in a garden, in a condition of innocence in which they enjoyed God's presence. Adam and Eve disobey the divine commandment, and thus turn away from God and come upon knowledge of good and evil. Lost innocence exiles human beings from the divine presence on account of the opposition that disobedience brings about between human beings and God and between human beings themselves. The story embodies the understandings of natural innocence, of the requirement that natural innocence be surpassed through self-cultivation, of self-assertion as the first moment of that process, of that moment as one in which the particular self finds itself able to turn away from the telos that is its own to center itself on itself, of the knowledge of good and evil that comes about in the experience and enactment of this possibility, and of the anguished contradiction that the self experiences as a consequence of its knowledge of good and evil. 'The story is the eternal history of humanity.'[32] It represents in narrative and seemingly historical terms a truth that pertains to the very roots of the condition of human existence.

Hegel has no hesitation interpreting the story of the Fall in existential and symbolic terms, and also in metaphysical or speculative terms, given the context of speculative reconceptualization to which the interpretation belongs. This is a point of great importance to which I will return in the concluding chapter. His interpretation also poses a problem. Hegel maintains that human self-actualization requires that the self transcend its natural immediacy. This demands a process through which the self pursues a relation to a telos that surpasses the self in its particularity. The particular self engages in this process by asserting itself. I have said that this self-assertion is essentially open to the possibility in which the self asserts its particularity against the telos that surpasses it and centers itself not on that telos but on itself, realizing the 'selfishness' of which Hegel speaks. Does Hegel say, and does his account require one to say, something stronger than this? Perhaps the first moment of self-assertion by the particular self must result in a focus that is self-centered. If this is a necessary developmental moment, then evil is unavoidable and necessary, if evil coincides with 'selfishness.' But an 'evil' that is in all ways unavoidable in a process like the one under consideration is really no evil at all. It is a necessary moment, perhaps in itself unfortunate, in the development of the good. And it would be hard to see how a moment like this could play the role that 'original sin' plays in Christian self-understanding and doctrine.

Many comments suggest this reading of Hegel's account. In the first volume of the *Encyclopedia*, for example, he expressly says, 'we must give up the superficial notion that Original Sin has its ground only in a contingent action of the first human pair. It is part of the concept of spirit, in fact, that man is by nature evil; and we must not imagine that this could be otherwise.'[33] Statements like this lead Paul Ricoeur to object that, in Hegel's account, 'There remains nothing of the injustice of evil or the gratuity of reconciliation.'[34] But if the 'evil' that Hegel identifies is necessary and in all ways unavoidable, it is something for which humans are not truly responsible. Hegel insists that the condition in which the self experiences the necessity of cultivation and self-transcendence is and must be one in which the self finds itself responsible.[35] And he clearly thinks that evil, as he accounts for it, can and must play, in a speculative reconstruction of the content of Christian doctrine, the role attributed to original sin. Part of Hegel's thinking seems to be that, if one must avoid thinking of original sin as 'a contingent action of the first human pair,' then the alternative he poses is the only one available. Perhaps the problem now under discussion points to the necessity of further thought concerning the relation of freedom and necessity, now in connection with the account of evil. That issue is extremely difficult. The position that Hegel takes on it may well call for serious, critical reconsideration. This is another matter I will discuss below.

At this moment, the issue of central importance is the claim that evil is to be understood as a kind of self-centeredness or 'selfishness' due to which the self stands in opposition to its universal telos, and thus to itself. That is to say, the opposition in question is not due to an external reality that approaches humanity from the outside and opposes itself to humanity. This opposition belongs to the human condition in an immanent way. 'It is therefore required that humanity should comprehend this abstract antithesis *within* itself.'[36] The experience of this opposition, as already noted, is one of anguish, indeed of limitless anguish. 'This is the deepest depth. Human beings are inwardly conscious that in their innermost being they are a contradiction, and have therefore an infinite *anguish* concerning themselves. Anguish is present only where there is opposition to what ought to be, to an affirmative.'[37] The anguish indicates that the opposition in which it is rooted ought to be overcome, and that overcoming that opposition would both respond to the deepest need of human nature and represent the deepest truth about human nature. But since the most basic feature of the condition in which humanity finds itself seems to be this very opposition, human beings are unable to find in themselves the possibility of responding to human nature's deepest need and realizing its deepest truth.

If so, then 'the resolution of this contradiction, must be represented as something that is in and of itself, it must be a presupposition for the subject.'[38] Human beings come to know that the opposition that introduces infinite anguish into human self-consciousness can be overcome only by finding that something presents itself to them as a reality in which that opposition has been overcome. 'This cognition must therefore *come* to it,'[39] to humanity. But the opposition in question is, most essentially, one between humanity and God. Self-opposition within human existence is a consequence of that. Therefore it is the overcoming of the opposition between humanity and God, or between God and human nature, that must present itself. This requires that 'the substantiality of the unity of divine and human nature comes to consciousness for humanity in such a way that a human being appears to consciousness as God, and that God appears to it as a human being.'[40] This is the necessity of what Christian theology understands as the Incarnation.

In an important book that should be widely read, James Yerkes points out the connection between Hegel's treatments of creation and of the Incarnation. 'The finite world and man as creature are posited by God as his "other"—given existence as his "other." Yet this positing as other is not the *final* truth about God's relation to the world, for he *also* overreaches the world as "other" to reconcile it to himself.[41] The moments of positing and overreaching otherness, that belong as such to the relation of God and creatures, are more concretely and most fully realized through the Incarnation. 'Speculatively and ontologically speaking, the incarnational principle of reconciliation points to the concept of God as the subsistent "cause" of all reality who "others" a world over against himself, while always at one and the same time overreaching and reconciling it to himself.'[42] In twentieth-century theology, Karl Rahner continues to link the ideas of creation and incarnation. 'If in the Incarnation the Logos enters into relationship with a creature, then it is obvious that the formal determinations of the Creator-creature relationship must also hold in *this* particular relationship.'[43] Rahner adds, 'In fact the whole of Christology could be seen as the unique and most radical realization of the relationship of God to what is other than himself,'[44] that is, to creatures. Hegel would agree, saying that the integration of relation-to-another and divine self-relatedness that the Incarnation represents is the most radical and therefore unique realization of the structure that belongs to the relation between God and creatures.

Hegel insists on the unique as well as the radical character of the Incarnation. The reconciliation of human kind with God that the Incarnation represents must appear to human beings with a kind of 'sensible certainty'; therefore it is necessary that the 'unity of divine and human nature must appear in *just one human being.*'[45] It will not do, he also insists, to consider that human being simply as a great teacher like Socrates, or even as a paradigmatic source of moral inspiration. Given the depth of the human need to which the Incarnation responds, one must think of Jesus as nothing less than God truly incarnate in a truly human being.

> In the church Christ has been called the 'God-man.' This is a monstrous compound, which directly contradicts both representation and understanding. But what has thereby been brought into human consciousness and made a certainty for it is the unity of divine and human

nature, implying that the otherness, or, as we also say, the finitude, weakness, and frailty of human nature, does not damage this unity, just as otherness does not impair the unity that God is in the eternal idea.[46]

The last of these statements suggests that the integration of relationship-to-another and divine self-relatedness that the Incarnation radicalizes, and that belongs more generally to the structure of the relation between God and creatures, recapitulates the dynamic that belongs to inner-trinitarian life. One might say that *finitum capax infiniti* is true because *infinitum capax finiti* is true, and that the ground of the latter truth resides in no less a place than the inner-trinitarian dynamic.

But of course if Jesus was not merely a teacher, he was nonetheless a teacher. One must consider him in relation to his sensible, historical presence, and also in relation to his teaching, as well as to the culminating events of his life. The teaching is supposed to convey, and the events are supposed to disclose, the fundamental reconciliation that the Incarnation represents. 'Since what is at issue is the consciousness of absolute reconciliation, we are in the presence of a new consciousness of humanity, or a new religion.'[47] In 1821, Hegel singled out three aspects of the teachings of Jesus that impart this new consciousness. The first is love. 'Love in Christ's sense [is]: (a) moral love of one's neighbor in the particular circumstances in which one is related to him; (b) the love that is the relationship, the bond among the apostles, who are one in love.'[48] This love is not something that the apostles practice along with their particular occupations. It is their occupation. '[They are] to make only this unity, this community in and for itself their goal—not the liberation of humanity [as] a political goal—and they are to love one another for its sake.'[49] This does not mean that the injunction to love one another for the sake of the community that results from such love fails to have political consequences. On the contrary, this love represents a reconciliation of human beings with each other, and thus a 'new consciousness of humanity,' that sets political relations on a new footing.

This leads to the second aspect of the teaching that Hegel identified in 1821, the requirement for 'breaking away in the negative sense from everything established.'[50] If the 'new consciousness of humanity' sets social and political relations on a new footing, then the order predicated on any earlier basis must be surpassed. Hegel asserts this emphatically in 1827. The new religion 'contains implicitly the characteristic of negating the present world. This is its polemical aspect, its revolutionary attitude towards all determinate aspects of that outer world, [all the settled attitudes] of human consciousness and belief.'[51] The final basis of this break with the established order, and the new consciousness that leads to it, appears in the third aspect of the teaching that Hegel discusses. This has to do with 'the proper definition and determinacy of the kingdom of God, i.e., with the relationship of Christ himself to God and of humanity to God and Christ.'[52] According to Hegel, the proclamation of the kingdom of God has to do with nothing other and nothing less than the reconciliation of divine nature with human nature, or of God with humanity, that the Incarnation exhibits, and the presence of God, through Christ, in and to the human beings who are gathered in the community that is the outcome of that reconciliation. This is the ground of the command that members of this community love one another for the sake of the community that results from that love, and order social and political life in a way that follows from the new consciousness of the reconciled nature of the relations of human beings with each other.

If the reconciliation of divine and human nature, or of God and humanity, is the final ground and center of the consciousness that the new religion conveys, then the events that belong to the life of Jesus, as well as the teachings of Jesus, must exhibit this central understanding. The culminating events of that life, for Hegel, exhibit that understanding in a most emphatic way. The death of Jesus is, on the one hand, 'a natural death, brought about by injustice, hatred, and violence.'[53] It is, however, at the same time the death of one to whose humanity God has joined Godself.

> But this humanity in God—and indeed the most abstract form of humanity, the greatest dependence, the ultimate weakness, the utmost fragility—is natural death. 'God himself is dead,' it says in a Lutheran hymn, expressing

the awareness that the human, the finite, the fragile, the weak, the negative are themselves a moment of the divine, that they are within God himself, that finitude, negativity, otherness are not outside of God and do not, as otherness, hinder unity with God. Otherness, the negative, is known to be a moment of the divine nature itself. This involves the highest idea of spirit.[54]

God shows Godself, in the death of Christ, to be united with the extremity of the finitude that determines human nature in its otherness from God. For this reason, the death of Christ is the culmination of the process of God's uniting Godself with human nature. The community that Christ gathered comes to understand this through coming to believe that the history of Christ culminates not only with his death, but with his death, resurrection, and ascension. 'The history of the resurrection and ascension of Christ to the right hand of God begins at the point where this history receives a spiritual interpretation. That is when it came to appear that this little community achieved the certainty that God has appeared as a human being.'[55] This certainty coincides with the consciousness that God, who has united Godself with human nature in a single human being and revealed Godself in doing this, dwells as Spirit within the community.

In the *Encyclopedia*, Hegel joins the ideas of the Resurrection and the indwelling of the Spirit closely together. In uniting Godself with Christ in Christ's death, God nonetheless 'keeps himself unchanged, and thus, as absolute return from that negativity, and as universal unity of universal and individual essentiality, has realized his being as the Idea of the spirit, eternal, but alive and present in the world.'[56] In the different iterations of the Lectures, Hegel discusses the indwelling of the Spirit in connection with an examination of the gathered community, the Church, and of its historical development. The community provides the context in which persons can encounter divine self-revelation. That is, the community is the setting in which persons can come to a consciousness of God as (1) creator, as (2) incarnate in Christ and united with Christ in Christ's death, and as (3) maintaining divine self-relatedness even in union with the extremity of human finitude, thus overcoming death and manifesting God's presence as Spirit in the community. At the same time, the community is the setting in which persons can come to a consciousness of themselves as (1) created, as (2) alienated from God on account of a fall into self-centered estrangement, and as (3) reconciled to God by an initiative that God takes, that is manifested in Christ, and that is fulfilled by God's indwelling as Spirit in the community. By implication, the consciousness that the community receives brings about an awareness of God as Trinity, and ultimately of the contrast between and the unity of the economic and the immanent Trinity. All other Christian teachings follow from and lead back to these central understandings.

The Church is the context in which it is possible for one to cultivate faith. Faith, in the first place, is personal certitude regarding the reconciliation of human beings with God as something that has been accomplished. 'Only by means of this faith that reconciliation is accomplished with certainty and in and for itself is the subject able and indeed in a position to posit itself in this unity. This mediation is absolutely necessary.'[57] In the second place, faith has to do with doctrine, with the teachings that the Church presents to its members regarding the reconciliation that faith acknowledges. Ultimately, this teaching has to do with the involvement of the triune God in the economy of creation and salvation. Its significance is first something that is felt, then expressed in the images, symbols, and conceptions, the representations, of the cultures in which doctrine is formed, and then further cultivated by developed and rationally autonomous thought. Through these processes doctrine is formed within and then preserved by the Church. 'The church is essentially a teaching church, by virtue of which there is a teaching office whose function is to expound doctrine.'[58] In presenting its members with doctrine, the Church gives form to faith and focuses feeling and thought properly on the central notion of reconciliation.

The Church gives form to faith not only through doctrinal understandings but also through sensible, sacramental signs. Baptism incorporates the person into the Church, and at the same time presents the Church to the person both as a community in whose life one participates and as a community that presents itself and its teachings to the person. '*Repentance* or *penitence* signifies that, through the elevation of human beings to the truth, which they now will, their transgressions are wiped out. Because they acknowledge the truth over against their evil and will the good—through repentance, that is to say—their evil comes to naught.'[59] Hegel believes that Christian teaching asserts both that evil, represented as the self-centered estrangement of human beings from God and from each other, has in itself been overcome, and that the individual needs to appropriate that overcoming. One does this through making the truth about the overcoming of evil one's own truth. Therefore the Church is concerned 'that this truth should become ever more identical with the self, with the human will, and that this truth should become one's volition, one's object, one's spirit.'[60]

In the Holy Communion one is able to experience the fullness of this truth. 'It is a question precisely of the conscious presence of God, of unity with God, the *unio mystica,* [one's] self-feeling of God, the feeling of God's immediate presence within the subject. This self-feeling, however, since it exists, is also a movement, it presupposes a movement, a sublation of difference, so that a negative unity issues forth. This unity begins with the host.'[61] Hegel mentions the Roman Catholic, Lutheran, and Calvinist understanding of sacramental presence. While respectful of each, he clearly prefers the second to the first and the third.

The faith, teachings, and sacramental practices of the Church enable persons to attain a personal sense of, an understanding of, and a practical experience of the reconciliation that the Church proclaims to its members. This reconciliation, however, takes fully concrete form only when extended to the world. The process that aims at that goal has three moments. It begins with the institution of the gathered community in which reconciliation and the freedom that results from reconciliation are experienced in an immediate way. Then, as the community develops, it differentiates itself from the world. This leads to a contradiction between the Church, where reconciliation and freedom is experienced in a heartfelt way, and the world that is found to be an unreconciled and unfree domain. This condition is surpassed to the extent that

this contradiction is resolved in the *ethical realm*, or
that the principle of freedom has penetrated into the

worldly realm itself, and that the worldly, because it has been thus conformed to the concept, reason, and eternal truth, is freedom that has become concrete and will that is rational. The institutions of ethical life are divine institutions—not holy in the sense that celibacy is supposed to be holy by contrast with marriage or familial love, or that voluntary poverty is supposed to be holy by contrast with active self-enrichment, or what is lawful and proper. Similarly, blind obedience is regarded as holy, whereas the ethical is an obedience in freedom, a free and rational will, an obedience of the subject towards the ethical. Thus it is in the ethical realm that the reconciliation of religion with worldliness and actuality comes about and is accomplished.[62]

In 1807, Hegel believed that one of the chief aims of a philosophical examination of religion was an overcoming of the separation between consciousness of the world and religious self-consciousness, and of the consequent sense that life is lived, as it were, in two parts, on the one hand in one's activity in the world, and on the other hand in one's religious conduct. He also maintained that a philosophical examination of religion undertakes the task of rethinking the religious representation in fully conceptual terms. And even earlier in his life, he envisioned a religious form that would contribute in a substantive way to overcoming the alienating fragmentation that had developed in contemporary cultural and social life, while at the same time preserving and enhancing the achievements regarding individual freedom that essentially characterize modernity. Through the development of his mature reflections on Christianity, Hegel came to believe that (1) he had defined the conditions needed for a conceptual rethinking of the religious representation in its consummate form, that (2) accomplishing that task is the final moment of overcoming a separation between consciousness of the world and religious self-consciousness, and that (3) realizing the aim of overcoming that separation contributes essentially to the constitution of a religious form that will operate in modern social and cultural life in a way that modernity demands.

Early in his career, Hegel determined that fundamental social and cultural, and in that sense practical problems required a theoretical achievement for their solution. He devoted the work of his mature life as a philosopher to the pursuit of that achievement. He maintained that to the extent that that pursuit was successful, to the same extent the practical matters that were its initial motivation were addressed, and that such matters are never, in the last analysis, lost to philosophical concern.

Chapter 6

Hegel's legacy: the problem

According to Karl Barth, the possibility that Hegel's thought might attain a new and substantial prominence in contemporary theological inquiry presents a problem and a promise. In this and the following chapter I will discuss issues related to each of these aspects that belong, according to Barth, to Hegel's legacy. In this chapter I will focus on some critical problems that do or at least may belong to Hegel's philosophical considerations of religion and Christianity. In the following chapter I will comment on positions that belong to Hegel's considerations of religion and Christianity that offer the productive possibilities for ongoing philosophical and theological work.

For the purposes of this chapter, it is important to be mindful of requirements that Hegel recognizes for critically assessing a philosophical position. If a position is genuinely philosophical, it is presented and supported in a rational and evidential manner. Then it will never do to deny a position simply by indicating that it is inconsistent with some other view that one finds desirable or even compelling. Such a procedure may show why I do not hold a position. It does nothing at all to show why I or anyone else should not hold that same position. A philosophical critique of a genuinely philosophical position must examine that position in an immanent way. One can do this by a direct assessment of the reasoning offered for a given position, or by an assessment of that position in relation to others belonging to the set of positions with which it is associated. Alternatively, in the course of developing an independent philosophical standpoint one may show how the reasoning that supports that standpoint counts against a given position, and perhaps how the standpoint in question preserves any truth that does belong to that position, thus confirming the comprehensiveness of that standpoint. One needs to observe these cautions in critically examining positions that Hegel offers regarding religion and Christianity, insofar as those positions are germane both to current philosophical and to theological concerns.

In this chapter I will develop aspects of the critical examination just mentioned. I will begin with some comments on specific aspects of Hegel's treatment of what I have called the Christian mysteries. Then I will turn to Hegel's understanding of the very idea of mystery. Next, I will consider what one might call an existential objection directed at Hegel's alleged failure adequately to understand religious practice in its specificity. Finally, I will consider what one might call an ethical objection directed at Hegel's alleged failure adequately to understand the prophetic role that religion and Christianity may play in incisive social critique.

I have already claimed, in agreement with Peter Hodgson, that Hegel presents an understanding of the Trinity that accords equal status to both the immanent and the economic Trinities, rather than prioritizing one dimension of the Trinity over the other in a problematic manner. I do not, however, maintain that Hegel presents this understanding in a thoroughly consistent or unambiguous manner. I have already noted that, in the *Phenomenology of Spirit*, Hegel says that, within what we must call the immanent Trinity, difference is simple and immediate and therefore otherness is as such not posited. And in the *Lectures on the Philosophy of Religion* he maintains that difference and otherness within the immanent Trinity do not possess the seriousness that spirit requires. But he also, in texts I have noted, attributes unqualified self-subsistence and actuality to God in God's triune self as such. There is an ambiguity in statements that Hegel makes about God that refer to the immanent and economic Trinities, and an account of that ambiguity is available. When Hegel discusses the triune God as spirit and focuses on the idea that the concept of spirit subsumes the concept of substance into itself, he asserts the unqualified self-subsistence and actuality of God in God's triune self. When Hegel discusses the triune God as spirit and focuses on the essential relation between the idea of spirit and the concepts of intersubjectivity, recognition, and therefore otherness and difference, he insists that intersubjectivity and recognition require difference and otherness in a robust sense, and then speaks as if there were what I have called a deficiency in the immanent Trinity in this regard.

Ewert Cousins would, I think, maintain that one might appeal to the notion of infinite fecundity that he finds in Bonaventure as a resource that would allow one to conceive of God as spirit, in Hegelian terms, without there being any need or even possibility of identifying a sense of privation within the immanent Trinity. I would add, more generally, that it is just for this reason that I think it is unfortunate that Hegel did not consider in a detailed way, as classical theology did, questions having to do with the nature of, identity of, and relations among the persons of the Trinity. It is just this consideration, I believe, that allows one to think carefully about questions having to do with community and unity within the triune God. Bernard Lonergan, whose work offers a difficult but elegant example of this consideration, is further able to show an analytical connection between the relations of persons within the immanent Trinity and the missions of persons within the economic Trinity, in view of the principle that 'although the external works of God are necessarily common to the three persons, the missions in the strictest sense are necessarily proper, since a divine person operates by reason of the divine essence but is not really and truly sent except by reason of a relation of origin.'[1] The demonstration that shows this connection, if successful, reinforces the assignment of equal status to the immanent and the economic Trinities, defines the relation between these two dimensions of the triune God, and supports an understanding of the contingency of creation.

As I previously noted, there is an ambiguity not only in statements about the Trinity that Hegel presents, but also in his account of the symbolism of the Fall. On the one hand, he insists that the occurrence of sin and evil is something for which responsibility must be imputed. On the other hand, he speaks of the self-centeredness in which evil consists as if it were a necessary moment in the dialectical development of finite spirit. I do not want to suggest that the problem of evil in its anthropological and theological dimensions is easily addressed. Nor do I want to chastise Hegel for presenting an ambiguity in his attempt at addressing this most vexing of problems. But the ambiguity is there, and it is a difficulty.

Paul Ricoeur, for whom this difficulty is especially serious, suggests an approach to dealing with it. He proposes that one trace back from the doctrine of original sin to the symbolic narratives and the symbols that represent the experience of a kind of original sin or evil, in order to determine the structure of the experience that those symbols and narratives disclose. This process shows, Ricoeur maintains, that evil or sin in an original sense is something that one does rather than a kind of entitative reality, and more specifically a kind of wandering or veering off course that precedes the full awakening of conscience. It is at the same time 'a power which binds man and holds him captive. In this sense, sin is not so much a veering as a fundamental impotence.'[2] Sin or evil has an essentially communal as well as an individual dimension. And it has a past. 'I do not begin evil; I continue it. I am implicated in evil.'[3] The Adamic myth unites these different features in the symbolic narrative that deals with the first ancestor, so as to disclose a structure belonging to the human condition at its roots.

An analysis of the kind that Ricoeur gives provides material that is quite valuable for the task of thinking through the problem of human evil and sin. If one undertakes that task with this material in hand, one has resources that allow one to begin to address an ambiguity of the kind I have attributed to Hegel. If one recognizes that the traditional symbolism depicts sin in its original sense as both an action and a condition that precedes my natality, a deed of my own and an impotence that grasps me, then one can begin to understand why attempts to understand this condition appeal both to the ideas of freedom and responsibility and to the ideas of inevitability and a kind of necessity. Hegel's attempt to integrate these ideas in a single understanding of original sin refers to the symbolic and narrative representations of the Fall, but does not in this instance take full account of the difficulties involved in restating in conceptual terms an integration of oppositions that receives its originating presentation in symbolic and narrative terms rather than in conceptual terms. This is in part because of the way in which Hegel privileges the doctrinal component of the religious representation.

Hegel's account of the Fall, especially in the 1820s, establishes the context in which he proceeds to consider the Incarnation.

I have already commented briefly on Hegel's treatment of the Incarnation, as well as of the life and teaching of Jesus. These comments support James Yerkes' view that 'Hegel is arguing that the entire event of Jesus of Nazareth is a religiously central *paradigmatic* event by which the truth of what ultimately *is* and the truth of the *meaning* of human existence are disclosed to human consciousness.'[4] In other words, the Incarnation and the Christological event as a whole are understood in relation to the purpose of making something known, of manifestation or revelation. This is the case for Hegel, I believe, in virtue of the fundamental importance of the concept of spirit and of the essential idea that spirit is self-manifesting. One may observe, however, that manifestation or revelation is not the only concept available for a theological definition of the significance of the Incarnation and of the Christological event. Indeed for one current author, the definition Hegel suggests 'is a theological reflection of the monopoly of epistemology in modern philosophy since Kant. The question, What can we know? seems to be the controlling *Fragestellung*. But when the question of knowledge becomes the central question in theology, then revelation as the answer to this question becomes the dominant category.'[5] Suppose, however, that another question, such as the question about overcoming estrangement, or about justification, becomes the central question. This does not set aside the category of revelation, but it does lead to interpreting the Incarnation and Christological matters generally more dominantly in soteriological terms.

I have no intention of trying to adjudicate or even more carefully to define the theological difference just indicated. One should point out, however, that the understanding of the Incarnation that Hegel espouses is not the only, and from some points of view not the preferred alternative. This also leads one to consider whether the central concept of spirit can be understood in a way that supports understandings of the Incarnation and of Christology that differ, in emphasis or in substance, from the ones that Hegel presents. These issues also have a bearing on the question of religious pluralism, which I will discuss in the next chapter.

To conclude this consideration of specific Christian mysteries, recall that Hegel links his understandings of the Resurrection and the indwelling of the Spirit in the gathered community closely together, and emphasizes the importance of both in discussing the cultic life of the Church. That is because the link and the emphasis that I have just mentioned, taken together, play a constitutive role in his understanding of the reconciliation of consciousness and self-consciousness that belongs to Christian religious consciousness and that identifies this as the consummate form of religious consciousness. Christ is raised up through the indwelling of the Spirit that informs the consciousness of the Christian community. That consciousness focuses on and integrates the moments of the process divine self-manifestation, and allows members of the community to be conscious of themselves and of the community itself in relation to that process. Given this understanding of the consummate form of religious consciousness, it is clear that, once again, Hegel is operating in the context that gives essential priority to what has just been called the question of knowledge, which in turn disposes Hegel to make the category of revelation, as he understands this, the dominant category that governs his interpretation of key Christian symbols and doctrines. One might well want to inquire if the basic categories and concerns that direct Hegel's interpretation of Christian symbols and doctrines can support understandings of the same that arise if one gives central emphasis to some other theological category, such as salvation or sanctification, in contrast to revelation.

While this question is very significant, it is not one I will pursue here. That is because another concern is of even greater significance, given Hegel's own claims about what he achieves through the speculative reenactment of the religious representation. That concern is regarding not specific Christian mysteries, but the very concept of mystery, as Hegel understands it.

Hegel commented explicitly on the concept of mystery in 1824 and 1827, in connection with the speculative understanding of the Trinity. In 1824 he says of the Trinity,

> It is the God who differentiates himself but remains
> identical with himself in the process. The Trinity is called
> the *mystery* of God; its content is mystical, i.e. speculative.
> But what is for reason is not a secret. In the Christian

religion one *knows*, and this is a secret only for the finite
understanding, and for thought that is based on sense
experience. [6]

In fact, Hegel is saying that there are two senses in which this
mystery, and by extension any mystery, is not a secret. First, it
is not hidden or undisclosed; it has been disclosed or revealed.
Second, the intelligibility of what has been disclosed is accessible
to reason, although not to the understanding. The understanding resembles thought that is simply based on sense experience
inasmuch as, for both, identity and difference are simply different from each other, they simply exclude each other. Thus,
since 'one' and 'three' are self-identical and therefore different
from each other, they exclude each other. To predicate one of
the other would be contradictory, which is to say senseless. But
reason comprehends the identity of identity and difference that
obtains even as it preserves the difference of each of these terms
from each other. 'Certainly when we say "Trinity" or "triune,"
the unfortunate formal pattern of a number series (1, 2, 3) comes
into play. Reason can employ all the *relationships* of the understanding, but only insofar as it destroys the *forms* of the understanding. And so it is with the Trinity.'[7] The relationships of the
understanding include, in this instance, numerical relationships.
The forms that determine the way in which the understanding
deals with those relationships include simple self-identity, simple difference, and exclusion. Reason employs the relationships
while overcoming the forms that determine those relationships
as they occur for the understanding. Thus where the understanding finds senseless contradiction, reason finds intelligibility. If this were not the case, Hegel seems to maintain, then the
mystery in question would be both disclosed on the one hand,
and wholly unavailable both to the understanding and to reason
on the other hand. But if that were so, then that which has been
disclosed would remain effectively undisclosed and spirit would
not be self-manifesting.

Hegel's language in the 1827 *Lectures* is, if anything, more
emphatic. There he insists that the speculative idea, the category in which the identity of identity and difference is radically grasped in a way that both acknowledges and surpasses

contradiction, is a mystery for the understanding but is nonetheless supremely rational. More specifically, 'The nature of God is not a secret in the ordinary sense, least of all in the Christian religion. In it God has made known what he is; there he is manifest. But he is a secret or mystery for external perception and representation, for the sensible mode of consideration and likewise for the understanding.'[8] Hegel thinks that examples of things that present themselves in a way that is contradictory to the understanding but that are known both spontaneously and philosophically to be rationally intelligible are in fact ready at hand. For instance, 'Life has certain needs and thus is in contradiction, but the satisfaction of the need annuls the contradiction. I am distinguished for myself in my drives and my needs. But life is the resolving of the contradiction, the satisfying of the need, giving it peace, though in such a way that the contradiction emerges once more.'[9] On account of needs I am related to things other than myself. This is a negation of my self-relatedness that places me in opposition to myself, in a condition of contradiction. But the need points beyond itself to its satisfaction and the concomitant restoration of self-relatedness. From a rational standpoint this is fully intelligible, although from the standpoint of the understanding one would have to say, 'This is inconceivable.' Even so, for the understanding

> the nature of God is inconceivable; but, as we already said, this is just the concept itself, which contains the act of distinguishing within itself. The understanding does not get beyond the fact of the distinction, so it says, 'This can't be grasped.' For the principle of the understanding is abstract identity with itself, not concrete identity, in accord with which these distinctions are [present] within a single [concept or reality].[10]

The understanding, operating with an abstract concept of identity, finds situations in which self-relatedness entails otherness, and thus both self-opposition and the overcoming of self-opposition, to be mysteries. Fully rational cognition finds in those same situations a radical consummation of intelligibility.

Hegel is concerned, as I have noted, to arrive at a position that avoids two claims that are, for him, basically erroneous: (1) the claim that we can have knowledge that God is but not knowledge of what God is, and (2) the claim that we can have knowledge of our relationship with God but not of God as such. The position at which he arrives and which avoids these errors asserts that 'God is none other than the idea, which determines itself and raises its determination to infinitude, and is only infinite self-determination.'[11] The 'idea,' in this case, is the ultimate category through which autonomous reason grasps and realizes the possibilities that belong to its own self-determining processes by radicalizing the comprehension of the identity and identity and difference through the warranted assertion of the infinite unity-in-difference of thought and being. The concept of the infinite unity-in-difference of thought and being is, as Anselm's version of the ontological argument showed in however imperfect a form, the concept of God. Through attaining and comprehending this concept, reason realizes its most essential possibilities. The discussion of mystery that Hegel develops follows from this assertion. He believes that he presents this concept in a way that shows its truth, and also entails the erroneous nature of the two other claims about knowledge of God previously mentioned. At the same time, his treatment of the concept of mystery seems to undermine the significance that belongs to that concept in the history of Christian religious thought and theology. Is it possible for one who adopts a Hegelian standpoint to preserve something of that significance? Are there reasons why one should do so?

A text that I cited from the *Phenomenology* in Chapter 2 is of importance for a critical consideration of Hegel in relation to these questions. There he says that to know that God is self-revealing is to know that God

is essentially a *self-conscious Being*. For there is something hidden from *consciousness* in its object if the object is an 'other' or something *alien*, and if it does not know it as *its own self*. The concealment ceases when absolute Being *qua* Spirit is the object of consciousness; for then the object has the form of a *Self* in relation to consciousness, i.e.

consciousness knows itself immediately in the object, or is manifest to itself in the object.[12]

Recall that the consummate form of religious consciousness integrates consciousness and self-consciousness. Consciousness has to do with something that stands over against it, and therefore is and can be hidden from it. Self-consciousness has to do with something through which it achieves self-relatedness. This is something that self-consciousness recognizes as another self, and therefore something in which it finds itself. Since self-consciousness finds itself in the other by recognizing the other as another self, the other, while necessarily independent, does not stand over against self-consciousness in a way that requires the other to be hidden. The other self is manifest to self-consciousness.

This at least is Hegel's claim. But are there additional aspects of the manifest nature of the other and independent self that, given Hegel's own account, should be acknowledged? For me to recognize you as another self is for me to be aware that I cannot have your experience of the world as my own experience. I can come to know about, perhaps a great deal about, your experience of the world. I can perhaps participate in your experience of the world. But I cannot have your experience of the world as my own experience. Therefore your experience of the world, and your identity in connection with that experience, are present to me, because I am aware of them. But they are present to me in virtue of a kind of absence that is blended with that presence. And it is precisely in virtue of the blend of presence with absence, or of disclosure or manifestation with hiddenness or reserve, that I do and can recognize you as a self who is other and independent.

I am maintaining, then, that Hegel's assertion regarding the manifest presence of the other and independent self to the self requires a dimension of reserve or concealment, absence in that sense, as a determination of that manifest presence. In this situation, presence and absence stand in contrast to each other, but not as contrasting alternatives, in the way in which your being absent from the room is the alternative to your being present in the room. Rather, presence integrates absence into itself so as to bring about the unity that is the manifestation of one independent self to another. An Hegelian comprehension of the identity of identity and difference is just what makes possible a conceptualization of this integration and its outcome. In turn a conceptualization of that outcome, namely, the actual nature of the manifest presence of one independent self to another, must preserve that integration.

To extend the conceptualization of the way in which human selves recognize, are manifest to, and are related to each other, to the relation between human beings and God is to employ a conceptual analogy. Hegel's analysis of the idea of God through the concept of spirit is supposed to show that the analogy is both possible and necessary. The analogy would suggest that a determining dimension of concealment or reserve belongs preeminently to divine self-manifestation or self-revelation.

Kenneth Schmitz has a comment related to this claim that I cite at length because of its importance for this discussion. He says that in view of the accounts of hierophanies belonging to their traditions,

> Jews, Christians, and Moslems came to attribute to
> the holy God a *mystery of excellence*. He was figured as
> too bright a light for clear sight, too precious a good
> to be measured or weighed. This central conviction
> characteristic of a certain classical understanding of
> these theistic faiths offers us a distinction between
> what I might call mystification and mystery. A state of
> mystification arises out of the darkness of ignorance
> due to the weakness of our faculties, the poverty of the
> object, or the obscurity of the medium. Mystery, on the
> other hand, arises out of the light of knowledge in the
> presence of that which excels every attempt to 'run it
> through,' to define it in concepts or embody it in words.
> The Hegelian dialectic may purge the presuppositions
> underlying the metaphysical theology associated with
> this sort of mystery, but that does not in itself invalidate
> its testimony to an extraordinary presence. . . . Such a
> presence would not be apprehended as indeterminate in
> the Hegelian sense, but its determinacy would be of an

order of actuality that stands free from all conceptual moments. Concepts would not comprehend it, but merely open out towards it.[13]

Note that what is at issue here is not unintelligibility, which would be a consequence of indeterminacy for Hegel, but a kind of excessive or hyper-intelligibility. To employ imagery for a moment, it is a kind of overwhelming light that, because it can be blinding, can be experienced as a kind of darkness. As an excessive intelligibility it exceeds concepts, which therefore do not fully comprehend it, but rather 'open out towards it.' But at the same time, as intelligibility, it does disclose itself essentially to conceptual thought, while simultaneously disclosing itself to conceptual thought as an actuality that both discloses itself and exceeds its own disclosure, thus maintaining in its self-disclosure a constitutive dimension of reserve or concealment. To appropriate this aspect of classical theology in the way I am suggesting is to develop an understanding that Hegelian categories have the unique capacity to express, because again one is speaking of an instance of the identity-in-difference of identity and difference. It is also an understanding that preserves in the Hegelian conception of divine self-revelation the integration of manifestation and concealment required if that conception follows from the extension of the concept of the mutual recognition that obtains between human beings to the relation between humans and God.

One can also reason to the position I am suggesting here by considering, once again, the relation between the religious representation and fully conceptual thought. As already noted, two of the essential components of the religious representation, images and narratives, are symbolic in nature. Symbols embody their referents and evoke responses to their referents. They also disclose and conceal. This is due to the manner in which analogies and metaphors operate in symbols. So for example, nightfall can be a symbol of death in a poem because of the metaphorical connection that one can establish between nightfall and death. The symbol discloses its referent through the medium of its constitutive metaphorical image. The disclosure, because it takes place through this medium, manifests and conceals at the same time. This is not to say that symbolic discourse discloses in way inferior to nonsymbolic expression. On the contrary, symbolic disclosure can be uniquely concrete and evocative. This is not in spite of but because of the operating metaphor which links symbolic disclosure with concealment.

The comments I have just made suggest that the integration of manifestation and concealment in symbolic disclosure is due to the form of the symbol. Indeed this is so. But one can also argue that, in the case of religious symbols, the integration pertains not only to form but also and essentially to content. This case can be more specifically made with regard to symbols that concern God. Take just one sort of case, that of theophanies, that is, events, objects, or persons supposed to be manifestations of God. Hegel and many of our contemporaries would say that the discourse used regarding theophanies is necessarily symbolic. Such discourse employs constitutive metaphors in order to represent something as a manifestation of God. Direct rather than symbolic discourse, the argument goes, cannot successfully do this. There are many reasons that can be given for this. The one that is important at the moment is that, on this account of theophanies, God's presence and action in the event, object, or person in question is not a directly given datum or range of data. God's presence and action are rather given in and through, but not as, data that are directly present in the item in question, and are accessible to those who are religiously engaged with that item and find it to be a theophany. Religious discourse needs to be able to convey this aspect of the nature of divine presence and action, and for that symbolism is required.

If these remarks are correct, the understanding that divine presence in theophanies is a kind of self-concealing or reserved presence, but a genuine presence at the same time, requires symbolic operators to be conveyed and belongs to the content, as well as the form of symbolic discourse. Hegel, of course, would call the sort of discourse to which I am now referring representational. He also insists that speculative thought surpasses the form but preserves the content of the religious representation. If so, then speculative thought must preserve the dimension of the content of religious discourse of which I am now speaking. This is of course possible only if the discourse that articulates speculative thought speaks in its own terms of divine presence as involving disclosure and reserve. But that is possible only if, for speculative thought itself, God genuinely reveals Godself, and discloses Godself as exceeding that disclosure. Speculative concepts regarding God must in this case be concepts that, if correct, genuinely have to do with God as God in Godself is and 'open out' to divine reality, rather than being concepts through which we come to know God with comprehensive finality.

The position that I am advocating is not a position that Hegel holds. According to Kathleen Dow Magnus, who has done some of the very best current work on the understanding and functions of symbolism in Hegel's philosophy, Hegel asserts 'that the real meaning of a symbol may be made fully explicit through philosophical reflection and speculation.'[14] On the view that I am presenting, to do this with reference to religious discourse, given the symbolic nature of the more basic components of religious discourse and the role that symbolism plays with regard to the form and the content of that discourse, would involve preserving in speculative terms the blend of disclosure and reserve that belongs to images, narratives, and indeed to theological but pre-philosophical discourse regarding God. The language that Hegel uses in his comments on mystery and speculative comprehension does not suggest that view. It rather suggests that speculative thought brings about a kind of fullness of comprehension that replaces what counts as mystery for the understanding. Notice that Hegel does not say that speculative comprehension abolishes mystery as such. Rather, he says that the significance that mystery has for the understanding is one thing, and its significance for speculative reason something notably different. The revisionist position that I am urging suggests a difference but also an essential continuity between the significance that mystery has for the understanding and for speculative reason.

I think that Hegel both should have and could have maintained the position I am presenting. An important reason why he should have is, once again, his view about the religious representation and its speculative comprehension. Paul Ricoeur speaks of this view by saying that absolute knowledge is 'the thoughtfulness of all of the modes that generate it.'[15] Speculative comprehension follows from and fulfills the standpoint of absolute knowing, and has the religious representation as an essential resource that generates it. If speculative comprehension is the mode in which one more successfully thinks the significance that belongs to religious representational thinking than is possible from within the representational dimension of thought, and if other claims I have made about that significance are true, then the position that I am presenting seems to be required. That Hegel did not himself arrive at this position is at least in part due to the fact that his hermeneutics 'is less and less a biblical hermeneutics and more and more hermeneutics of Christian dogmatics.'[16]

But is it possible that Hegel not only did not but also could not have taken the position I recommend? Does that position contradict other positions that he held, including some positions most basic and central to his philosophy? I concede that it is possible to make a case that this is so, and not a few philosophers who concern themselves with Hegel would want to do that. But I do not think that this is so. The position I recommend does not entail that we can have knowledge only of our relation to God but not of God as such, or that we can have knowledge that God is but not knowledge of what God is, at least given Hegel's understanding of what that position means. The deepest problem regarding the compatibility of Hegel's philosophical commitments with the view I recommend has to do with the understanding of absolute knowing as the final and ultimate reconciliation of rational consciousness and self-consciousness. From the standpoint of that reconciliation, the relation of consciousness to its object is a relation to something that is other and independent, and a relation that is and is known to be a self-relation. If the other discloses itself as exceeding its self-disclosure, such that manifestation has reserve as a defining component of itself, is not self-relation violated? This question perhaps demands a book length study. I am going to offer only the briefest of responses. But I think not. The situation I describe is rather one that preserves both the self-related unity of rational self-consciousness and the relation of that same self-consciousness to an object that is genuinely independent and other. That, I believe, is the proposition that can receive more than plausible support. Reflection on this proposition, and the problem to which it responds, would be an important part of philosophical and theological inquiry that would appropriate Hegel as an essential resource and also aim at rehabilitating the notion of religious mystery.

The comments that Hegel makes regarding mystery all belong to a consideration of the nature of speculative comprehension of God. The development of that comprehension is supposed to be the final, perfecting moment of the reconciliation of consciousness and self-consciousness achieved in the consummate religion. As previously noted, that reconciliation requires the integration of consciousness of God and cultic practice. Only in that integration does the speculative comprehension that finalizes that reconciliation find its necessary ground. Since philosophical comprehension follows from and also involves a focus on a kind of integration of theory and practice, one can appropriately turn a critical eye to Hegel's understanding not only of cultic life, but also of religious practice more generally.

That practice has two aspects. There is, on the one hand, the cultivation of the religious dimension of the life of the individual. There is, on the other hand, conduct that extends the values of the infinite dignity of the free individual in a community of free individuals to the institutions of the family, civil society, and the state. Critical reflection is available in connection with each of these aspects.

The cultivation of the religious dimension of individual life takes place as the individual personally appropriates the truth that the Church presents. This process has two sides, in that the truth is present to the individual in two different ways. 'First it is [present] as intuition, faith, feeling—as the felt witness of the Spirit like a flame of fire. But it is supposed to be present and presupposed; thus it must be developed from the concentration and interiority of feeling into representation as something immediately present.'[17] The inner faith and the affective life of the individual develop through personal identification with the understanding of reality that prevails in the community. This is in part but importantly due to the symbols used to convey that understanding, and to participation in the sacramental life of the Church, which leads to the 'self-feeling of God, the feeling of God's immediate presence within the subject.'[18] At the same time, the Church does and must express the truth that it presents in doctrines that are presupposed and that the community conveys to individuals through the instruction it offers. The cultivation of the religious life of the individual includes a distinctly cognitive side. The individual receives, affirms, and comes more deeply to understand the significance of the essential teachings that determine the mind of the community.

Thus the religious development of the individual includes an inward and affective and a more cognitive and conceptual side. Through participation in the process that includes both of these sides the individual comes to be more concretely situated in the life of the community and at the same time finds the value and dignity of his or her particular individuality reinforced. One may ask, however, if there is not a notable incompleteness to this account of individual religious development, and if some of Hegel's most basic claims about the consummate religion do not suggest this. Kierkegaard would answer the first of these questions affirmatively, although he does not seem to consider the second. Hegel maintains, as previously discussed, that the central conception that Christianity puts forward is reconciliation, and that this reconciliation is the deepest significance of the Incarnation. The Incarnation expresses the understanding that the reconciliation of the estrangement between God and humankind has been achieved from the divine side of that estrangement, and therefore definitively. At the same time, the individual is set the task of personally appropriating this achievement and of making it his or her own. It is not an exaggeration to say that, on the basis of Hegel's views concerning Christian self-understanding, the Church exists for the sake of presenting this two-sided conception of reconciliation as something that both has been accomplished as such and is to be accomplished in the condition of the individual.

It is also more than plausible to say that the task of bringing about in the condition of one's life, or if you prefer of receiving in the condition of one's life, the reconciliation of God and humankind that God is supposed from the divine side to have definitively accomplished, is not a one time thing that the individual achieves and then is done with. Indeed there are good reasons to say that the individual who undertakes this task must always find it to be one that he or she is on the way toward accomplishing and never one that is fully accomplished.

Kierkegaard argues for this view by developing the idea of appropriation in connection with the notions of objective and subjective reflection. Briefly, objective reflection aims exclusively at understanding the object itself, whether it is of a conceptual or a historical nature, on which one is focused. This aim calls on one to abstract from a consideration of one's relation to the object so that one can attend to the thing on its own terms. Subjective reflection has to do not precisely with conceptual or historical matters but with existence possibilities, possibilities to which one might commit oneself in the conduct of one's own existence. Here the question of one's concern is precisely that of one's relation to the possibility under consideration. To reach an affirmation through the process of subjective reflection is to commit one's oneself to the possibility and to make it one's own. Making an existence possibility one's own on account of a voluntary commitment is what Kierkegaard means by appropriation.

The locus classicus for Kierkegaard's discussion of appropriation is the consideration of subjective truth in the *Concluding Unscientific Postscript*. There, as is well known, he presents a definition of truth understood in association with subjectivity, which he also calls a definition of faith. '*An objective uncertainty, held fast through appropriation with the most passionate inwardness, is the truth*, the highest truth there is for an *existing* person.'[19] There are a number of issues that this definition directly or indirectly presents concerning objective and subjective truth, objective and subjective reflection, and certainty, which I am not going to take up here. I have argued elsewhere that Kierkegaard plausibly held, and certainly should have held, a far more nuanced and dialectical position about the relations between objective and subjective reflection and truth than is commonly attributed to him.[20] Additionally, one need not at all maintain the very positions that Kierkegaard either did hold or is supposed to have held on those matters in order to develop his concept of appropriation in the way I intend. Through appropriation, he maintains, one holds fast to an existence possibility. That is, one determines one's existence in the light of that possibility. It is in this manner and only in this manner that one makes an existence possibility one's own. To say this is to say that appropriation coincides with the task of self-becoming, of becoming the self that I am and that I am capable of becoming in the world. In turn, to even admit that self-becoming is a task that an individual can undertake is to affirm that it is a task that is ever before one as a task to be accomplished rather than a task that one can ever claim to have accomplished. That is because it must be at least possibly the case that at any new moment in time there is something further to be done in pursuit of this task. To put the point somewhat simplemindedly, when can I ever say that I have done all that can be done toward the end of becoming the self that I am and can be, and can now choose to turn to my leisure? If it were even possible for me to make that choice, then actually making it would be a way of pursuing the task of self-becoming, in however paradoxical a manner.

Hegel would fundamentally disagree with Kierkegaard's claim that Christianity presents the individual not with doctrine but with the communication of an existence possibility. Hegel could not disagree with the claim that Christian doctrine does communicate an existence possibility to the individual. Like Kierkegaard after him, Hegel understands Christianity centrally in relation to the idea of the Incarnation. Certainly, for Hegel, Christianity presents this idea in doctrinal form. The significance of this doctrine has to do with the two-sided understanding of reconciliation mentioned earlier. The individual who is receptive to that significance must find it to be both an intelligible sense and an existence possibility. After all, the significance of the doctrine, according to Hegel, is that reconciliation between God and humankind has come about through divine initiative and is therefore a condition that the individual is called on to realize, or is a condition whose realization the individual is called on to allow, in his or her life.

Endeavoring to determine one's existence in relation to this existence possibility certainly does or at least can engage feeling and focus understanding. But the process itself is as such not an affective one, and not an intellectual one, and not both together. It tends toward the integration of all dimensions of the self: body and spirit; feeling, will and mind; the private and the social components of life. At its core is an effort at a kind of conversion of the self, a turning away from the self-centeredness that Hegel indeed does identify with sin, for the sake of a fundamental self-transcendence. The most essential determinants of the process are persistence, renewal, and trust. Persistence is required because this process must be extended from some to all parts of life and from moment to moment. Renewal is required because the very fact that one needs to undertake this process indicates that one's efforts will predictably be imperfect in constancy. Trust is required because, even though this task may require every effort of the self, full progress comes about not so much on account of those efforts but because of the grace of a possibility that one receives.

Kierkegaard accuses Hegel of failing in an essential way to understand the full measure of the task of religious appropriation. There are good reasons to think that Hegel does think of the religious cultivation of the individual essentially in affective and intellectual terms, and does overlook the significance of the existence possibility that Christian doctrine does pose given Hegel's own interpretation of the Incarnation. There is also every reason to hold that the idea of appropriation can be incorporated into the framework that Hegel builds with his speculative interpretation of Christianity, given the role that his understanding of the relation of infinite and finite spirit plays in that interpretation. That incorporation does not leave the Hegelian framework unchanged. But arguably the outcome of putting Hegel and Kierkegaard into critical dialogue with each other in the way I am presently suggesting is a philosophical and theological position that is more substantive and more defensible than the result of considering either figure simply apart from the other. And in fact, this outcome would retrieve Hegel's recognition, in 1807, that concrete religious consciousness integrates the acknowledgment of finitude and the awareness of a specific sort of self-transcendence.

While religious practice certainly emphasizes the cultivation of the individual, it is not confined to this. There is also, for Hegel, a substantively ethical and social dimension to religious practice. It is of emphatic significance for the consummate religion. This is due to the essential recognition that Christianity gives to the freedom of the individual. 'In religion human beings are free before God. Because they make their will conform to the divine will, they are not opposed to the highest will but rather have themselves within it; they are free because in the cultus they have achieved the sublation of the rupture.'[21] Divine recognition of the individual as a self gives the individual a very basic experience of his or her freedom and of its infinite value. The union of the individual's will with the divine will disposes the individual freely to affirm what is true and to consent to what is good. But freedom of course cannot be confined to inner experience. One must be able to realize one's freedom in the conduct of one's life. The individual who conducts his or her life toward the end of realizing freedom is in turn a socially situated individual, one who participates in a social community in which individuals receive from others and accord to others recognition of their freedom. Moreover, even if the individual's most basic experience of freedom occurs in the context of the relation of the self to God, the social community to which I just referred does not coincide exclusively with the religious community. Reconciliation, following as it does from recognition, both grounds the experience and actuality of freedom and requires its extension throughout the wider society. 'What is required, therefore, is that this reconciliation should be accomplished in the worldly realm.'[22]

The 'worldly realm,' in this instance, is the domain that Hegel calls ethical life. Ethical life includes the various institutions, practices, and interactions that comprise the family, civil society, and the state. It is within this domain that the individual cultivates his or her life and strives to realize his or her freedom. The institutions, practices, and interactions that make up this domain are, of course, normative. Those norms, laws, and customs, are in the condition in which they should be, that is to say they are rational, in that, and inasmuch as, conformity to them makes possible the realization of the freedom of each one and of everyone in society in a concrete and genuine way. Given this situation, the legitimacy of those norms, and of the rights and duties that follow from them, will command rational affirmation, and the applicability of those norms, rights, and duties to each one and to all will command rational consent. This, again, is because of the relation of those norms, rights, and duties to the ability of individuals to realize their freedom as members of a community of free individuals, and because of the infinite value of human freedom itself.

Recall that, for Hegel, individuals experience and understand the infinite value of human freedom in a most basic way in the context of a properly formed sense of the relationship with God, and thus within the context of the particular community that forms the experience of that relationship. It is in view of this experience and understanding that individuals are disposed to affirm the infinite value of freedom, and to consent to the applicability to each one and to everyone, including of course the self, the conditions that freedom requires. There are three consequences of this.

First, if it is within the context of the relation with God, as understood by the consummate religion, that individuals acquire a most basic sense of the infinite value of human freedom, then religious consciousness in its consummate form is the source from which 'the principle of freedom has penetrated into the worldly realm itself, and that the worldly, because it has been thus conformed to the concept, reason, and eternal truth, is freedom that has become concrete and will that has become rational.'[23] This development of freedom in the world does not occur only or even chiefly on account of processes that occur within the historical religious community. But the independent social processes that foster this development, and that lead to the institutions of modern social life, realize a principle whose origin resides in Christian religious consciousness. Second, while social and civic obligations are and must be understood to be distinct from religious obligations, Christian religious consciousness contributes to the legitimation of the social and civic obligations in its definition of their final source. 'It is in being thus related to religion that state, laws, duties and all alike acquire for consciousness their supreme confirmation and their supreme obligatoriness, because even the state, laws, and duties, are in their actuality something determinate which passes over into a higher sphere and so into that on which it is grounded.'[24]

Third, the believer who is disposed, ultimately on account of religious self-awareness, to affirm and conform to the customs and the laws of those dimensions of social life that freedom requires, will understand the conduct that promotes the establishment of and the stability of those customs and laws as a kind of religious act. 'To that extent ethical life is the most genuine cultus. But consciousness of the true, of the divine, of God, must be directly bound up with it.'[25] In the absence of this consciousness the conduct in question is not fully informed. Given this consciousness one can and should see conduct that promotes laws and institutions that establish freedom in social life as a genuine religious act, indeed as a most substantive realization of the most basic principle of Christian religious consciousness.

Of course religious consciousness need not be properly formed, and societies need not be rationally governed.

> People who do not know that human beings are free in
> and for themselves live in a benighted state regarding
> their constitution as well as their religion. There is
> *one* concept of freedom in religion and state. This one
> concept is the highest concept that human beings have,
> and it is made real by them. A people that has a bad
> concept of God, also has a bad state, bad government, and
> bad laws.[26]

The consummate religion, then, is the ultimate source of the principle of freedom that comes to realization through the independent processes that belong to social history and that bring about modernity. It makes a basic contribution to the legitimation of the normative dimension of modern civilization. It encourages persons to conduct their lives in ways that promote the establishment and the stability of the personal and civic freedom that is the central achievement of modernity. And as the most recent citation indicates, it is a resource for a critique of arrangements or understandings in religion or society that fall short of the principle of freedom that the central Christian concept of reconciliation presents, whether those arrangements or understandings develop outside of or within the existing institutional structure of Christianity.

That critique would address situations in which, one might say, modernity falls short of itself. It would understand the existing state of affairs that determines a prevailing social order in relation to a comprehension of the fundamental actuality of that same social order, the essentially intelligible condition that belongs to that same social order insofar as it fully realizes the possibilities that belong authentically to it. In that condition the social order attains genuine actuality and is fully true to itself. The truth in question is, of course, a normative truth that grounds a critique of factual circumstances on account of which a social order falls short of or is not fully true to itself. Hegel does and can understand a critique of this sort and can also understand the consummate religion as having a role in relation to this critique.

But it is one thing to understand the possibility of a social critique that assesses modernity, or any prevailing social order, in terms of circumstances on account of which it fails to realize its own most authentic possibilities. It is another thing to understand the possibility of a critique that assesses the legitimacy or worth of a social order in even more fundamental terms. For example, the critique of capitalism that Marx presents is not an assessment that measures existing social circumstances against the intelligible social actuality that emerges with the more perfect realization of authentic capitalist possibilities. It is a critique of capitalism as such. That critique is neither utopian, nor is it one that appeals to norms whose relevance to the social order in question is debatable. It appeals to the idea of contradiction. 'A contradiction is a feature of some system which is dysfunctional for the system, yet which is an essential feature of the system.'[27] Contradictions 'are dysfunctional for the system itself, yet they can be abolished only along with the system itself. Hence they can stand as objective reasons why the system should be superseded.'[28]

My purpose in referring to this is not, in this place, to endorse some version of this critique. It is rather to suggest that the claim that there are conditions on account of which such a critique is in rational terms legitimately possible is at least a plausible claim. Marx develops that claim by appealing to an understanding of contradiction that clearly derives from Hegel. But he also insists on an essentially critical revision of the Hegelian idea of reason. And indeed it is at least a question as to whether one can understand the rational possibility of a critique of the sort now being mentioned in the light of the basic principles that belong to Hegel's philosophy, given his insistence on the essential connection between reason and actuality. Again, to say this is not to say that Marx succeeds and Hegel fails. But it is at least possible that Marx or someone else has shown or can show that a critique of a type now being mentioned is in rational terms legitimate as a possibility. If so, and if the basic principles of Hegel's philosophy do not allow for a recognition of that possibility, then that needs to be taken into account in an assessment of the successes and the limitations of Hegel's achievement.

But the consummate religion may pose an even farther ranging and more fundamental question. Christianity presents, as Hegel notes, the idea and the symbol of the kingdom of God. That idea or symbol is linked to the 'absolute reconciliation' that Christianity proclaims, which presents 'a new consciousness of humanity, or a new religion.'[29] Hegel goes on to say,

> The kingdom of God, the new religion, thus contains implicitly the characteristic of negating the present world. This is its polemical aspect, its revolutionary attitude towards all the determinate aspects of that outer world, [all the settled attitudes] of human consciousness and belief. So what is at issue is the drawing of those who are to achieve the consciousness of reconciliation away from present actuality requiring of them an abstraction from it. The new religion is itself still concentrated and does not actually exist as a community, but has its vitality rather in that energy which constitutes the sole eternal interest of its adherents who have to fight and struggle in order to achieve this for themselves, because it is not yet coherent with the world consciousness and is not yet in harmony with the condition of the world.[30]

The proclamation of the kingdom of God is an implicit negation of the world in which it is proclaimed. That proclamation, because it has not yet led to the formation of a community and has not become harmonious with the condition of the world, is revolutionary in relation to the world and calls on its hearers to abstract themselves from the world in order to achieve a new consciousness of reconciliation. But when the community forms, and when principle that animates the self-understanding of the community becomes available to the world, and when independent historical processes bring the world into harmony with that principle, then the proclamation ceases to have revolutionary potential and then its hearers are invited to participate in the institutions of ethical life as a kind of perfection of the religious cultus.

But perhaps the idea or symbol of the kingdom of God does have the revolutionary potential that Hegel attributes to it, and does not lose that potential so easily. Could it be that that symbol suggests the essentially problematic character not only of the world order in which it was originally proclaimed, but also of any social order that has or could come about in world history? What sort of critique does that possibility suggest? What does that possibility suggest about the role of theology in the development of social critique? How does one understand, in philosophical terms, the principles that determine the intelligibility of this sort of critique? Can one show, on the basis of those principles, that such critique is legitimate as a rational possibility? In addition, what role does or might the symbol of the kingdom of God play in relation to the sort of social critique that appeals in a radical way to the idea of contradiction, or to some current instance of the sort of social critique that Hegel more obviously recommends, that appeals to the contrast between existence and intelligible actuality?

I state the issues very intentionally as questions. They are questions that emerge from a consideration of one essential dimension of Hegel's philosophical reflections on religion and Christianity. Along with questions that emerge in considering his treatment of specific Christian mysteries, of the very concept of mystery, and of the cultivation of the religious life of the individual, they represent possible avenues along which critical reflection in philosophy and theology might develop, insofar as that reflection involves an effort to understand and assess Hegel's philosophical achievement.

Chapter 7

Hegel's legacy: the promise

Writing in 1970 on the political and theological significance of Hegel's philosophical achievement, Michael Theunissen asserted that 'In the two hundredth year of the anniversary of his birth, Hegel is more contemporary than ever.'[1] This is due, Theunissen believes, both to active and rich developments in scholarly research on Hegelian texts and to a 'living Hegelianism' present in ongoing philosophical inquiry. My aim in this chapter is to suggest that Hegel's philosophical conceptualization of religion and Christianity offers important, indeed essential, resources for ongoing inquiry in theology and philosophy of religion on our contemporary scene. This is not to deny the need to take up those resources in a critical manner. The previous chapter dealt with just that necessity. It is to assert that a critical but genuine appropriation of resources that Hegel's philosophy offers has outcomes of fundamental importance for current philosophical and theological investigation.

My remarks in this chapter will develop four considerations. First, I will comment on the general model that Hegel offers for inquiry into religious phenomena. Then I will discuss the approach to understanding religious discourse that Hegel proposes. This discussion will deal with the differentiated nature of religious discourse, the role of contemporary theology in relation to Hegel's philosophical proposal about understanding discourse concerning God, and the need for interrelated but specifically different approaches to understanding religious discourse in general. I will, in the third place, turn again to the question of a Hegelian analysis of transcendence. Finally, I will make some remarks on Hegel's views concerning Christianity and the religions of the world, for the sake of approaching the question of pluralism and religious truth.

A review of some matters discussed in previous chapters shows that Hegel presents a valuable model that guides inquiry of various sorts that concern religious life, be that inquiry undertaken under the rubric of theology, philosophy, or religious studies. According to that model, inquiry that deals with any form of religious life must aim at understanding the nature of the object and telos with which persons and communities who participate in that form of life take themselves to be involved. In asserting this proposition, Hegel employs a theistic idiom. He maintains, however, that the proposition holds for all forms of religious life. To reiterate a claim noted earlier, one cannot understand a mode of religious involvement without understanding the object with which persons and communities take themselves to be involved, the telos that religious involvement approaches.

That said, it is still the case that understanding religious life more concretely involves understanding the nature of a sacred object and telos in connection with its presence to religiously involved persons and communities. Hegel insists on this. He also introduces a most significant nuance into the idea of what I am calling religious involvement. Such involvement, he maintains, has an essential and necessary discursive aspect. At the same time, religious involvement is not to be understood precisely as a discourse. Religious involvement includes a dimension that is essential, essentially related to religious discourse, but at the same time different from and relatively independent of that discourse. This dimension also needs to be acknowledged and understood. Hegel understands this dimension of religious involvement in what one might call experiential terms, in connection with the sense of immediate certainty and with feeling. Comments in the previous chapter suggest that it might be preferable to understand this dimension of religious involvement in terms of the ideas of practice, self-becoming and appropriation, and to discuss religious affectivity in the context of that understanding. But it is still the case that Hegel proposes that we understand religious involvement in connection with its discursive aspect and in terms of a distinct and relatively independent dimension that such involvement concretely requires.

Moreover, Hegel insists that we recall that the religiously involved individual is socially situated. This means that understandings of religious life must focus on the individual and at the same time must not be individualistic in nature. Persons enact religious involvement while participating in the lives of religious communities. That participation has the activities that belong to the cultus as one of its constitutive dimensions. Another constitutive dimension comes about as a consequence of the relations that religiously involved persons and groups have with the larger social and civic domain to which they belong.

Thus, on the terms that belong to Hegel's project, a comprehensive inquiry into religious life in some or other form would focus on the conception of sacred reality that informs that mode of religious life. That inquiry would consider the object and telos of religious involvement in connection with the concrete and differentiated manner in which persons approach that object, and find in language the ability to relate to that object in a discursive manner. That inquiry would understand religious life in what one might call, and in what Hegel does call, both theoretical and practical terms. The understanding of religious life in practical terms would take account of the specifically religious activities that fund the lives of persons and communities, and also the relations between specifically religious persons and communities and the social, cultural, and political worlds in which they participate. Rather obviously, specific investigations in theology, philosophy of religion, and religious studies make specific and thus incomplete contributions to the comprehensive goal that this model for understanding religious life proposes. That is necessarily the case. A well-formed division of labor must belong to intellectual pursuits as well as to all aspects of the human enterprise. Still, the model for understanding religious life that one can form through considering Hegel's philosophical reflections on religion and Christianity is an important reminder of the many interrelated concerns that need to be addressed in developing that understanding. It also guards against the supposition that addressing any one of those concerns eliminates the need to consider the others. This model is, among other things, a counsel against reductionism or the fallacy of misplaced concreteness in the study of religion.

Of course, Hegel pays more attention to some of the aspects of religious life that I just mentioned than he does to others.

He pays a great deal of attention to religious discourse in his considerations of the religious representation. The positions that he defends in these considerations continue to be of essential importance for inquiry in philosophy of religion and theology in a number of ways.

In the first place, Hegel recognizes the differentiated nature of religious discourse, and thus the necessity of a multiplicity of interrelated but different approaches to understanding religious discourse. Symbols operate in religious discourse at a very basic level. Religious discourse develops in a variety of ways as a discourse that takes up and elaborates the significance of fundamental symbols belonging to a religious tradition. Hegel takes those elaborations to be essentially narrative in form, and speaks in his own way of symbolic narratives as myths and sacred histories. Later writers, such as Ricoeur, add that discourses belonging to a variety of genres take up and develop symbolic operators basic to a religious tradition.[2] This realization takes a step forward from, and is not at all a step away from, the proposal about the importance of symbolism for an essential dimension of the religious discourse that Hegel takes to be originary. An implication of this proposal is that approaches to understanding the meaning of this discourse need to be appropriate to a discourse that is symbolic and poetic in character.

At the same time, participation in the discursive tradition of a religious community can and does lead persons to raise basic questions about the consciousness of the world and of the divine that the discourse proposes. Those questions, as they develop, come to demand responses of a conceptual nature. As this occurs, religious discourse itself develops a conceptual dimension. Doctrine develops as a component of religious understanding and self-understanding. The importance of this component of religious understanding differs for different religious traditions. For the Christian tradition its importance is manifest. Hegel argues that this significance is not simply a historical contingency. Without conceptual or doctrinal formulations, questions that allow for no other sort of answer go unanswered, understanding is denied or truncated, and the intellect is left unsatisfied. One may fault Hegel because of the way he privileges the doctrinal over what he considers the symbolic and narrative components of religious discourse or the religious representation. At the same time, he argues in a powerful way that discourse of a conceptual or doctrinal nature plays a role in the development and articulation of religious understanding that is essential and can be played in no other way.

The privileged role that Hegel assigns to the doctrinal component of the religious representation is the basis for his claim regarding what is required in order to understand discourse about God. A comment on this claim leads to a remark about the role of contemporary theology in relation to Hegel's philosophical proposal. In remarks that deal specifically with Christianity, Hegel suggests that an understanding of church doctrines concerning God and the world in relation to God is the necessary and essential condition of the possibility of attaining knowledge of God in Godself, rather than knowledge that affirms that God is but does not deal with what God is, or knowledge having to do with our relation to God but not with God as such. Hegel believed that the pursuit of this understanding and the attainment of this knowledge is a task that belongs to philosophy. In fact, on more than one occasion he expressed the belief that, in his day, that task belonged to philosophy in a special way, to the extent that theology had abandoned that task. He said in 1821, for example, that

> Religion must take refuge in philosophy. (For [the theologians of the present day], the world [is] a passing away into [subjective reflection because it has as its] form merely the externality of contingent occurrence.) But philosophy, [as we have said, is also] partial: [it forms] an isolated order of priests—a sanctuary—[who are] untroubled about how it goes with the world, [who need] not mix with it, [and whose work is to preserve] this possession of the truth. How things turn out [in the world] is not our affair.[3]

As Hegel saw things, theologians in his day, commonly although not universally, had come to believe that rational cognition is essentially restricted to the finite world, the domain of 'contingent occurrence.' This means that any supposed knowledge of

God would take on the form of 'subjective reflection,' and thus be limited to considerations of our relations to God, or at best to affirmations of the claim that God is, as contrasted with assertions concerning what God is. Genuine philosophy overcomes the erroneous belief about the nature of cognition just mentioned, and thus offers itself as a place where religion can take refuge. But philosophy has its own limitations. The philosopher is in the business of inquiring into, attaining, and preserving truth. The philosopher is not trying to affect the course of the world. Thus the philosopher is not in the business of directly addressing the problems that arise in the world in the absence of religious truth. Assuming possession of that truth, philosophers can only preserve it and wait for better days, when persons whose business it is to address those problems want to avail themselves of it.

On our contemporary scene, I think it is very difficult to imagine philosophy playing the role that Hegel assigns to it. A philosopher might consider claims regarding the Trinity, the Incarnation, or the Resurrection and the indwelling of the Spirit, as those are interpreted by some other philosopher, for instance Hegel, for the sake of assessing some basic philosophical position that that philosopher puts forward in his interpretation of those claims. It is hard to conceive of a contemporary philosopher, acting precisely in his or her role as a philosopher, examining such claims simply in terms of questions about their meaning and truth. This means that part of the role that Hegel assigned to philosophy in his day must in our day be taken up by theology, if it is to be taken up at all. Today, only theologians can fulfill an important part of the philosophical project that Hegel defines.

Hegel invites today's theologians to undertake that project. He argues that the conditions of the possibility of undertaking that project are in place. He urges today's theologians to undertake that project, by arguing that only if this is done can the possibilities of reason be fulfilled and the demands of reason be satisfied. He requires that theologians equip themselves with the philosophical and other resources necessary for undertaking this project. Doing this in a contemporary way would bring about a new integration of philosophy and theology without absorbing either discipline into the other. The invitation that

Hegel extends to today's theologians is a kind of anticipation of Bernard Lonergan's twentieth-century proposal regarding an integration of strictly philosophical considerations of God and the theological specialization that Lonergan calls systematics.[4]

But of course, any suggestions one might draw from Hegel about what I am calling an integration of philosophy and theology must be considered in the light of his proposal concerning the speculative reconceptualization of the religious representation. And it is quite possible to be critical of that proposal. For instance Raymond Keith Williamson, who is very sympathetic to Hegel, nonetheless believes that the speculative comprehension of the religious representation is supposed to replace obscurity with absolute clarity regarding the nature of God in and for Godself, whatever Hegel might suggest about preserving rather than annulling mystery. This makes faith or trust unnecessary, and that is unacceptable. 'Religious faith can never be turned into knowledge in that sense, and no endeavor, such as that undertaken by Hegel, can avoid the language of representation.'[5] Indeed, Williamson seems to claim, the obscurity regarding the divine nature that is due precisely to the form of the religious representation is an essential component of the understanding of divine transcendence that belongs to the content of the representation. So if speculative comprehension overcomes the form of the religious representation, it leaves behind, by implication at least, this aspect of the content of the religious representation. Appealing to Fackenheim, Williamson says that

> the truth of religious faith is that of 'a relation *between* the divine and the human, in which the divine is both *other* than the human and yet *inwardly related* to it,' and unless this truth is retained in philosophic thought, then Hegel's claim that the absolute religion contains the truth, but in an inadequate form, cannot be correct; and if this truth is retained in philosophic thought, then the form in which it is expressed in absolute religion must be true as well.[6]

Williamson seems to make a convincing case. But one must remember just what the fundamental problem is with the form of the religious representation, according to Hegel. Recall that

in 1827, while discussing the possibility that concepts can function as representations, Hegel says, 'But to the extent that they
are not analyzed internally and their distinctions are not posited
in the way in which they relate to one another, they belong to
[the realm of] representation.'[7] Representations convey meanings that have to do with differences and relations. The religious
representation conveys meanings that have to do with the difference between the world and God and the relation between the
world and God. But to the extent that the conveyance of these
meanings is formally representational, they are 'not analyzed
internally': the differences and relations 'are not posited,' they
do not receive explicit statement, analysis, and comprehension.
Thus something that belongs to the content of the representation is and must be unthought due to the form of the representation. And the something in question is most basic. It has to
do with the way in which the world is simultaneously different
from and related to God, and with the manner in which God is
simultaneously both different from and related to the world, that
is to say with the very being of the world and of God respectively. These are not matters that representational thinking can
address. Only genuinely conceptual thinking can address them.
To the extent that some development in the history of thought
does successfully address these matters, for example a theology,
it has ceased to be exclusively representational and become to
some degree, perhaps to a very great degree, genuinely conceptual. Speculative thinking can address these matters fully, in that
speculative thinking radicalizes the possibilities of conceptual
thinking by thinking through the very categories of difference,
relation, identity, unity, and other related categories, autono-
mously, systematically and down to their roots.

It is one thing to say that one can explicitly address questions about the difference between and the relation between the
world and God and God and the world through the resources
of speculative but not of representational thinking. It is another
thing to say that doing that replaces the obscurity that belongs
to representational thinking with fully clear and fully adequate
comprehension. The first statement does not entail the second. I
concede that Hegel often does or at least seems to associate these
views. But those who appropriate the resources that Hegel offers

for the sake of ongoing philosophical and theological inquiry need not do so. It is necessarily the case that some specific sort of obscurity that does belong to what Hegel calls representational thinking is surpassed in speculative comprehension. But that in of itself does not mean that speculative comprehension coincides with fully clear and adequate cognition. I tried to discuss why that might be in the comments on speculative thought and mystery in the previous chapter. Hegel does seem to make a powerful case for the importance and the necessity of attaining comprehension regarding the issues of the difference and the relation between the world and God and God and the world, and the specific but essential shortcoming that belongs to religious thought insofar as that thought is exclusively representational and thus incapable of addressing these issues and achieving that comprehension.

If this is so, then Williamson cannot be right in maintaining that the true lesson to be learned from Hegel has to do with the difference between symbols and myths that are taken literally and symbols that myths that are recognized for what they are, 'broken myths.' Williamson believes that the Hegelian concept of spirit itself, when applied to God, is a symbol rather than a philosophical concept in the strict sense. He says that 'no linguistic expression or concept devised by finite man can embrace ultimate reality: all our expressions and concepts are nothing more than signs and symbols—"myths"—that can serve as suggestive models of the truth of that reality.'[8] This is too hasty. What would it be for a concept to 'embrace' a reality? This is itself an image in need of conceptual understanding. According to Hegel a concept, the content of an act of understanding, can and does have to do with a reality on its own terms, rather than through the mediation of a constitutive and metaphorical image. That does not entail that the act of understanding in question comprehends the reality it intends with full, unqualified clarity and adequacy. Only conceptual thinking can deal adequately and critically with the matters of relation and difference, and the issues associated with them. If our thinking about God and the world is in the last analysis confined to operating with symbols and broken myths, then we cannot think adequately about the difference between and the relation between God and the world.

I agree with Williamson that 'Hegel's philosophy of religion is characterized by ambiguity; it is very understandable that a variety of interpretations have been imposed upon it, not least that which sees Hegel as having, either unintentionally or deliberately, moved away from Christianity.'[9] I have already tried, although briefly, to comment on aspects of ambiguity in Hegel's interpretation of Christianity. But the problematic aspects of Hegel's philosophy of religion and Christianity do not reside in the most essential claims he makes concerning the possibility and necessity of a philosophical reconceptualization of the religious representation. The lesson to be learned from Hegel is not that, in the last analysis, all our discourse and thought about God is mythological and symbolic. The lesson is rather that both symbolic and genuinely conceptual discourse and thought about God are possible and necessary, and that thought can be genuinely conceptual thought without entailing claims about utter clarity and adequacy and about fully overcoming mystery in a robust sense of that word. I believe that a return to the understanding of analogical predication, which speaks of concepts that are truly concepts rather than images, symbols, or metaphors, and also truly analogical, rather than univocal or equivocal, would assist in clarifying this lesson.

If the case I have just tried to present is correct, then Hegel offers to contemporary philosophy of religion and theology the idea of a twofold hermeneutic of religious discourse. That hermeneutic would approach religious discourse with the recognition that that discourse integrates contrasting dimensions. It would endeavor to understand religious discourse insofar as that discourse operates with constitutive symbols and elaborates those symbols through a variety of literary genres, including narration. And it would endeavor to understand that discourse insofar as it presents or suggests understandings that have to do in the last analysis with the very being of the world and of God. Borrowing and adapting language from Paul Ricoeur, I will call the first of these endeavors a hermeneutics of the poetic dimension of religious discourse.[10] Robert Neville speaks of a 'metaphysical hermeneutic,'[11] an expression that I find most helpful in referring to the second endeavor just mentioned, and of speaking of the lesson I noted above. Hegel shows that religious discourse presents contemporary philosophers and theologians with the conditions of the possibility and necessity of a hermeneutic of its poetic dimension and of a metaphysical hermeneutic that would address questions having to do with the being of the world and of God, and that would develop or recover the categories that would allow one to pursue understanding of the fundamental Christian doctrines that have to do with those questions.

Karl Rahner suggests a specific theological issue that seems to call for a metaphysical hermeneutic of the sort that Hegel recommends, although he rejects the idea that Hegel might be helpful in considering that issue. In discussing the doctrine of the Incarnation, Rahner asserts that 'God can become something, he who is unchangeable in himself can *himself* become subject to change *in something else*.'[12] He notes that 'The formal truth of the oneness of God is not denied by the doctrine of the Trinity.'[13] Then he adds that

> The mystery of the incarnation must lie in God himself:
> in the fact that he, through unchangeable 'in himself',
> can become something 'in another'. The immutability
> of God is a dialectical truth like the unity of God. These
> two truths only—de facto—retain their validity for us
> when we think at once of the other two truths (of the
> trinity and the incarnation). But *we* cannot think and may
> not think of either as prior to the other.[14]

Rahner concludes his remark by saying, 'This we can and must affirm, without being Hegelians. And it would be a pity if Hegel had to teach Christians such things.'[15] I do not know why Rahner is compelled to say this, given that he is speaking about dialectical truths, and about the being that a thing has 'in-itself' as contrasted with the being 'in another' of that same thing. Hegel seems precisely the philosopher who can help us learn to think carefully and well with categories like these, and to use them in the pursuit of and in the articulation of understanding.

I truly do not know if this proposal that Rahner presents regarding an understanding of the Incarnation is supportable. I present it as a hypothesis, and offer the additional hypothesis that, if this belief or one that resembles it is supportable, its productive formulation and defense would employ Hegelian categories and distinctions.

In addition to a specific theological issue like the one I just mentioned, the very basic issue of divine transcendence is just the sort of issue to which a metaphysical hermeneutic is suited. I have already given a somewhat extensive discussion of this issue in relation to Hegel's understanding of creation. There, I tried to show the plausibility of an understanding of Hegel's position concerning the relation between God and the world that preserves the idea of divine transcendence, by responding to criticisms of Hegel in this regard made on his contemporary scene and on our contemporary scene. Now, even though I refer again to criticisms of Hegel, I want to argue directly that he provides and employs resources that make possible a plausible and powerful understanding of divine transcendence. Providing and employing these resources is a key contribution of the metaphysical hermeneutic that Hegel's philosophical comprehension of religion and Christianity recommends.

Recall that, for Hegel, one comes to an understanding of the nature of the being of the world and of God by understanding the most fundamental ways in which the world differs from God and is related to God, and by understanding the most fundamental ways in which God differs from and is related to the world. God differs from the world in that God is unqualifiedly self-subsistent and self-determining. Hegel conceptualizes this understanding by maintaining that God is absolute substance and absolute spirit. Absolute, in this context, means 'not relative.' God is not substance and spirit in any relative or qualified sense, but in an utterly unqualified manner. If so, then God is unqualifiedly self-subsistent and self-determining. The being of the world, in turn, is at its roots a received being, a kind of 'borrowed being,' Hegel says at one point, and thus most fundamentally determined by divine creativity.

This means, as previously noted, that the world has the being that is its own wholly in the context of its relation to God. The relation of the world to itself, to put the point in terms that the Hegelian analysis suggests, is wholly encompassed by the relation of the world to something other than itself, namely by the relation of the world to God. God in turn is, as creator of the world, related to the world. At the same time, since God is absolutely self-subsistent and self-determining, God's relation to the world is wholly encompassed by God's relation to God's own self. To put this point in terms the Hegelian analysis suggests, God's creation of the world belongs without reservation to God's unqualified and eternal self-determination.

According to William Desmond, the last statement about divine self-determination, if we affirm it, makes it impossible for us to recognize that 'as creatures, we ourselves are derivative, and hence not on a par with the origin.'[16] There must be, Desmond maintains, an essentially asymmetrical relation between creator and creatures. In view of this necessary asymmetry,

> we as derived beings cannot be identified with the
> origin, otherwise we would be underived and absolutely
> original, or else self-derived, or perhaps an expression
> of the ultimate's own self-derivation. In so far as Hegel
> does not respect the being of asymmetrical difference that
> follows from the very essence of being created, he moves
> ambiguously in these directions, and especially the last
> possibility.[17]

I fully agree with Desmond regarding the necessarily asymmetrical relations that must obtain between creator and creatures. But the statements I have most recently made about differences and relations between God and the world, which are strongly supported by texts from Hegel's published and unpublished writings, and which employ essentially Hegelian conceptions, assert an essential asymmetry. According to those statements, what one might call a fundamental ontological autonomy in God has as its compliment a fundamental ontological heteronomy in creatures. The differences and relations whose integration comprises what one might call the unity of God and the world are such that a most basic and unsurpassable ontological asymmetry obtains within that unity.

However this does not in and of itself resolve the issue. Insofar as one claims that creation belongs to divine self-determination, as Hegel does and as I have suggested, might one not then say that creatures are themselves a dimension, indeed a necessary dimension, of self-determining divine life, and for that reason not 'other' than God in the way that ontological asymmetry would require?

If this is a problem for Hegel, it is, according to Wolfhart Pannenberg, a problem that is widely shared.

> For as long as the freedom of God is thought of as a
> faculty of the divine being, who is asserted to be free,
> but who is himself the basis of the act of freedom, then
> the act of God's freedom is bound to appear either as
> something additional and external to his being, or as
> an expression of his being, his power, and thus as a
> manifestation of his self-identity, that is, as a necessity
> inherent in it. The traditional theological doctrine of
> God has no solution to this dilemma. Hegel shares with
> it the acceptance of an absolute being which already
> exists before the act of divine freedom. . . . One can
> scarcely reproach Hegel for taking the doctrine of God
> held in theology in a more strictly literal fashion than it
> did itself, by trying to think the freedom of God as the
> expression of his being, which was supposedly prior to its
> freedom, so that freedom was a manifestation of God's
> being. One may be justified in feeling unhappy at this,
> but the reproach must be directed in the first instance not
> at Hegel, but to the insoluble problem which exists here
> in the traditional doctrine of God, and which he did not
> succeed in removing.[18]

I do not readily disagree with Wolfhart Pannenberg. But in this case, there is an option in the history of theology, one of whose representatives is Aquinas, to which he does not refer. Aquinas speaks of divine freedom by speaking of God's will, just as he speaks of divine knowledge by speaking of God's intellect. Ordinarily 'intellect' and 'will' denote faculties. But this is not and cannot be the case regarding God. It cannot be the case because God is pure, unqualified, self-subsistent act of being. There can be no potency in such a being. But faculties are potencies. Therefore God's intellect, and for present purposes more importantly God's will, cannot be faculties that belong to

God. Rather, God's intellect and God's will are identical with God's being. I must say that I have an intellect and that I have a will. Aquinas maintains that God is God's intellect and that God is God's will. So the 'act of divine freedom' is not an expression of God's being. It is God's being.

It would be too weak to say that this is a position that Hegel can hold. It is a position that he does and must hold. According to Hegel, God is, as substance, unqualifiedly self-subsistent, and as spirit, unqualifiedly self-determining and self-manifesting. The first claim requires, if the matter is raised at all, that there is no potency in God. Taken in conjunction with the second claim, it requires that God's being be identical with God's self-determination and self-manifestation.

Now take these positions in conjunction with the assumption of a trinitarian doctrine that presents, in relation to the different persons of the Trinity, an otherness that is 'serious,' to use Hegel's word, with the implication that there is no deficiency in the being of God in and for itself with regard to the concept of recognition that the idea of spirit presents. It would be very easy to develop the outlines of such a doctrine on the basis of resources that Bonaventure offers, or for that matter on the basis of resources that Aquinas offers, and in the light of principles essential to Hegel's speculative philosophy. Given this, creation is not required for the unlimited and unqualified actuality of the being of God, given a conception of that being through the ideas of substance and spirit. At the same time, God is the creator of the world. Since God is unqualifiedly self-determining, being creator belongs to God's self-determining being. Moreover, since God is God's freedom, God determines Godself from all eternity to create the world. Because of God's own eternal, self-determining freedom, God cannot fail to create the world. But the full actuality of God's self-determining being still does not require creation. Therefore creation doe not represent any sense of 'the ultimate's own self-derivation,' to use Desmond's language, required by a deficiency in divine being considered apart from creation. If so, then the being of God is, in God's connection with the world, still utterly self-subsistent, self-determining, and self-related, whereas the being of the world is at its roots received and thus entirely encompassed by the relation of the world to God. The asymmetry in relations between God and the world that I previously asserted is retained and demonstrated.

This, of course means, that, in the relations that there are between God and the world, the otherness of God and the world from each other is preserved. But this needs a stronger statement. God is emphatically transcendent in connection with the world in that God, in God's relation with the world, is unqualifiedly self-subsistent, self-determining, and self-related, and inasmuch as, on the account I have developed, the being of God is infinitely and unqualifiedly actual apart from a consideration of God as creator, even though, on account of the eternal identity of God's being with God's freedom, we cannot conceive of God truly unless we conceive of God as creator. This transcendence is necessarily associated with the most profound immanence, just because the very being of the world depends at its roots on the presence in and to the world of God. This gives us a conception of divine transcendence that derives its power in part but essentially from the integration of the concepts of transcendence and immanence that it requires.

Would Hegel recognize his own thinking in this conception? Because I think Williamson is right in attributing ambiguities to Hegel's philosophical theology, I do not believe that, for us, an unambiguous answer to this question is possible. It is hard for us to know what we should say, and of course we will never know what Hegel would have said. But he certainly would have recognized that the fundamental principles that belong to the conceptions of divine transcendence that I have sketched are ones that genuinely belong to his own speculative philosophy, and are principles that he at least sometimes employed as I have employed them. Therefore one can argue that it would have been right for Hegel to recognize this conception as a plausible implementation of those principles. Moreover, it is those principles themselves that, in philosophical terms, render this conception itself plausible, while at the same time allowing elements of that conception to be derived by way of an appropriation of aspects of classical theology. That the principles of Hegel's philosophy open out to appropriations of classical theology and make possible the development of a powerful as well as plausible conception of divine transcendence indicates the productive role those principles can play in contemporary philosophical and theological inquiry.

There is still one more step to be taken in this consideration of a Hegelian formulation of the conception of divine transcendence. This step makes the integration of the concepts of transcendence and immanence that belongs to that conception even more emphatic. I pointed out in Chapter 2, by way of appealing to the *Phenomenology*, that for Hegel the historical and social self-production of humanity is to be understood as the historical production of reason and human self-understanding. To be somewhat more concrete, the history of humanity is the history of our relating to and transforming nature so that developing human needs can be satisfied and so that human life can both continue and flourish. It is simultaneously the history of our relating to ourselves by forming and transforming the social relations that obtain among us, so that we may become able and better able to produce and distribute what we need and want, govern our social lives, experience and articulate meaning, and live in ways in which it is good for us to live and as we ought to live. The process is long, laborious, and hardly even. If there are steps forward, there are many steps back and many steps that lead nowhere at all and finally are abandoned. But over the very long run, Hegel maintains, the steps forward prevail in however halting a way, so that a kind of progress can be discerned in human history.

As we develop the ability to do the things just mentioned, humanity develops itself. Human history is the history of the social self-production of humanity. Developing the ability to do the things just mentioned involves learning how to do them and developing the ability more efficiently and effectively to learn how to do them. The social self-production of humanity is to be interpreted as the historical production of thought and understanding. Historically produced understanding is, in its most essential aspect, human self-understanding. As we work on and transform nature, and as we form and transform social relations, we are doing what we as human beings uniquely can do. Humankind is becoming what humankind is and can be in the world. We human beings are becoming ourselves. As we learn how to do these things and learn to learn more effectively, we are learning about the historically realized capacities that belong to us as human beings. We are developing through our own activities, producing, our understanding of ourselves.

A moment of the production of our understanding of ourselves is the production of an understanding of understanding itself. Indeed it is possible to say, and Hegel would say, that the understanding of understanding itself is the most radical moment of our self-understanding. We are most basically the human beings that we are, a species capable of historical, social self-production, insofar as we can and do learn how to do the things that our self-production requires. If for this reason thought and understanding belong most basically to human beings, then the most basic moment in human self-understanding is the understanding of understanding. For the sake of referring to thought and understanding in its fullest and most authentic form, Hegel uses the term 'reason.' Given this, one can say that the history of the social self-production of humankind is the history of the production of reason. The fullest development of reason requires comprehension of rational understanding itself. Philosophy has this as its goal, insofar as philosophy is, in the most substantial possible sense, thinking about thinking. Therefore philosophy, precisely in this sense, belongs to the pinnacle of human self-understanding.

We understand things by understanding the differences and relations that determine the identities of those things. We understand ourselves by understanding our identities in connection with the different individuals with whom we are associated in relations of recognition. We understand the state by understanding the identity that belongs to the state in virtue of its difference from and relations to the institutions of the family and civil society. We understand rational cognition by understanding the differences and relations that obtain between understanding, dialectic, and reason. We understand the being of God and of the world by understanding the differences and relations that most fundamentally obtain between God and the world.

From 1807 on, Hegel maintained that the social world, the context that belongs to and that allows for the formation of what it means to be human, presents in every moment of its development some representation of the divine. Divine reality is supposed to differ from human reality and is supposed to be the absolute reality to which human reality stands in a most fundamental relation. Therefore, human self-understanding most fundamentally comes about with reference to an understanding of the differences and relations that obtain between human beings and divine reality. The latter understanding, of course, takes form in the light of the consciousness of the nature of divine reality that persons have attained, however restricted or substantial that consciousness might be.

Thus Hegel cites with approval a statement that Karl Friedrich Göschel made in *Aphorismen über Nichtwissen und absolutes Wissen im Verhähtnisse zur christlichen Glaubenserkenntnis*, a book that Hegel most favorably reviewed in 1829.

> The question, What is man? stands in such reciprocity
> with the question, What is God? that with one the other
> would also be answered,—for with both questions we are
> really asking nothing other than, *What is God in relation to
> man? What is man in relation to God?*[19]

Hegel goes on to insist that the claims made in the text just cited stand opposed to the view that our knowledge extends to knowledge of our relation to God but not to God in Godself. That is because, he maintains, we can only have knowledge of our relation to God if we have knowledge of the God to whom we are related. Furthermore, if God stands in relation to human beings, then that is a characteristic that belongs as such to God's being. Thus, to understand 'God in relation to man' is to understand God as such.

Moreover, any human self-understanding that is formed in the context of an understanding of our relation to God and God's relation to us is, to the extent of the adequacy of the understanding of those relations, a kind of participation in divine self-knowledge.

> God, as being in Godself, is knowledge of Godself
> in Godself—Self-consciousness of God; as being in
> others, God is self-knowing outside of Godself—the
> consciousness of God—in the world, in individual beings
> as creatures of God.[20]

God's being is identical with God's self-knowledge. Our consciousness of God, again to the extent that at least some adequacy belongs to that consciousness, is a kind of presence of divine self-knowledge in us. Additionally, our consciousness of God undergoes historical development. Therefore one can say that the presence of divine self-knowledge in us develops in us. This of course has as its correlate the development of human self-understanding. If so, then human self-understanding develops along with the development of the divine self-knowledge that is present in us. This does not entail that the knowledge that God has of Godself as such develops in us. It is our participation in divine self-knowledge that develops, just as our self-understanding develops along with it. But the participation is a real participation, Hegel maintains.

According to Hegel, we arrive most fully and decisively at knowledge of God in the light of revelation. It is in virtue of the revelation that determines the consummate religion that we know God as self-manifesting subject, that is, as spirit. Hegel believes that human self-understanding is perfected as a correlate of the proper and perfected understanding of this revelation. Nonetheless, any consciousness of God that is in any way adequate is to that extent a participation in divine self-knowledge, a moment of the presence of divine self-knowledge in us. Moreover, divine self-knowledge coincides with divine being. And human self-understanding develops as a correlate of the development of human consciousness of God. Thus divine self-knowledge and divine being are present in and to human beings in history, in correlation with the development of human self-understanding.

This idea intensifies the concept of divine immanence that stands in a reciprocal relationship with the concept of divine transcendence, and thus the concept of transcendence as well. God is present in and to all creatures as the creator and conserver of the being of creatures. God is historically present in and to human beings in that the consciousness of God that stands in most fundamental correlation with human self-understanding is a participation in divine self-knowledge. Through this participation divine self-knowledge, which is to say divine being, is present in or related to itself in us. With these ideas in mind, consider once again the propositions that Hegel derives from Göschel and asserts in the *Encyclopedia*.

> God is God only insofar as he knows himself: his self-knowledge is, further, a self-consciousness in man and man's knowledge *of* God, which proceeds to man's self-knowledge *in* God.

Human knowledge of God coincides with a kind of presence of divine self-consciousness in human beings and in human history, that is to say, with a kind of divine indwelling. This in turn leads to the human self-understanding that is possible in virtue of our knowledge of the relation in which we stand to God, which of course is inseparable from knowledge of God. Taken together, these statements, I believe allow one to say that to come upon and develop a fundamental and genuine self-understanding is to encounter God within us, whether that is or is not recognized. At the same time, God is God only insofar as God knows Godself. That is to say, divine self-knowledge coincides with the being that belongs to God on account of Godself alone. Then that self-knowledge is, 'further,' a presence of divine self-consciousness in human beings.

Of the many questions that must arise in view of the preceding remarks I will consider only one. Hegel assigns Christianity the status of the consummate religion because he identifies Christianity as the religion of revelation. He always associates that revelation most centrally with the Incarnation, and insists that this revelation is unique. At the same time, some explicit consciousness of God develops throughout the course of human history, and Hegel holds that such a consciousness indicates the presence in and to human beings of divine self-knowledge. Does this not suggest that revelation is available in a variety of religions, and argue against identifying any one of them as the consummate religion?

Peter Hodgson responds affirmatively to this question in his discussion of Hegel's treatment of 'Determinate Religion' in the different iterations of the *Lectures*. Under the heading 'Determinate Religion,' Hegel discusses particular historical religious traditions and forms of life, as contrasted with discussions of the essential 'Concept of Religion,' on the one hand, and with

'The Consummate Religion' on the other hand. Because this book deals with the treatment of Christianity in Hegel's philosophy of religion I have barely given a nod to the discussion of determinate religion. Nor is this the occasion for a substantive treatment of the issue. Hodgson gives a thoroughly informed and excellent discussion of the matter in *Hegel and Christian Theology* that I most strongly recommend, even though I will disagree with the response Hodgson gives to the question just mentioned.

Along with Walter Jaeschke, Hodgson maintains that, in fact, in the discussion of 'Determinate Religion' Hegel presents a typology of religious forms rather than a history of religion in the strict sense.

> To be sure, religion is fundamentally historical, but its historicality follows from the historicality of the human spirit. Since there is no single history of the human spirit, there cannot be a single, unified history of religion. At best, what we can attain is a history of religions, or better, histories of religions—diversity of histories that cannot be organized under a single, encompassing philosophical conceptuality. Hegel's claim to do this is falsified by his actual achievement in the successive lectures, which should have made it clear that the objective of a logical construction of the history of religion cannot be attained. What Hegel gives us is a typology of shapes in which spirit appears in religious history and by which it develops, but these shapes need not, indeed cannot, be linked to a unitary history directed to a common goal.[21]

Hodgson believes that the implication of a typological account of determinate religions, as he understands it, is that one cannot claim that any single religion is the consummate religion. He takes this belief to find confirmation in contemporary interreligious dialogue, and to be the logical outcome of Hegel's speculative philosophy of religion, Hegel's own interpretation of that outcome notwithstanding.

> The concept of religion comes to completion in different ways in a diversity of historical shapes. God disperses

Godself into the world as absolving spirit and is known in the mode of dispersal rather than finality. The claim for a single perfect or final religion is as specious as the claim for a single savior figure. Hegel's philosophy of religion really shows why in history God is revealed and encountered only in the mode of dispersal.[22]

The interpretation of Hegel's treatment of determinate religions as a typology is entirely plausible, and the claim about the impossibility of a consummate religion may seem to follow from that. But recall Hegel's reason for referring to Christianity as the consummate religion. He maintains that the Incarnation, God's uniting of Godself with a single human being, exhibits the fullest possible self-manifestation of God as spirit. He also holds that this can occur only once, since this revelation must present itself as something that is given to, and thus that stands over against, all other human beings. Should one find that argument less than fully convincing, another is available. According to Hegel the Incarnation exhibits, let us say, the fullness of divine self-revelation. If any revelation exhibits the fullness of revelation, it can be the only one that does so, since if there were two or more, each would differ from the other and therefore would be, by way of contrast with the others, other than full. Two revelations would not be like two glasses of water. Two different glasses of water can be completely full. Two different revelations cannot be. One can criticize this argument by questioning the legitimacy of the concept of 'the fullness of revelation.' But if one has a reason to maintain the legitimacy of the concept, then the argument stands. And if one has any reason to maintain that the Christological event exhibits the fullness of revelation, then something like Hegel's claim that the central revelation that Christianity receives is consummate in nature becomes to that extent plausible.

Further, Hodgson's argument about the very possibility of identifying Christianity as the consummate religion follows from an understanding of the Christological event as a paradigmatic disclosure, to use Yerkes' terms. They at least implicitly affirm what Schubert Ogden calls an understanding of the Christ event as an event that 'in no way constitutes the possibility of salvation but only *represents* it.'[23] Ogden argues for a position on religious truth according to which it is at least possible that a plurality of religions can present that truth in an essentially normative fashion.[24] He says that this position requires the Christological understanding just mentioned. The position is quite similar to the one that Hodgson recommends. But if there are reasons to prefer an alternative Christological understanding, this position is imperiled.

This, however, in no way settles the question about religious truth and pluralism. Since Hegel maintains that any consciousness of God that is in any way adequate participates to that extent in divine self-knowledge, he implies that a diversity of forms of religious consciousness at least can present religious truth. Moreover, one needs to distinguish between the revelation that Christianity receives, and the reception of that revelation. It may sometimes or often be the case that the reception on the part of Christendom of the revelation that has been given to it falls far short of that revelation itself. In that case, it is at least possible that other religious traditions sometimes or often present, quite independently, the truth about, or some aspect of the truth about, God and humanity far more fully than historical Christianity does.

There seem to be two implications of the preceding discussion. First, Hegel's own view regarding the relation between Christianity and other religions challenges contemporary philosophers and theologians who are so minded to define a position that both allows for a conception of Christianity as the consummate religion, or as least as defined by a consummate revelation, and understands the conditions of the possibility of the truth of a diversity of religious standpoints. Hegel's view also offers some important resources for an inquiry concerned with that position. It is unquestionable that contemporary empirical and linguistic resources for inquiry concerning comparative religions are vastly superior to those available in Hegel's day. But the conceptual resources he offers are still productive for that inquiry.

Second, in concrete terms the question about religious truth and pluralism, when integrated with the question concerning the relation of Christianity to other religions, cannot be resolved exclusively in philosophical terms. As indicated above, this question requires the adjudication of alternative Christologies, and this is a theological issue. Previously I proposed that basic aspects of the program that Hegel outlines for a speculative philosophy of religion can, today, be undertaken only by theologians. Now I propose that at least one basic question that arises on the contemporary scene in the light of Hegel's philosophy of religion, can be resolved only if theological inquiry does and is allowed to contribute to that resolution.

These comments indicate at least some aspects of the essential contribution that theological inquiry can make to the line of thought that Hegel developed in philosophy during his lifetime. Other comments, in this chapter and through this book, suggest the productive role that Hegelian philosophy can play in contemporary inquiry in philosophy of religion and theology. In addition, Hegel issues challenges. He challenges us to inquire substantively and comprehensively into the phenomenon of religion; to respond fully in our inquiry to the complexity of religious discourse, integrating existential, poetic, and conceptual dimensions in the interpretation of that discourse; to recover the metaphysical conceptuality that alone makes it possible to address the matters with which philosophy and theology most centrally deal; and to probe in all its complexity the difficulty of issue of the nature of religious truth.

The resources that Hegel offers to contemporary inquiry and the challenges that he presents to us are both aspects of the promise that Barth foresaw in the possibility that Hegel's thought might assume a prominent place in contemporary theological investigation. They point to an effort not only directed toward understanding diverse conceptual possibilities, but also and even more importantly at coming to terms with truth. That, Hegel maintained, is the goal that must, in the last analysis, orient inquiry, and that we always need to be pressing toward. Certain interpretations notwithstanding, he never conceived of anything like an end of philosophy or of rational inquiry, a condition in which truth had been attained in a way that made further efforts at seeking it dispensable. Thought and inquiry must be ongoing. To the extent that thought and inquiry are not concerned with truth they fall short of their best possibilities. To the extent that an effort at coming to terms with the truth does orient thought and inquiry, they aim at the goal that Hegel believed to be most noble and most necessary. There are reasons to join him in this view. After all, he was not alone in believing that it is truth that frees us.

Notes

Introduction

1. Karl Barth, *Protestant Theology in the Nineteenth Century* (trans. Brian Cozens and John Bowden; Grand Rapids, Michigan/Cambridge, U.K.: 2002), p. 370.
2. Ibid., p. 406.
3. Ibid., p. 382.
4. Ibid., p. 381.
5. Ibid., p. 405.
6. Ibid., p. 376.
7. Ibid., p. 407.
8. G. W. F. Hegel, *The Encyclopedia Logic* (trans. T. F. Geraets, W. A. Suchting, and H. S. Harris; Indianapolis/Cambridge: Hackett, 1991), p. 6. G. W. F. Hegel, *Werke* (eds. E Moldenhauer and K. M. Michel; 20 vols; Frankfurt: Suhrkamp, 1986), vol. 8, p. 17.
9. Hegel, *Encyclopedia I*, p. 11; *Werke*, vol. 8, pp. 23–24. Italics in the original texts.
10. Hegel, *Encyclopedia I*, p. 12; *Werke*, vol. 8, p. 24.
11. Terry Pinkard, *Hegel: A Biography* (Cambridge: Cambridge University Press, 2000).
12. Jacques D'Hondt, *Hegel in His Time: Berlin, 1818–1831* (trans. John Burbidge; Peterborough and Lewiston: Broadview Press Ltd., 1988).
13. Peter Hodgson, *Hegel and Christian Theology* (Oxford: Oxford University Press, 2005), pp. 3–72.
14. Hegel's early writings on religion and Christianity are collected in Herman Nohl (ed.), *Hegel's Theologische Jugendschriften* (Tübingen: J. C. B. Mohr, 1907). English translations of these writings appear in Peter Fuss and John Dobbins (ed. and trans.), *Hegel: Three Essays, 1793–1795* (Notre Dame, Ind.: University of Notre Dame Press, 1984), and T. M. Knox and Richard Kroner, *Friedrich Hegel: Early Theological Writings* (New York: Harper, 1961).
15. *Early Theological Writings*, p. 68. Nohl, p. 153.
16. *Three Essays*, pp. 115–116, translation modified. Nohl, p. 87.
17. *Three Essays*, p. 112. Nohl, p. 87.
18. *Three Essays*, p. 108. Nohl, p. 80.

Notes

19. *Three Essays*, p. 114. Nohl, p. 85.
20. *Early Theological Writings,* p. 174. Nohl, p. 144.
21. See *Early Theological Writings*, pp. 145–151. Nohl, pp. 214–219.
22. *Early Theological Writings*, p. 232. Nohl, p. 282.
23. *Early Theological Writings*, p. 182. Nohl, p. 244.
24. H. S. Harris, *Hegel's Development: Towards the Sunlight, 1770–1801* (Oxford: Clarendon Press, 1972), p. 326.
25. G. W. F. Hegel, *Vorlesungen über die Philosophie der Religion* (Walter Jaeschke [ed.]; 3 vols; Hamburg: Felix Meiner Verlag, 1983–85, 1993–95). G. W. F. Hegel, *Lectures on the Philosophy of Religion* (Peter C. Hodgson [ed.]; R. F. Brown, P. C. Hodgson, and J. M. Stewart with the assistance of H. S. Harris [trans.]; 3 vols; Berkeley and Los Angeles: University of California Press, 1984–87; Oxford: Oxford University Press, 2006). Subsequent citations from the *Lectures,* unless otherwise noted, will be to the 1993–95 German edition and the 1984–87 English translation.
26. Hodgson, *Hegel and Christian Theology*, p. 4.

Chapter 1

1. G. W. F. Hegel, *The Difference Between Fichte's and Schelling's System of Philosophy* (H. S. Harris and Walter Cerf [eds. and trans.]; Albany: State University of New York Press, 1977), p. 89; *Werke*, vol. 2, p. 20.
2. *Phenomenology*, p. 46; *Werke*, vol. 3, p. 68.
3. See *Phenomenology*, p. 47; *Werke*, vol. 3, pp. 69–70.
4. *Phenomenology*, p. 49; *Werke*, vol. 3, p. 71.
5. *Phenomenology*, p. 48; *Werke*, vol. 3, p. 71.
6. *Phenomenology*, p. 49; *Werke*, vol. 3, p. 72.
7. *Phenomenology*, p. 54; *Werke*, vol. 3, p. 78.
8. *Phenomenology*, p. 56; *Werke*, vol. 3, p. 80.
9. *Phenomenology*, p. 53; *Werke*, vol. 3, p. 78.
10. *Phenomenology*, p. 49; *Werke*, vol. 3, p. 72.
11. Ibid.
12. *Phenomenology*, p. 50; *Werke*, vol. 3, p. 73.
13. *Phenomenology*, p. 105; *Werke*, vol. 3, p. 138.
14. *Phenomenology,* p. 105; *Werke*, vol. 3, p. 139.
15. *Phenomenology*, p. 104; *Werke*, vol. 3, p. 138.
16. These comments only briefly refer to the important concept of 'life' that emerges in the transition from the dialectic of 'Understanding' to the introductory comments on self-consciousness in the *Phenomenology,* and that Hegel develops in those comments. It is not possible to more fully comment on this significant concept in the context of these remarks on absolute knowing.
17. See *Phenomenology*, pp. 109–110; *Werke*, vol. 3, pp. 143–144.
18. *Phenomenology*, p. 106; *Werke,* vol. 3, p. 140.

Notes

19. See *Phenomenology*, pp. 111–112; *Werke*, vol. 3, pp. 145–147. Robert R. Williams, *Recognition: Fichte and Hegel on The Other* (Albany: State University of New York Press, 1992), pp. 149–160, gives an alternative translation of and a most insightful commentary on this text.

20. *Phenomenology*, p. 142; *Werke*, vol. 3, p. 181.

21. *Phenomenology*, p. 110; *Werke*, vol. 3, p. 145.

22. *Phenomenology*, pp. 263–264; *Werke*, vol. 3, p. 325.

23. *Phenomenology*, p. 263; *Werke*, vol. 3, p. 324.

24. *Phenomenology*, p. 219; *Werke*, vol. 3, p. 273.

25. *Phenomenology*, p. 279; *Werke*, vol. 3, p. 342.

26. Joseph C. Flay, *Hegel's Quest for Certainty* (Albany: State University of New York Press, 1984), p. 224.

27. *Phenomenology*, p. 411; *Werke*, vol. 3, p. 497.

28. Quentin Lauer, *A Reading of Hegel's Phenomenology of Spirit* (New York: Fordham University Press, 1976), p. 232.

29. This statement, while true, does not fully represent the complexities of Hegel's understanding of rational knowing. For a fuller discussion in relation to the *Phenomenology* see Martin J. De Nys, 'Dimensions of Absolute Knowing,' *The Review of Metaphysics*.

30. Stephen Houlgate, *Freedom, Truth, and History: An Introduction to Hegel's Philosophy* (London and New York: Routledge, 1991), pp. 45, 57.

31. G. W. F. Hegel, *Philosophy of Right* (trans. T. M. Knox; Oxford: Oxford University Press, 1967), p. 10; *Werke*, vol. 7, p. 24.

32. *Phenomenology*, p. 488; *Werke*, vol. 3, p. 586.

33. Hegel, *Philosophy of Right*, p. 11; *Werke*, vol. 7, p. 26.

34. *Phenomenology*, p. 413; *Werke*, vol. 3, p. 498.

35. Ibid.

36. *Phenomenology*, p. 410; *Werke*, vol. 3, p. 495.

37. *Phenomenology*, p. 415; *Werke*, p. 501.

38. *Phenomenology*, 'Foreword,' p. xxvii.

39. G. W. F. Hegel, *The Encyclopedia Logic* (trans. T. F. Geraets, W. A. Suchting, and H. S. Harris; Indianapolis/Cambridge: Hackett, 1991), p. 56; *Werke*, vol. 8, p. 81.

40. Hegel, *Encyclopedia Logic*, p. 50; *Werke*, vol. 8, p. 74.

41. Hegel, *Encyclopedia Logic*, p. 50; *Werke*, vol. 8, p. 73.

42. Hegel, *Encyclopedia Logic*, p. 125; *Werke*, vol. 8, p. 169.

43. Hegel, *Encyclopedia Logic*, p. 126; *Werke*, vol. 8, p. 169.

44. Hegel, *Encyclopedia Logic*, p. 128; *Werke*, vol. 8, p. 172.

45. Hegel, *Encyclopedia Logic*, p. 129; *Werke*, vol. 8, p. 173.

46. Hegel, *Encyclopedia Logic*, p. 130; *Werke*, vol. 8, p. 174.

47. Hegel, *Encyclopedia Logic*, p. 131; *Werke*, vol. 8, p. 176.

48. Hegel, *Encyclopedia Logic*, p. 131; *Werke*, vol. 8, p. 177.

49. Hegel, *Encyclopedia Logic*, p. 52; *Werke*, vol. 8, p. 76.

50. Hegel, *Encyclopedia Logic*, p. 54; *Werke*, vol. 8, p. 78.

51. Ibid.

Notes

Chapter 2

1. Hegel, *Phenomenology*, p. 410; *Werke*, vol. 3, p. 495.
2. Hegel, *Phenomenology*, p. 396; *Werke*, vol. 3, p. 479.
3. Hegel, *Phenomenology*, p. 398; *Werke*, vol. 3, p. 482.
4. Hegel, *Phenomenology*, pp. 398, 399; *Werke*, vol. 3, pp. 482, 483.
5. Hegel, *Phenomenology*, p. 400; *Werke*, vol. 3, pp. 483, 484.
6. Hegel, *Phenomenology*, p. 405; *Werke*, vol. 3, p. 489.
7. Hegel, *Phenomenology*, p. 405; *Werke*, vol. 3, p. 490.
8. Ibid.
9. Hegel, *Phenomenology*, p. 408; *Werke*, p. 493.
10. Flay, *Hegel's Quest for Certainty*, p. 222.
11. Ibid., p. 223.
12. Ibid.
13. *Phenomenology*, p. 409; *Werke*, vol. 3, p. 494.
14. Emil Fackenheim, *The Religious Dimension in Hegel's Thought* (Bloomington and London: Indiana University Press, 1967), p. 66.
15. Flay, *Hegel's Quest for Certainty*, p. 385.
16. Jean Hyppolite, *Genesis and Structure of Hegel's Phenomenology of Spirit* (trans. Samuel Cherniak and John Heckman; Evanston: Northwestern University Press, 1974), p. 536.
17. Hegel, *Phenomenology*, p. 412; *Werke*, p. 497.
18. Hyppolite, *Genesis and Structure*, p. 538.
19. I follow Quentin Lauer in translating '*Die offenbare Religion*' as 'the religion of revelation.' See *A Reading of Hegel's Phenomenology of Spirit*, p. 234, n. 4.
20. Hegel, *Phenomenology*, p. 455; *Werke*, vol. 3, p. 547.
21. Ibid.
22. Hegel, *Phenomenology*, p. 458; *Werke*, vol. 3, p. 551.
23. Ibid.
24. Hegel, *Phenomenology*, p. 459; *Werke*, vol. 3, p. 552.
25. Ibid.
26. Ibid.
27. Hegel, *Phenomenology*, p. 461; *Werke*, vol. 3, p. 554.
28. Hegel, *Phenomenology*, p. 462; *Werke*, vol. 3, pp. 555–556.
29. Hegel, *Phenomenology*, p. 462; *Werke*, vol. 3, p. 556.
30. Hegel, *Phenomenology*, p. 464; *Werke*, vol. 3, p. 557.
31. Hegel, *Phenomenology*, p. 465; *Werke*, vol. 3, p. 559.
32. See ibid.
33. Hegel, *Phenomenology*, pp. 465–466; *Werke*, vol. 3, p. 560.
34. Hegel, *Phenomenology*, pp. 466–467; *Werke*, vol. 3, p. 561.
35. Cyril O'Regan, *The Heterodox Hegel* (Albany: State University of New York Press, 1994), p. 294.
36. Hegel, *Phenomenology*, p. 467; *Werke*, vol. 3, p. 561.
37. Hegel, *Phenomenology*, p. 467; *Werke*, vol. 3, p. 562.

Notes

38. Hegel, *Phenomenology*, p. 468; *Werke*, vol. 3, p. 562.

39. Hegel, *Phenomenology*, p. 468; *Werke*, vol. 3, pp. 562–563.

40. H. S. Harris, *Hegel's Ladder* (2 vols; Indianapolis/Cambridge: Hackett, 1997), vol. 2, p. 684.

41. Hegel, *Phenomenology*, p. 470; *Werke*, vol. 3, p. 564.

42. Hegel, *Phenomenology*, p. 471; *Werke*, vol. 3, p. 566.

43. Hegel, *Phenomenology*, p. 472; *Werke*, vol. 3, p. 567.

44. Hegel, *Phenomenology*, p. 474; *Werke*, vol. 3, p. 569.

45. Ibid.

46. Hegel, *Phenomenology*, p. 473; *Werke*, vol. 3, p. 568.

47. Hegel, *Phenomenology*, p. 475; *Werke*, vol. 3, p. 571.

48. Hegel, *Phenomenology*, p. 475; *Werke*, vol. 3, p. 570.

49. Hegel, *Phenomenology*, p. 483; *Werke*, vol. 3, p. 579.

50. Hegel, *Phenomenology*, p. 478; *Werke*, vol. 3, p. 573.

51. Lauer, *A Reading of Hegel's Phenomenology of Spirit*, p. 254.

52. Hegel, *Phenomenology*, p. 474; *Werke*, vol. 3, pp. 568–568.

53. Hegel, *Phenomenology*, p. 461; *Werke*, vol. 3, p. 554.

54. Hegel, *Phenomenology*, p. 467; *Werke*, vol. 3, p. 561.

55. Hegel, *Phenomenology*, p. 475; *Werke*, vol. 3, p. 570.

56. Ibid.

57. H. S. Harris, *Hegel's Ladder II*, pp. 719, 747.

58. Merold Westphal, *History and Truth in Hegel's Phenomenology* (Atlantic Highlands: Humanities Press, 1979), p. 194.

59. See Martin J. De Nys, 'Mediation and Negativity in Hegel's Phenomenology of Christian Consciousness,' *The Journal of Religion*, 66 (1986), pp. 46–67.

Chapter 3

1. Georg Wilhelm Friedrich Hegel, *Lectures on the Philosophy of Religion*, vol. 1, p. 116. G. W. F. Hegel, *Vorlesungen über die Philosophie der Religion*, Teil 1, p. 33.

2. Ibid.

3. Ibid.

4. Hegel, *Lectures*, vol. 1, p. 163; *Vorlesungen*, Teil 1, pp. 72–73.

5. Hegel, *Lectures*, vol. 1, p. 161; *Vorlesungen*, Teil 1, p. 71.

6. Ibid.

7. Ibid.

8. Hegel, *The Encyclopedia Logic*, p. 109; *Werke*, vol. 8, p. 149.

9. See *The Encyclopedia Logic*, p. 110; *Werke*, vol. 8, p. 149.

10. Hegel, *The Encyclopedia Logic*, p. 112; *Werke*, vol. 8, p. 153.

11. Hegel, *The Encyclopedia Logic*, p. 114; *Werke*, vol. 8, p. 155.

12. Hegel, *Lectures*, vol. 1, p. 136; *Vorlesungen*, Teil 1, pp. 50–51.

13. Hegel, *The Encyclopedia Logic*, p. 47; *Werke*, vol. 8, p. 70.

14. Ibid.

15. Hegel, *Lectures*, vol. 1, pp. 136–137; *Vorlesungen*, Teil 1, p. 51.
16. Hegel, *Lectures*, vol. 1, p. 122; *Vorlesungen*, Teil 1, p. 39.
17. Hegel, *Lectures*, vol. 1, p. 126; *Vorlesungen*, Teil 1, p. 43.
18. Hegel, *Lectures*, vol. 1, p. 127; *Vorlesungen*, Teil 1, p. 43.
19. Walter Jaeschke, 'Philosophical Theology and Philosophy of Religion,' in *New Perspectives on Hegel's Philosophy of Religion* (ed. David Kolb; Albany: State University of New York Press, 1992), p. 4.
20. Ibid., p. 3.
21. Hegel, *The Encyclopedia Logic*, p. 46; *Werke*, vol. 8, p. 68.
22. Hegel, *Lectures*, vol. 1, p. 386; *Vorlesungen*, Teil 1, p. 282.
23. Hegel, *Lectures*, vol. 1, pp. 386–387; *Vorlesungen*, Teil 1, p. 282.
24. Hegel, *Lectures*, vol. 1, p. 386; *Vorlesungen*, Teil 1, p. 282.
25. Hegel, *Lectures*, vol. 1, p. 388; *Vorlesungen*, Teil 1, p. 284.
26. Hegel, *Lectures,* vol. 1, p. 389; *Vorlesungen,* Teil 1, p. 284.
27. Hegel, *Lectures*, vol. 1, p. 389; *Vorlesungen*, Teil 1, p. 285.
28. Hegel, *Lectures*, vol. 1, p. 390; *Vorlesungen*, Teil 1, p. 285.
29. Hegel, *Lectures*, vol. 1, p. 390; *Vorlesungen*, Teil 1, p. 286.
30. Hegel, *Lectures*, vol. 1, p. 391; *Vorlesungen*, Teil 1, p. 286.
31. Hegel, *Lectures*, vol. 1, p. 395; *Vorlesungen*, Teil 1, p. 290.
32. Hegel, *Lectures*, vol. 1, p. 393; *Vorlesungen*, Teil 1, p. 289.
33. Hegel, *Lectures,* vol. 1, p. 397; *Vorlesungen*, Teil 1, p. 293.
34. Hegel, *Lectures*, vol. 1, pp. 397–398; *Vorlesungen*, Teil 1, p. 293.
35. Hegel, *Lectures*, vol. 1, p. 398; *Vorlesungen*, Teil 1, p. 293.
36. Hegel, *Lectures*, vol. 1, p. 399; *Vorlesungen*, Teil 1, p. 294.
37. Hegel, *Lectures*, vol. 1, p. 400; *Vorlesungen*, Teil 1, p. 295.
38. Ibid.
39. Paul Ricoeur, *Figuring the Sacred* (ed. Mark Wallace; trans. David Pellauer; Minneapolis: Fortress Press, 1995), p. 223.
40. Ibid.
41. Hegel, *Lectures*, vol. 1, p. 442; *Vorlesungen*, Teil 1, p. 330.
42. Ibid.
43. Hegel, *Lectures*, p. 443; *Vorlesungen*, Teil 1, pp. 332–333.
44. Hegel, *Lectures*, vol. 1, p. 446; *Vorlesungen*, Teil 1, p. 334.
45. Hegel, *Lectures*, vol. 1, pp. 446–447; *Vorlesungen*, Teil 1, pp. 334–335.
46. Georg Wilhelm Friedrich Hegel, 'Reason and Religious Truth: Hegel's Forward, to H. Fr. W. Hinrich's *Die Reigion im inneren Verhältnisse zur Wissenschaft*,' in *Beyond Epistemology: New Studies in the Philosophy of Hegel* (ed. Frederick G. Weiss; The Hague: Martinus Nijhoff, 1974), p. 228; *Werke*, vol. 11, p. 43.
47. Hegel, *Lectures*, vol. 1, p. 289; *Vorlesungen*, Teil 1, p. 184.
48. Hegel, 'Reason and Religious Truth,' p. 238; *Werke*, vol. 11, p. 58.
49. Hodgson, *Hegel and Christian Theology*, p. 46.
50. Hegel, *Lectures*, vol. 1, p. 280, n. 37.
51. Hodgson, *Hegel and Christian Theology*, p. 65.
52. Hegel, *Lectures*, vol. 1, p. 127; *Vorlesungen*, Teil 1, p. 43.
53. Hegel, *The Encyclopedia Logic*, p. 20; *Werke*, vol. 8, p. 35.

Notes

54. Hegel, *The Encyclopedia Logic*, p. 74; *Werke*, vol. 8, p. 104.
55. Hegel, *Lectures*, vol. 1, pp. 131–132; *Vorlesungen*, Teil 1, pp. 47–48.
56. Hegel, Lectures, vol. 1, p. 84; *Werke*, Teil 1, p. 4.
57. Hodgson, *Hegel and Christian Theology*, p. 126.

Chapter 4

1. See John Burbidge, 'Is Hegel a Christian?' in *New Perspectives in Hegel's Philosophy of Religion* (ed. David Kolb; Albany: State University of New York Press, 1992), pp. 93–94.
2. Hodgson, *Hegel and Christian Theology*, p. 258.
3. William Desmond, *Hegel's God, A Counterfeit Double* (Aldershot and Burlington: Ashgate Publishing, 2003), p. ix.
4. Hegel, *Lectures,* vol. 1, p. 302; *Vorlesungen*, Teil 1, p. 206.
5. Hegel, *Lectures*, vol. 1, p. 401; *Vorlesungen*, Teil 1, p. 296.
6. Ibid.
7. Ibid.
8. Stephen Crites, 'The Golgotha of Absolute Spirit', in *Method and Speculation in Hegel's Phenomenology* (ed. Merold Westphal; New Jersey: Humanities Press, 1982), p. 54.
9. Ibid.
10. Hegel, *Lectures*, vol. 1, p. 369; *Vorlesungen*, Teil 1, pp. 268–269.
11. Hegel, *Lectures*, vol. 1, p. 370; *Vorlesungen*, Teil 1, p. 269.
12. Hegel, *Lectures*, vol. 1, pp. 373–374; *Vorlesungen*, Teil 1, p. 272.
13. Hegel, *Lectures*, vol. 1, p. 176; *Vorlesungen*, Teil 1, p. 85.
14. Hegel, *Lectures*, vol. 1, p. 323; *Vorlesungen*, Teil 1, p. 226.
15. Hegel, *Lectures*, vol. 1, p. 371; *Vorlesungen*, Teil 1, p. 270.
16. Hegel, *Lectures,* vol. 1, p. 369; *Vorlesungen*, Teil 1, p. 268.
17. Hegel, *Lectures*, vol. 1, p. 421; *Vorlesungen*, Teil 1, p. 314.
18. Hegel, *The Encyclopedia Logic*, p. 26; *Werke*, vol. 8, pp. 47–48.
19. Hegel, *Lectures*, vol. 1, p. 424; *Vorlesungen*, Teil 1, p. 316.
20. Hegel, *Lectures*, vol. 1, p. 427; *Vorlesungen*, Teil 1, pp. 318–319.
21. G. W. F. Hegel, *Lectures on the Proofs of the Existence of God* (ed. and trans. Peter C. Hodgson; Oxford: Clarendon Press, 2007), p. 111.
22. Hegel, *Lectures*, vol. 1, p. 424; *Vorlesungen*, Teil 1, p. 316.
23. Hegel, *Lectures on the Proofs of God's Existence*, p. 112.
24. See Martin J. De Nys, 'God, Creatures, and Relations: Revisiting Classical Theism,' *The Journal of Religion* (2001), pp. 595–614, for a full discussion of this and other assertions about Aquinas in the following comments.
25. Hodgson, *Hegel and Christian Theology*, p. 49.
26. Hegel, *Lectures*, vol. 1, p. 432; *Vorlesungen*, Teil 1, p. 322.
27. Ibid.
28. Ibid.
29. Hegel, *Lectures*, vol. 1, p. 432; *Vorlesungen*, Teil 1, pp. 322–333.
30. Hegel, *Lectures*, vol. 1, p. 432; *Vorlesungen*, Teil 1, p. 323.

31. G. W. F. Hegel, *Hegel's Philosophy of Mind* (trans. William Wallace and A. V. Miller; Oxford: Clarendon Press, 1971), p. 310; *Werke*, vol. 10, p. 389.

32. Hegel, *Philosophy of Mind*, p. 311; *Werke*, vol. 10, pp. 389–390.

33. Hegel, *Philosophy of Mind*, p. 312; *Werke*, vol. 10, p. 391.

34. Desmond, *Hegel's God*, p. 124.

35. Ibid., p. 128.

36. Ibid., p. 134.

37. Ibid., p. 88.

38. Ibid., p. 134.

39. Ibid., p. 92.

40. Ibid.

41. Ibid., p. 180.

42. Eberhardt Jüngel, *God's Being Is in Becoming: The Trinitarian Being of God in the Theology of Karl Barth* (trans. John Webster; Edinburgh: T&T Clark Ltd., 2001), p. xxv.

43. Hodgson, *Hegel and Christian Theology*, p. 252.

44. Hegel, *Lectures*, vol. 1, pp. 176–177; *Vorlesungen*, Teil 1, p. 85.

45. Hegel, *Hegel's Philosophy of Mind*, p. 298; *Werke*, vol. 10, p. 374.

46. Hegel, *Lectures on the Proofs of the Existence of* God, p. 126.

47. Hegel, *Lectures*, vol. 1, p. 126; *Vorlesungen*, Teil 1, p. 43.

Chapter 5

1. Hegel, *Lectures*, vol. 3, p. 185; *Vorlesungen*, Teil 10, p. 119.

2. Hegel, *Lectures*, vol. 3, p. 186; *Vorlesungen*, Teil 10, p. 120.

3. Hegel, *Lectures*, vol. 3, p. 250; *Vorlesungen*, Teil 10, p. 178.

4. Hegel, *Lectures*, vol. 3, p. 251; *Vorlesungen*, Teil 10, p. 179.

5. Hegel, *Lectures*, vol. 3, p. 165; *Vorlesungen*, Teil 10, p. 100.

6. Hegel, *Lectures*, vol. 3, p. 163; *Vorlesungen*, Teil 10, p. 99.

7. Hegel, *Philosophy of Mind*, p. 299; *Werke*, vol. 10, p. 375.

8. Hodgson, *Hegel and Christian Theology*, p. 134.

9. Dale Schlitt, *Divine Subjectivity: Understanding Hegel's Philosophy of Religion* (London and Toronto: Associated University Presses, 1990), p. 181.

10. Ibid., p. 183.

11. Dale Schlitt, *Experience and Spirit: A Post-Hegelian Philosophical Theology* (New York: Peter Lang, 2007), p. 68.

12. Hegel, *Lectures*, vol. 3, p. 292; *Werke*, Teil 10, p. 216.

13. Hegel, *Lectures on the Proofs of God's Existence*, p. 54.

14. Desmond, *Hegel's God*, p. 106.

15. Ibid.

16. Hodgson, *Hegel and Christian Theology*, p. 131.

17. Hegel, *Lectures*, vol. 3, pp. 273–274; *Werke*, Teil 10, pp. 198–199.

18. Ewert Cousins, *Bonaventure and the Coincidence of Opposites* (Chicago: Franciscan Herald Press, 1978), p. 102.

Notes

19. Ibid., p. 105.
20. Ibid., p. 102.
21. Ibid., p. 238.
22. Ibid., p. 239.
23. Hegel, *Philosophy of Mind*, p. 300; *Werke*, Teil 10, p. 376.
24. Hegel, *Lectures*, vol. 3, p. 299; *Vorlesungen*, Teil 10, p. 223.
25. Ibid.
26. Ibid.
27. Hegel, *Lectures*, vol. 3, p. 299; *Vorlesungen*, Teil 10, p. 224.
28. Hegel, *Lectures*, vol. 3, p. 306; *Vorlesungen*, Teil 10, p. 229.
29. Hegel, *Lectures*, vol. 3, p. 305; *Vorlesungen*, Teil 10, p. 228.
30. Hegel, *Lectures*, vol. 3, p. 307; *Vorlesungen*, Teil 10, p. 230.
31. Hegel, *Lectures*, vol. 3, p. 300; *Vorlesungen*, Teil 10, p. 224.
32. Hegel, *Lectures*, vol. 3, p. 106; *Vorlesungen*, Teil 3, p. 42.
33. Hegel, *The Encyclopedia Logic*, p. 63; *Werke*, vol. 8, p. 90.
34. Paul Ricoeur, 'The Hermeneutic of Symbols: I,' *Conflict of Interpretations*, p. 313.
35. See *Lectures*, vol. 3, p. 298; *Vorlesungen*, Teil 3, p. 223.
36. Hegel, *Lectures*, vol. 3, p. 305; *Vorlesungen*, Teil 3, p. 228.
37. Hegel, *Lectures*, vol. 3, p. 305; *Vorlesungen*, Teil 3, p. 229.
38. Hegel, *Lectures*, vol. 3, p. 213; *Vorlesungen*, Teil 3, p. 144.
39. Hegel, *Lectures*, vol. 3, p. 110; *Vorlesungen*, Teil 3, p. 46.
40. Hegel, *Lectures*, vol. 3, p. 312; *Vorlesungen*, Teil 3, p. 236.
41. James Yerkes, *The Christology of Hegel* (Missoula: Scholars Press, 1978), p. 169.
42. Ibid., p. 171.
43. Karl Rahner, *Theological Investigations*, vol. I (trans. Cornelius Ernst; New York: Crossroad, 1982), p. 163, n. 1.
44. Ibid., p. 176, n. 1.
45. Hegel, *Lectures*, vol. 3, p. 313; *Vorlesungen*, Teil 3, p. 238.
46. Hegel, *Lectures*, vol. 3, pp. 315–316; *Vorlesungen*, Teil 3, p. 239.
47. Hegel, *Lectures*, vol. 3, p. 317; *Vorlesugnen*, Teil 3, p. 241.
48. Hegel, *Lectures*, vol. 3, p. 118; *Vorlesungen*, Teil 3, pp. 53–54.
49. Hegel, *Lectures*, vol. 3, p. 118; *Vorlesungen*, Teil 3, p. 54.
50. Hegel, *Lectures*, vol. 3, p. 119; *Vorlesungen*, Teil 3, p. 54.
51. Hegel, *Lectures*, vol. 3, p. 318; *Vorlesungen*, Teil 3, p. 241.
52. Hegel, *Lectures*, vol. 3, p. 121; *Vorlesungen*, Teil 3, p. 56.
53. Hegel, *Lectures*, vol. 3, p. 322; *Vorlesungen*, Teil 3, p. 245.
54. Hegel, *Lectures*, vol. 3, p. 326; *Vorlesungen*, Teil 3, pp. 249–250.
55. Hegel, *Lectures*, vol. 3, p. 326; *Vorlesungen*, Teil 3, p. 249.
56. Hegel, *Philosophy of Mind*, p. 300; *Werke*, Teil 10, p. 376.
57. Hegel, *Lectures*, vol. 3, p. 332; *Vorlesungen*, Teil 3, p. 255.
58. Hegel, *Lectures*, vol. 3, p. 334; *Vorlesungen*, Teil 3, p. 257.
59. Hegel, *Lectures*, vol. 3, pp. 336–337; *Vorlesungen*, Teil 3, p. 259.
60. Hegel, *Lectures*, vol. 3, p. 337; *Vorlesungen*, Teil 3, p. 260.

61. Hegel, *Lectures*, vol. 3, pp. 337–338; *Vorlesungen*, Teil 3, p. 260.
62. Hegel, *Lectures*, vol. 3, p. 342; *Vorlesungen*, Teil 3, pp. 264–265.

Chapter 6

1. Bernard Lonergan, *The Triune God: Systematics* (ed. Robert M. Doran and H. Daniel Mousour; trans. Michael Shields; Toronto: University of Toronto Press, 207), p. 436.
2. Paul Ricoeur, *The Conflict of Interpretations*, p. 283.
3. Ibid., p. 284.
4. James Yerkes, *The Christology of Hegel*, p. 175.
5. Carl Braaten, *Justification: The Article by Which the Church Stands or Falls* (Minneapolis: Fortress Press, 1990), pp. 71–72.
6. Hegel, *Lectures,* vol. 3, p. 192; *Vorlesungen*, Teil 3, p. 125.
7. Hegel, *Lectures*, vol. 3, p. 192; *Vorlesungen*, Teil 3, p. 126.
8. Hegel, *Lectures*, vol. 3, p. 280; *Vorlesungen*, Teil 3, p. 205.
9. Hegel, *Lectures*, vol. 3, p. 282; *Vorlesungen*, Teil 3, p. 207.
10. Hegel, *Lectures*, vol. 3, p. 283; *Vorlesungen*, Teil 3, p. 208.
11. Hegel, *Lectures*, vol. 3, p. 76; *Vorlesungen*, Teil 3, p. 14.
12. Hegel, *Phenomenology*, p. 459; *Werke*, vol. 3, p. 552.
13. Kenneth Schmitz, 'The Element of Mystery in the Conception of God,' in *The Challenge of Religion*, pp. 71–72.
14. Kathleen Dow Magnus, *Hegel and the Symbolic Mediation of Spirit* (Albany: State University of New York Press, 2001), p. 50.
15. Paul Ricoeur, 'The Status of *Vorstellung* in Hegel's Philosophy of Religion,' in *Meaning, Truth, and God* (ed. Leroy Rouner; Notre Dame & London: University of Notre Dame Press, 1982), p. 86.
16. Ibid., p. 85.
17. Hegel, *Lectures*, vol. 3, p. 334; *Vorlesungen*, Teil 3, p. 257.
18. Hegel, *Lectures*, vol. 3, p. 337; *Vorlesungen*, Teil 3, p. 260.
19. Soren Kierkegaard, *Concluding Unscientific Postscript to Philosophical Fragments*, vol. 1 (ed. and trans. Howard V. Hong and Edna H. Hong; Princeton: Princeton University Press, 1992), p. 203.
20. See Martin J. De Nys, 'Faith, Self-Transcendence, and Reflection,' *International Journal for Philosophy of Religion* 51 (2002), pp. 121–138 (125–128).
21. Hegel, *Lectures*, vol. 1, p. 452; *Vorlesungen*, Teil 1, p. 339.
22. Hegel, *Lectures*, vol. 3, p. 340; *Vorlesungen*, Teil 3, p. 263.
23. Hegel, *Lectures*, vol. 3, pp. 341–342; *Vorlesungen*, Teil 3, p. 264.
24. Hegel, *Philosophy of Right*, p. 166; *Werke*, vol. 7, p. 417.
25. Hegel, *Lectures*, vol. 3, p. 446; *Vorlesungen*, Teil 3, p. 334.
26. Hegel, *Lectures*, vol. 1, p. 452; *Vorlesungen*, Teil 1, p. 340.
27. Andrew Collier, *Marx* (Oxford: Oneworld Publications, 2004), p. 54.
28. Ibid., p. 55.

29. Hegel, *Lectures*, vol. 3, p. 317; *Vorlesungen*, Teil 3, p. 241.
30. Hegel, *Lectures*, vol. 3, p. 318; *Vorlesungen*, Teil 3, p. 241.

Chapter 7

1. Michael Theunissen, *Hegels Lehre vom absoluten Geist as theologisch-politischer Traktat* (Berlin: Walter de Gruyter, 1970), p. vii.
2. See Paul Ricoeur, *Figuring the Sacred*, pp. 37–41.
3. Hegel, *Lectures*, vol. 3, p. 162; *Vorlesungen*, Teil 3, pp. 96–97.
4. See Bernard Lonergan, 'Philosophy of God and the Functional Specialty Systematics,' in *Collected Works of Bernard Lonergan: Philosophical and Theological Paper, 1965–1980* (ed. Robert C. Croken and Robert Doran; Toronto: University of Toronto Press, 2004), pp. 156–218.
5. Raymond Keith Williamson, *Introduction to Hegel's Philosophy of Religion* (Albany: State University of New York Press, 1984), p. 300.
6. Ibid., pp. 295–296. Williamson cites Fackenheim, *The Religious Dimension in Hegel's Thought*, p. 186.
7. Hegel, *Lectures*, vol. 1, p. 401; *Vorlesungen*, Teil 1, p. 296.
8. Williamson, *Introduction*, p. 303.
9. Ibid., p. 302.
10. See Paul Ricoeur, *Figuring the Sacred*, pp. 221–223.
11. Robert Neville, *God the Creator* (Albany: State University of New York Press, 1992), p. xix.
12. Karl Rahner, 'On the Theology of the Incarnation,' in *Theological Investigations*, vol. IV (trans. Kevin Smyth; New York: Crossroad, 1982), p. 113.
13. Ibid., p. 114.
14. Ibid.
15. Ibid.
16. William Desmond, *Hegel's God*, p. 128.
17. Ibid.
18. Wolfhart Pannenberg, *The Idea of God and Human Freedom* (trans. R. A. Wilson; Philadelphia: The Westminster Press, 1973), p. 173.
19. Hegel, *Werke*, vol. 11, p. 363, my translation.
20. Ibid., p. 368. My translation.
21. Peter Hodgson, *Hegel and Christian Theology*, p. 218.
22. Ibid., p. 238.
23. Schubert Ogden, *Is There Only One True Religion Or Are There Many* (Dallas: Southern Methodist University Press, 1992), p. 84.
24. See ibid., pp. 79–104.

Bibliography

Barth, Karl, *Protestant Theology in the Nineteenth Century* (trans. Brian Cozens and John Bowden; Grand Rapids, Michigan/Cambridge, U.K.: Eerdmans, 2002), p. 370.

Braaten, Carl, *Justification: The Article by Which the Church Stands or Falls* (Minneapolis: Fortress Press, 1990).

Burbidge, John, 'Is Hegel a Christian?' in *New Perspectives in Hegel's Philosophy of Religion* (ed. David Kolb; Albany: State University of New York Press, 1992).

Collier, Andrew, *Marx* (Oxford: Oneworld Publications, 2004).

Cousins, Ewert, *Bonaventure and the Coincidence of Opposites* (Chicago: Franciscan Herald Press, 1978).

Crites, Stephen, 'The Golgotha of Absolute Spirit', in *Method and Speculation in Hegel's Phenomenology* (ed. Merold Westphal; New Jersey: Humanities Press, 1982).

D'Hondt, Jacques, *Hegel in His Time: Berlin, 1818–1831* (trans. John Burbidge; Peterborough and Lewiston: Broadview Press Ltd., 1988).

De Nys, Martin J., 'Dimensions of Absolute Knowing,' *The Review of Metaphysics* (2008) 555–576.

—'Faith, Self-Transcendence, and Reflection,' *International Journal for Philosophy of Religion* 51 (2002), pp. 121–138.

—'God, Creatures, and Relations: Revisiting Classical Theism,' *The Journal of Religion* (2001), pp. 595–614.

—'Mediation and Negativity in Hegel's Phenomenology of Christian Consciousness,' *The Journal of Religion*, 66 (1986), pp. 46–67.

Desmond, William, *Hegel's God, A Counterfeit Double* (Aldershot and Burlington: Ashgate Publishing, 2003).

Fackenheim, Emil, *The Religious Dimension in Hegel's Thought* (Bloomington and London: Indiana University Press, 1967).

Flay, Joseph C., *Hegel's Quest for Certainty* (Albany: State University of New York Press, 1984).

Harris, H. S., *Hegel's Development: Towards the Sunlight, 1770–1801* (Oxford: Clarendon Press, 1972).

—*Hegel's Ladder* (2 vols; Indianapolis/Cambridge: Hackett, 1997).

Hegel, G. W. F., *The Difference Between Fichte's and Schelling's System of Philosophy* (H. S. Harris and Walter Cerf [eds. and trans.]; Albany: State University of New York Press, 1977).

Bibliography

Hegel, G. W. F., *The Encyclopedia Logic* (trans. T. F. Geraets, W. A. Suchting, and H. S. Harris; Indianapolis/Cambridge: Hackett, 1991).

—*Friedrich Hegel: Early Theological Writings* (eds. T. M. Knox and Richard Kroner; New York: Harper, 1961).

—*Hegel: Three Essays, 1793–1795* (ed. and trans. Peter Fuss and John Dobbins; Notre Dame, Ind.: University of Notre Dame Press, 1984).

—*Hegel's Philosophy of Mind* (trans. William Wallace and A. V. Miller; Oxford: Clarendon Press, 1971).

—*Hegel's Theologische Jugendschriften* (ed. Herman Nohl; Tübingen: J. C. B. Mohr, 1907).

—*Lectures on the Philosophy of Religion* (Peter C. Hodgson [ed.]; R. F. Brown, P. C. Hodgson, and J. M. Stewart with the assistance of H. S. Harris [trans.]; Berkeley and Los Angeles: University of California Press, 1984–87; Oxford: Oxford University Press, 2006).

—*Lectures on the Proofs of the Existence of God* (ed. and trans. Peter C. Hodgson; Oxford: Clarendon Press, 2007).

—*Phenomenology of Spirit* (trans. A. V. Miller; Oxford: Clarendon Press, 1977).

—*Philosophy of Right* (trans. T. M. Knox; Oxford: Oxford University Press, 1967).

—'Reason and Religious Truth: Hegel's Foreword, to H. Fr. W. Hinrich's *Die Reigion im inneren Verhältnisse zur Wissenschaft*,' in *Beyond Epistemology: New Studies in the Philosophy of Hegel* (ed. Frederick G. Weiss; The Hague: Martinus Nijhoff, 1974).

—*Vorlesungen über die Philosophie der Religion* (Walter Jaeschke [ed.]; 3 vols; Hamburg: Felix Meiner Verlag, 1983–85, 1993–95).

—*Werke in zwanzig Bänden* (Eva Moldenhauer and Klaus Michel [eds.]. vol. 2; Frankfurt: Suhrkamp, 1986).

Hodgson, Peter, *Hegel and Christian Theology* (Oxford: Oxford University Press, 2005).

Houlgate, Stephen, *Freedom, Truth, and History: An Introduction to Hegel's Philosophy* (London and New York: Routledge, 1991).

Hyppolite, Jean, *Genesis and Structure of Hegel's Phenomenology of Spirit* (trans. Samuel Cherniak and John Heckman; Evanston: Northwestern University Press, 1974).

Jaeschke, Walter, 'Philosophical Theology and Philosophy of Religion,' in *New Perspectives on Hegel's Philosophy of Religion* (ed. David Kolb; Albany: State University of New York Press, 1992).

Jüngel, Eberhardt, *God's Being Is in Becoming: The Trinitarian Being of God in the Theology of Karl Barth* (trans. John Webster; Edinburgh: T&T Clark Ltd., 2001).

Kierkegaard, Soren, *Concluding Unscientific Postscript to Philosophical Fragments*, vol. 1 (ed. and trans. Howard V. Hong and Edna H. Hong; Princeton: Princeton University Press, 1992).

Lauer, Quentin, *A Reading of Hegel's Phenomenology of Spirit* (New York: Fordham University Press, 1976).

Bibliography

Lonergan, Bernard, 'Philosophy of God and the Functional Specialty Systematics,' in *Collected Works of Bernard Lonergan: Philosophical and Theological Paper, 1965–1980* (ed. Robert C. Croken and Robert Doran; Toronto: University of Toronto Press, 2004), pp. 156–218.

—*The Triune God: Systematics* (ed. Robert M. Doran and H. Daniel Mousour; trans. Michael Shields; Toronto: University of Toronto Press, 2007).

Magnus, Kathleen Dow, *Hegel and the Symbolic Mediation of Spirit* (Albany: State University of New York Press, 2001).

Neville, Robert, *God the Creator* (Albany: State University of New York Press, 1992).

O'Regan, Cyril, *The Heterodox Hegel* (Albany: State University of New York Press, 1994).

Ogden, Schubert, *Is There Only One True Religion Or Are There Many* (Dallas: Southern Methodist University Press, 1992).

Pannenberg, Wolfhart, *The Idea of God and Human Freedom* (trans. R. A. Wilson; Philadelphia: The Westminster Press, 1973).

Pinkard, Terry, *Hegel: A Biography* (Cambridge: Cambridge University Press, 2000).

Rahner, Karl, 'On The Theology of the Incarnation,' in *Theological Investigations*, vol. IV (trans. Kevin Smyth; New York: Crossroad, 1982).

—*Theological Investigations*, vol. I (trans. Cornelius Ernst; New York: Crossroad, 1982).

Ricoeur, Paul, *Figuring the Sacred* (ed. Mark Wallace; trans. David Pellauer; Minneapolis: Fortress Press, 1995).

—'The Status of *Vorstellung* in Hegel's Philosophy of Religion,' in *Meaning, Truth, and God* (ed. Leroy Rouner; Notre Dame & London: University of Notre Dame Press, 1982).

Schlitt, Dale, *Divine Subjectivity: Understanding Hegel's Philosophy of Religion* (London and Toronto: Associated University Presses, 1990).

—*Experience and Spirit: A Post-Hegelian Philosophical Theology* (New York: Peter Lang, 2007).

Theunissen, Michael, *Hegels Lehre vom absoluten Geist as theologisch-politischer Traktat* (Berlin: Walter de Gruyter, 1970).

Westphal, Merold, *History and Truth in Hegel's Phenomenology* (Atlantic Highlands: Humanities Press, 1979).

Williamson, Raymond Keith, *Introduction to Hegel's Philosophy of Religion* (Albany: State University of New York Press, 1984).

Yerkes, James, *The Christology of Hegel* (Missoula: Scholars Press, 1978).

Index

Index

Index

self-relatedness 19, 39–40, 43, 49, 56, 88, 90–1, 98, 102, 110, 125, 127, 139, 141
self-revelation 112, 127, 142–3, 180
self-transcendence 43, 59, 122, 151
Socrates 111, 124
speculative thinking 13, 51, 87–9, 146–7
Spinoza, Baruch 95–6
Spirit 19–24, 27–8, 31–3, 43–5, 49–52, 55–9, 61–2, 72, 89–90, 96–7, 104, 108–11, 113, 118, 127–8, 136, 142, 147, 151, 163, 172, 180
"Spirit of Christianity and its Fate" (Hegel) 7
subjective reflection 149, 163
symbolic disclosure 144

teleology 62
telos 119–21, 159
theophany 144
Theunissen, Michael 158

thinking 45, 85
Tholuck, F. A. G. 95
Tillich, Paul 70, 72
transcendence 12–13, 43, 54, 82–3, 89, 100, 102, 106–7, 173–4, 177
Trinity 12, 51, 59, 71, 78–9, 100, 110–12, 116–17, 119, 128, 133, 137–8, 163, 168, 172
truth 2, 13, 19–20, 36, 68, 147, 149, 181, 183
"Tübingen Fragment" (Hegel) 5–6
Tübingen, University of 4–5

unhappy consciousness 49
unio mystica 129

Westphal, Merold 58
whole of wholes 101–2
Williamson, Raymond Keith 164–7, 173
worldly realm 152

Yerkes, James 123, 180